HOWARD
BOOKS

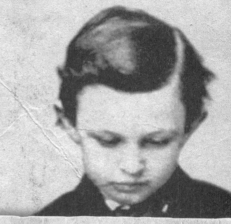

Stories of Our
Most Admired President

ABRAHAM
LINCOLN
A MAN OF
Faith and Courage

HOWARD BOOKS
A DIVISION OF SIMON & SCHUSTER
New York   London   Toronto   Sydney

JOE WHEELER

Our purpose at Howard Books is to:
+ *Increase faith* in the hearts of growing Christians
+ *Inspire holiness* in the lives of believers
+ *Instill hope* in the hearts of struggling people everywhere

Because He's coming again!

Published by Howard Books, a division of Simon & Schuster, Inc.
1230 Avenue of the Americas, New York, NY 10020
www.howardpublishing.com

Library of Congress Cataloging-in-Publication Data
Wheeler, Joe L., 1936–
    Abraham Lincoln, a man of faith and courage : stories of out most admired president / Joe Wheeler.
        p. cm.
    Includes bibliographical references.
1. Lincoln, Abraham, 1809–1865—Religion. 2. Presidents—United States—Biography. I. Title.
E457.2.W55 2008
973.7092—dc22
[B]
                                        2007038947

ISBN 13: 978-1-4165-5096-9
ISBN 10:   1-4165-5096-8

10 9 8 7 6 5 4 3

For information regarding special discounts for bulk purchases, please contact: Simon & Schuster Special Sales at 1-800-456-6798 or business@simonandschuster.com.

Edited by Jeff Gerke
Cover design by Michael J. Williams, www.mwillustration.com
Interior design by John Mark Luke Designs
Cover image by The Collection of Keya Morgan, LincolnImages.com, NYC

Scripture quotations marked KJV are taken from the *Holy Bible*, Authorized King James version.

Contents

CONTENTS

Why was Lincoln so great that he overshadows all other national heroes? He really was not a great general like Napoleon or Washington; he was not such a skilled statesman as Gladstone or Frederick the Great; but his supremacy expresses itself altogether in his peculiar moral power and in the greatness of his character.

Washington was a typical American. Napoleon was a typical Frenchman, but Lincoln was a humanitarian as broad as the world. He was bigger than his country—bigger than all the presidents together.

We are still too near his greatness, but after a few centuries more our posterity will find him considerably bigger than we do. His genius is still too strong and too powerful for the common understanding, just as the sun is too hot when its light beams directly on us.

—LEO TOLSTOY

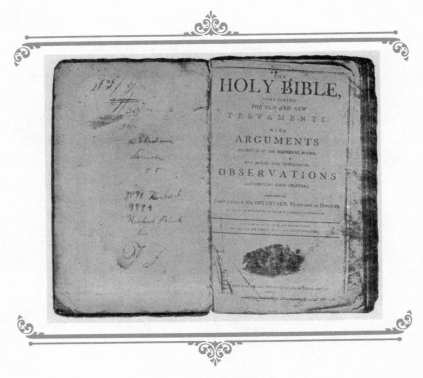

Thomas Lincoln's Bible

Introduction

As, in spite of some weaknesses, Republicanism is the sole hope of a sick world, so Lincoln with all his foibles, is the greatest character since Christ.

—JOHN HAY *(U.S. Secretary of State)*

"Which presidents are kids most interested in reading about?"

I was standing in the children's section of a local chain bookstore. I'd asked the lady at the information desk to take me to books about presidents.

She looked at me as though I'd come from another planet. "Who else—Lincoln and Washington."

"Any runners-up?"

"Nope. Nobody else in sight."

I had figured as much. Now I was just doing an informal survey. "Well," I said, "between Lincoln and Washington, which one do they ask about most?"

She laughed. "There's no contest. It's Lincoln by a country mile."

"Hmm," I said. I'd gotten the same answer from elementary and middle school librarians.

Apparently more books have been written about Lincoln than about all the rest of our presidents put together. More poems have been written about Lincoln than about all the other presidents put together. More quotations originating with Lincoln are in circulation than for all the rest of our presidents put together, and that's not even counting the vast number of other quotations that are *attributed* to him. More anecdotes associated with Lincoln exist than for all the rest of our presidents put together. We have more stories told by Lincoln than we have from all the rest put together.

For many years I have made a living collecting stories into anthologies. So it is with professional wonder that I survey the multitude of stories about Lincoln, true and otherwise, that have been written about him. Far more of these tales exist about Lincoln than for all the rest of the presidents put together. Abraham Lincoln is and was an epic, legendary figure in American history.

Three of our national holidays—Presidents' Day, Memorial Day, and Thanksgiving—are directly tied to Lincoln. Nor is his fame restricted to the United States. Lincoln is the one American who is revered around the world. He is, indeed, the only universally beloved American.

Our son Greg is an advertising copywriter. He tells us that one of the absolutes in advertising is this: *No matter what the product, just tie Lincoln to it and it's guaranteed to sell.*

Nor does this fascination seem about to fade any time soon. Interest in Lincoln has done nothing but build since his presidency. With untold millions of words written about him, it is logical to assume that there couldn't be anything new to discover. And yet new Lincoln biographies continue to pour out of publishing houses. Momentum will only compound as we near 2009 (the two-hundredth anniversary of his birth) and 2011 to 2015 (the hundred-fiftieth anniversary of the Civil War years).

AN ENDURING LEGACY

As a historian of ideas I have long been fascinated by biographical history. One of my central questions has been the exploration of why the vast majority of historical luminaries flicker out before another generation comes on the scene and why others endure. Fame itself has been reduced to fifteen minutes in our time. For a name to survive in the national consciousness for two generations is abnormal, three generations is a miracle.

Yet each new generation has found and continues to find something special in the sixteenth president, something no one wants to live without.

What that something might be has never been more aptly summed up than by Lloyd Lewis in his landmark book *Myths after Lincoln.* Lewis postulated that a nation doesn't really consider itself to be a nation until someone, against all odds, emerges from the mass and stands out against the sky. Many there are who tread the stages of their age acclaimed by thousands and appear to be heroes. Yet in the leveling field of death and with the perspective time brings, almost all crumble into the dust of forgottenhood. It takes almost superhuman qualities to survive—admired, honored, and loved—from generation to generation to generation, to evolve at last into imperishable myth, Lewis says.

For ninety years America vainly struggled to produce such a towering figure of myth. Neither Jackson nor Jefferson made it. Not even Washington, who was too austere, "too cold in his perfections to claim anything more than their formal reverence and sober admiration." Besides, Lewis notes, all those heroes lived too long, and by no stretch of the imagination could their passing be construed as mysterious, miraculous, or sacrificial.

All that changed in April of 1865:

It was not until Lincoln had been assassinated and his body seen firsthand by 1,500,000 people, that something truly miraculous took place. As they saw him stretched to his giant's length in the coffin, they remembered with awe how cool and strong he had seemed through those four years of terror, now miraculously ended. Remembering how he had been abused during his lifetime, and how even his friends had mistaken his patience for weakness, the people began to revere him. Seeing his body go back to the common soil amid such sobbing pomp, they understood in full that he had sacrificed himself for them. Dimly, but with elemental power, they felt he had died out of love for the people.

Under him the nation had become for the first time one, all questions of its division settled, its unity cemented in blood. More than that, the nation was at last a great world power. With Lincoln as leader the young Republic had defied Europe. Under him four million Negro slaves had been set free. To have done what he had done, it seemed that he must, perforce, have been superhuman.[1]

Lewis noted that by the end of the war Lincoln was already the chief American hero. His assassination (and he was the first American president to be murdered) elevated him into the pantheon of mythology overnight. Now, as was true with other heroes who had died for others, his betrayer was elevated into the mythology of archvillains. Balder had his Loki, Arthur his

Mordred, and Jesus His Judas. Now Lincoln's John Wilkes Booth displaced Benedict Arnold as the ultimate American villain.[2]

The catalyst for all this was perhaps the longest funeral in world history. For fourteen days the slow funeral train meandered 1,700 miles from the White House to Oak Ridge Cemetery in Springfield, Illinois. Hardly ever was there a moment without booming guns. Even in the middle of the night and during torrential rainstorms, grieving Americans waited faithfully by the tracks to see it pass at a somber twenty miles per hour. In cities, more than a million and a half people filed by the casket to take one last look at their fallen leader. Out of a U.S. population of 31 million, well over 7 million saw the train or the catafalque. That's nearly one in every four living Americans.

Thus the myth of Abraham Lincoln was born.

But the true miracle is what has happened since. Ordinarily in biographical history, every hero is shown to have offsetting flaws detracting from his or her greatness. But for almost a century and a half now, scholars have hammered away at the Lincoln monolith in an almost desperate search for significant character flaws or fissures. *And they have not found them.*

This is why millions continue thronging the Lincoln trail. Here, parents introduce their children to a real hero as a counterbalance in an age teeming with pseudoheroes.

WHY I WROTE THIS BOOK

I mentioned before that I am a professional anthologist and a historian of ideas. Over a span of seventeen years I have compiled and edited sixty-four books, forty-eight of them being story anthologies. The best known of these are the Christmas in My Heart, Heart to Heart, Great Stories Remembered, Forged in the Fire, and The Good Lord Made Them All series. My academic journey includes a masters in history from Pacific Union College, a masters in English from Sacramento State University, and a PhD in English (History of Ideas emphasis) from Vanderbilt University. I have also been a lifelong appreciator and student of Abraham Lincoln and the stories written about him.

As a homeschooled child, I was encouraged to become a voracious reader, to gobble up entire libraries. I burrowed into history, religion, literature, mythology, nature, story, folk tales, anthropology, true-life adventure, and biography—*especially* biography. Though I reveled in make-believe worlds, there was something comfortable, something with foundations under it, about the true stories of people who did such extraordinary things that no one has ever been able to obliterate their memories.

I ended up reading every biography that interested me at all. Especially was I intrigued by the lives of American presidents. However, without even knowing what I was doing or why, I winnowed down to five the ones who intrigued me: Washington, Jefferson, Lincoln, and both Roosevelts. Jefferson lacked staying power. Teddy Roosevelt intrigued me because of his rambunctious children and his love of the outdoor world. FDR (Roosevelt the Second) fascinated me because, through radio, his voice was part of the sound track of my childhood.

As the years passed, however, and I continued my long, steep learning curve, Jefferson and the two Roosevelts fell away in my interest, leaving me with only two mythical figures: Washington and Lincoln.

For thirty-four years I taught English in the academic setting. I taught at the junior high, senior high, junior college, college, and adult-education levels. During those years I sired nine paperback libraries in attempts to get young people into reading. Where my collections included books about the presidents, they were Washington and Lincoln—but mostly Lincoln.

Eighteen years ago, I entered into the stage of my life when I began anthologizing stories. *Abraham Lincoln, A Man of Faith and Courage* is my sixty-fourth book. From that vantage point one thing is clear: where stories about presidents are concerned, readers invariably choose Lincoln.

I finally realized that while I admire and revere Washington, it stops there. He is a model for many fine qualities, but with me, at least, he remains only a model to be venerated. Not so with the sixteenth president. There is something about Abraham Lincoln that makes me *love* him. I cannot explain it; I know only that it's there.

And this is the real reason I wrote this book. I wanted to learn, by total immersion into Lincoln biography, whether my hero worship, my love for Lincoln, could survive exhaustive scholarship. After reading some sixty Lincoln books, both biography and history, and writing this book to its completion, I can say that it did survive and in fact has been strengthened.

This book is not a definitive biography of Lincoln. Writing such a thing would take a lifetime. What I have endeavored to create is a Lincoln book for the masses: people of all ages, from children to senior citizens, from those who know almost nothing about Lincoln to those who are Lincoln scholars. No matter where you are in life's journey, I hope you'll decide that climbing aboard this Lincoln Concord stagecoach might end up being one of the most interesting rides of your life.

As we move through this book, we'll be concentrating on the two aspects of his life story that fascinate me most: his faith and his courage.

Welcome aboard.

PART ONE

THE WORLD AND FAITH OF

Abraham Lincoln

Lincoln during the Civil War

Abraham Lincoln's grandfather, killed by Indians in Kentucky; the boy is Thomas Lincoln

ABRAHAM
Lincoln's World

*Biographies, as generally written, are not only misleading, but false. The author
makes a wonderful hero of his subject. He magnifies his perfections, if he has any,
and suppresses his imperfections. History is not history unless it is the truth.*

—ABRAHAM LINCOLN

Abraham Lincoln was permitted to live only fifty-six years. Yet had he been
given the opportunity to choose any fifty-six-year period from the thousands
of years of recorded history, chances are he'd have chosen 1809 to 1865.
These were quite possibly the fifty-six most exciting years our world has ever
known.

As we set out to examine Abraham Lincoln's life, it might be helpful
to take a quick look at the world in which he lived and made such a lasting
impact.

THE INDUSTRIAL REVOLUTION

Lincoln was born at the intersection of two ages: the colonial and the industrial. The old ways were dying out and were being replaced by newfangled
inventions and mysterious automated processes.

For thousands of years the fastest form of land transportation had been
the horse. In 1858, land travel's last hurrah was the overland stage. What an
experience it must have been to have boarded that great Concord stagecoach
with its gleaming metal and wood accoutrements. At the head of the coach,
restlessly snorting their eagerness to hit the roads, were six magnificent
horses. When the driver snapped his whip, the stage leaped into motion.
As the horses galloped out of St. Louis, hundreds of bystanders enviously
watched it streak by. "Would you believe," one of them said in wonder, "that

only twenty days from now those folk will step down onto the streets of Los Angeles in California, 2,600 miles away!"

"'That the most direct way there is?" his neighbor might have asked.

"Nope. But it's the only one that'll get them there in twenty days without being scalped by Indians on the warpath."

In those days, getting mail across vast distances was always a problem. In 1860, William Russell and Alexander Majors bankrolled and organized the Pony Express. Their intrepid riders raced across the country from St. Louis, Missouri, to Sacramento, California, changing horses 119 times along the way—that was, if Indians hadn't attacked the stations before they got there. In spite of all obstacles, including blistering heat, sandstorms, ice storms, snowstorms, rainstorms, and Indian attacks, those courageous riders still averaged an almost unbelievable twelve miles an hour.

Then there was travel by sea. For millenia the fastest means of sea travel was the sailing ship. In the middle of the nineteenth century, as always, there were but two alternatives: oars and sails, neither of which resulted in much speed.

It's doubtful that a more beautiful sailing ship was ever constructed than that legendary windjammer the *Flying Cloud*. She sailed from Boston clear around Cape Horn, on the southern tip of South America, to come up to the coast of California. Travelers wanting to get from Boston to California overland were faced with a long wagon-train ride that was iffy at best and ran the risk of attack by marauding Indians. Ship travel, then, dangerous as the storms might be, offered more favorable odds. Still, it was a 19,000-mile-long voyage (only 5,000 miles shorter than traveling clear around the world). Even so, in 1854, the *Flying Cloud* broke the time record by making the voyage in eighty-nine days and eight hours.

Impressive as such feats may be, the Overland Stage, the Pony Express, and the *Flying Cloud* were swan songs from a dying age. The Industrial Revolution was beginning, and steam engines were changing everything.

Though Isaac Newton had come up with the concept of steam locomotion way back in 1680, it didn't move out of the theoretical into the practical until 1801. That's when Richard Trevithick, a Cornish mine captain, built the first steam locomotive. George Stephenson took it to the next level. By 1830, when Lincoln was twenty-one, the railroad age had begun in America. From that time on, faster and faster locomotives were built, and more and more track was laid. People then traveled by horse or coach only when rail transportation wasn't available.

For the first time in human history, time became relevant. Unless a train arrived and departed at a specific time, how could travelers know when to be at a station? So clocks became important and time zones became necessary. The modern age was dawning.

Steam changed sea and river travel, too. Until then, sailing ships had arrived in port "whenever." The vagaries of wind and weather made more precise timetables impossible. As for river travel, it was possible to float downstream with a current but it was nearly impossible to travel the other direction against a current. Mark Twain immortalized for us the practice of mules towing boats upstream on rivers.

But now steam engines were propelling sea and river vessels. By the time Lincoln was born, steamboats were beginning to appear on lakes and rivers. A few years later, more powerful engines would make it possible for steamboats to travel against the current up rivers such as the Mississippi, Missouri, and Ohio. On the high seas, in 1838, the British steamer the *Great Western* crossed the Atlantic Ocean in an unprecedented fifteen days. By 1850, the crossing time had been reduced to ten days. Timetables now became crucial for sea travel as well as rail.

Abraham Lincoln had no way of knowing that his world was changing so rapidly as he grew up in a frontier time warp. Nine years before Lincoln was born, Alessandro Volta had discovered how to create electricity, which would change the world much more dramatically than steam had done. When Lincoln was five, the circular saw was invented. By the time he was twenty, the trickle of technological change had swelled into a torrent: the electric motor, photographic negatives, acetelyne, carpet power looms, rubber, ozone, thermodynamics, the hydroelectric crane, the first form of an electric light bulb, rayon, tungsten steel, the passenger elevator, the lawnmower, electrical incandescent light, the practical storage battery, and the discovery of petroleum in Titusville, Pennsylvania, and the subsequent oil boom. All of these represent just a few of the inventions and discoveries that would revolutionize Lincoln's world during his lifetime.

When Lincoln was born, America was almost totally an agricultural nation. But technology began to change there, too. The cotton gin (1793), the Deere steel plow (1833), the McCormick reaper (1834), and the grain elevator (1842) would make seismic changes in farm productivity.

CHANGES AT HOME

The home life of Mary Todd, the future Mrs. Lincoln, would change, too. During her lifetime came the development of the icebox (1803), the canning process (1810, 1819) and Mason canning jars (1858), and the sulfur match (1827). With the sulfur match it was no longer necessary to keep a fire burning day and night. Now a fire could be started whenever anyone wanted one. More inventions that transformed domestic life during this period were Howe's sewing machine (1843), Singer's continuous-stitch sewing machine (1851), and the cold-storage machine. And what a difference a simple little thing like a safety pin (1849) would make in a mother's life!

For company and special occasions, party hostesses could now offer Ghirardelli's chocolate (1851), potato chips (originally called "Saratoga chips," 1853), strawberry shortcake (1855), and dessert out of a hand-cranked ice cream machine (1846); children could enjoy chewing gum (1848).

Customs and fashions were changing as well. At the dinner table, the two-pronged fork was changing to four prongs, and good manners required not using it with the left hand anymore but moving it to the right.

In 1800, only eighteen years before Mary Todd's birth and for the first time in fashion history, a shoe for the right foot was contoured differently from one for the left foot. Trousers began to replace breeches in Paris by 1821, and by 1823, men were transitioning to trousers in America as well. In 1830, stiff white collars would begin to make men's social occasions miserable, while in the same year it became fashionable for women's sleeves to expand enormously. During the 1850s, women sometimes dared to wear those scandalous items of attire called "bloomers." More prosaically, in California's mining camps, more and more men were wearing Levi Strauss's utilitarian creation—jeans.

THE ART OF HEALING—AND KILLING

Sadly, medical science was not advancing at the same rate. Men and women of the nineteenth century were morbid about disease and death, and for a very good reason: no one—least of all doctors—seemed to know what caused disease. More to the point: no one knew what caused one patient to recover and another to die. All people knew was that when a disease hit a given community, some lived and some died. Doctors took credit for the former and blamed God for the latter. Terrible visitations such as cholera took 4,000 lives in New York and the Carolinas in 1831 and 1832. Smallpox killed 13,000 Indians in 1838. And in 1843, yellow fever ravaged the Mississippi Valley, to the tune of 13,000 lives.

Those who could afford doctors were often worse off than those who could not, as misdiagnosis was almost a given, pills were often as big as cherries, nostrums might contain almost anything, and the favorite all-purpose remedy of the day was bleeding the patient with leeches. Not even the high and mighty were spared. When sixty-seven-year-old George Washington contracted "quinsy" (acute laryngitis) on December 13, 1799, his solicitous doctors bled him four times, inflicted garglings of molasses, vinegar, and butter on him, and for good measure plastered a blister of cantharides on his throat. Not surprisingly, he was dead by the next day.

Neither did doctors understand what germs were, what an antiseptic was, or why they should want to keep anything sanitary. On the frontier, baths were rare. One might take a bath or two during the summer months and none at all during the rest of the year. And when baths *were* given—well into the early twentieth century—chances were that the entire family, beginning with the oldest adult and ending with the smallest child, would climb into the same little tub and wash in water that got filthier with each immersion. The folk saying, "Don't throw the baby out with the bath water," resulted from documented incidents of babies drowning in bath water so filthy that no one had noticed they'd slipped under the surface.

The average man in the nineteenth century would go through three wives in a lifetime. Nobody seemed to know why women died so often in childbirth. In the middle of the century, the Hungarian physician Ignaz Philipp Semmelweis (1818–1865) discovered that there was a simple reason why so many mothers died of a particular childbirth complication, puerperal fever: neither doctors nor midwives bothered to wash their hands between patients. The result was that they would carry death on their hands as they moved from one patient to another.

The medical profession so ridiculed Semmelweis for his "theory" that he died young (of a broken heart, some say). It would not be until half a century later that the medical profession would correct the mistake that continued unnecessarily to take the lives of millions of women. Today, women have not only caught up with men in terms of longevity but now outlive men by seven or eight years.

Sadly, though the science of healing had improved little, the science of killing was improving at a dizzying rate. The Lincoln era saw the development of shrapnel (1784), the torpedo (1805), the breech-loading rifle (1811), the steam warship (1814–1815), the Samuel Colt revolver (1833), nitroglycerin (a high explosive, 1833), the Smith and Wesson quick-firing revolver (1854), the exploding artillery shell (which replaced the solid cannon ball, 1860), the fast-firing Winchester repeater rifle (1860), the Gatling gun (an early machine gun so deadly that some prophesied it would make war obsolete, 1861), the rifle-bore cannon (1862), and ironclad warships (1862). Indeed, it was these new killing technologies that would make the Civil War so terrible, especially because the technology of *saving* lives was still so primitive.

ECOLOGICAL CONDITIONS

Ecologically, the United States of the nineteenth century was on the road to unmitigated disaster. So vast did the continent appear at the time that people assumed it would take a thousand years to populate it. Consequently, since the land was perceived as both "inexhaustible" and "cheap," they could with impunity do anything to it they wanted—from neglecting to rotate their crops to chopping down entire forests, from poisoning streams and rivers to damaging beyond recovery irreplaceable natural resources. In the words of Henry Steele Commager:

> The American rarely expected to stay put and had little interest in building for the future. It was easier to skim the cream off the soil, the forests, the mines. . . . For this self-indulgence he paid a high price, and his descendants a higher. Dazzled by the concept of infinity, prodigal of the resources of nature and of his own resources, greedy and reckless, he did more damage in a century than nature could repair in a thousand years.[1]

POLITICAL CONDITIONS

Politically, America had never become one nation. The founding fathers had been against slavery. Indeed they had held a high view of human rights in general. But knowing that bringing up the slavery issue at the very beginning would have cost them any chance at nationhood, they left it alone, and so it became a ticking time bomb for later generations to deal with.

The global climate was changing with regard to slavery. In 1807, the British abolitionist William Wilberforce and his associates pushed a bill through Great Britain's Parliament against slavery. Denmark abolished it in 1792. The French colonies abolished it in 1794. In 1807, Britain's Parliament abolished the slave trade itself. But none of this caused Americans to take a stand against it.

The early history of America was plagued by an ever-present migraine that sabotaged any chances that America might become a united people: slavery. As we shall see, never in Lincoln's lifetime did he experience a day without being impacted by being a citizen of a hybrid nation—half free and half slave.

Cultural Expectations

Lincoln's generation was incurably optimistic. Having never known national defeat, anything seemed possible to these Americans. Even in grinding poverty, the common assumption was that "tomorrow" life would get better and wealth would come sooner or later. Most Americans were more religious than devout. They made hard work into essentially an eleventh commandment. In their minds, shiftlessness was considered to be on a par with cowardice. Whatever increased wealth was thus automatically good.

Fair play was expected of every boy and man. Those who violated that code were expelled from society's good graces. Since most frontier people were unable to read or write, the oral tradition was valued, and storytelling became almost a fine art. Women controlled both education and religion and thus dictated the standards of literature and art.

Paradoxically, Americans on the frontier venerated laws and honor and in general lived by Puritan standards. Purity and female virtue were venerated; chastity was a given. In their minds there was a crystal-clear demarcation between right and wrong. The Bible was universally read and was considered the basic storehouse of society's allusions. Terms such as truth, justice, loyalty, reverence, virtue, and honor were not mere abstractions to them. They were the very fabric of day-to-day life.

This, in brief, was Abraham Lincoln's world.

Pigeon Creek, the Indiana church the Lincolns attended

THE FAITH OF
Abraham Lincoln

*Probably it is to be my lot to go on in a twilight, feeling and reasoning
my way through life, as questioning, doubting Thomas did. But in
my poor maimed, withered way, I bear with me as I go on a
seeking desire for a faith that was with Him of olden time, who,
in His need, as I in mine, exclaimed, "Help Thou my unbelief."*

—ABRAHAM LINCOLN

The morning this manuscript was to be handed over to the publisher, I
chanced to speak with a Navy chaplain friend of mine. When I told him I
was writing a book on the faith of Abraham Lincoln, a faraway look came
into his eyes.

"A number of years ago," he said, "when I was in high school, my history
teacher spent an entire hour telling us the story of Abraham Lincoln's life.
We were all fascinated. When he asked if any of us had any questions, I
raised my hand.

"'Yes?'

"'Uh . . . I'm just a bit curious. You've told us the story of Lincoln's life
but you didn't say anything about God. I've always understood Lincoln was a
very spiritual man. What do you know about that part of his life?'

"There was a long, long silence. Finally he kind of sputtered, 'Well, I
don't know anything about *that!*'"

What that teacher said is so typical of today's secularized take on who
Lincoln was. The modern American culture wants to remove Lincoln's Christianity from his personality altogether. You can see this even in collections
of Lincoln quotations: the spiritual dimension of Lincoln's life is consistently

shortchanged. The same is true in Lincoln biographies and American history textbooks and films.

Certain scholars have taken unwarranted liberties with even well-documented accounts of Lincoln's faith, such as those dealing with the Emancipation Proclamation. Regarding that document Lincoln said, "I made a solemn vow before God, that if General Lee was driven back from Pennsylvania, I would crown the result by the declaration of freedom for the slaves." This precise wording of the quotation, including the reference to Lincoln's vow before God, is corroborated in the diaries of Gideon Welles, then secretary of the Navy, and Salmon Chase, then secretary of the treasury. And yet we see modern scholars changing "I made a solemn vow before God" to "I made a solemn resolve."

Indeed, it sometimes appears that there is a calculated conspiracy to take the life story of the greatest American and pare away most everything that has to do with his high moral character and spiritual walk. Except, of course, anything that tends to debunk it and portray Lincoln as irreligious or an infidel.

All this would be funny were it not so sad. To accept the qualities that have made Lincoln immortal—his courage, integrity, kindness, generosity, gentleness, strength, tact, empathy, mercy, humility, and lack of prejudice—but be unwilling to reference his faith in God, without which these qualities would be but pale shadows of what they came to be, is ridiculous.

And so in this book we will not be minimizing Lincoln's faith in God.

Yet we must simultaneously avoid the other extreme. We must not portray Lincoln as what he was not. To skew his portrait by oversanctifying or orthodoxizing would be just as bad as underemphasizing his faith and would invalidate everything else we say about him.

And so I have sought to strike a balance when it comes to portraying the faith of our sixteenth president.

VERIFYING WHAT LINCOLN ACTUALLY SAID ABOUT HIS FAITH

A problem Lincoln biographers face has to do with authenticating what Lincoln actually said. There is a vast number of Lincoln quotations floating around that cannot be authenticated. Some of them might have helped create a false view of the man's faith—in one direction or the other. In this book I've made every attempt to include only genuine, verifiable quotations, especially regarding his faith. Where there is the slightest doubt, I qualify it with the word "attributed." This does not mean he didn't say it, only that authenticating it has proved difficult.

For instance, one reality we face is that Lincoln, when referring to the Deity, almost invariably uses derivatives of God as the Father of us all—often the "Living God" or "Providence." Rarely does he use "Christ" or "Jesus." Consequently, we are including in this book only those few references to "Christ" that are verifiable.

A Survey of Abraham Lincoln's Faith

With these qualifiers noted, let's take a few pages to explore Abraham Lincoln's spiritual journey. Beginning in chapter three we will be studying Lincoln's life in a chronological fashion, but for the purposes of this book I thought it would be useful to isolate his faith for a moment and look at it alone, apart from the noise and tumult of his fascinating life story.

Note that you may see certain quotations used in more than one spot: here and in later chapters. This was sometimes necessary to support the differing emphases in the diverse sections. Note also that you may encounter in this chapter a name or term that is not familiar to you. In most cases these will be further defined in later chapters.

The Kentucky/Indiana Years (1809–1830)

Child psychologists tell us that half of what we learn in life comes by the time we're six and that our sails are usually set for life by the age of twelve. Therefore these early years of Abraham Lincoln's life—from his birth in 1809 to the time he'd turned twenty-one—are crucial to his faith and to our story.

What we discover is that two women—both unassuming, dedicated, loving, and devout—made possible Abraham Lincoln as we know him: Nancy Hanks Lincoln (Abe's mother) and Sarah Bush Johnston Lincoln (who became Abe's stepmother), interconnected both in spirit and faith, accomplished this quietly, moment by moment, patiently answering each of young Abe's questions as it came. They were never too busy to grant him that bullion of the universe—time.

In those several little log cabins in which they lived, cabins almost devoid of furniture and printed material, the oral tradition ruled supreme. And the Bible had center stage. Thomas, Abe's father, did his best to keep it there. The Bible was generally the only textbook in the so-called blab schools Abe would attend, ever so briefly, during his first eighteen years of his life.

The Bible was so central to Abe's formative years that years later, listeners could detect the rhythmic beat of King James Bible English in his greatest speeches as president, making them sound almost biblical. Though there were certain interruptions, Abraham Lincoln's love affair with the Bible would continue for the rest of his life.

The New Salem Years (1831–1837)

Between the ages of twenty-one and twenty-seven, Abraham Lincoln lived in New Salem, Illinois. These six brief but momentous years—the Vanity Fair of his life—would prove to be a time of searching, of disengaging from Mother and Father, and of extending the tendrils of his mind. He focused on gaining mentors, seeking counsel and wisdom in his quest for meaning, and finding answers to his questions.

During these years he continued to grow intellectually and broaden his literary horizons, most significantly into Shakespeare. But this was also a phase in Lincoln's life during which God ceased to hold center stage of his life. His spiritual growth all but stopped in these years.

The Early Springfield Years (1837–1849)

During these thirteen years, when Lincoln was aged twenty-eight to forty, he would so immerse himself in politics that for a while it would substitute for his lost relationship with God. When he finally returned to Springfield from Washington in 1849, he was a beaten man. He was finding his political religion hollow and without sustaining power. This was the beginning of his wilderness years.

The Awakening (1850–1853)

Lincoln was forty-one when his son Eddie died of consumption (tuberculosis). This was a monumental blow to Abraham Lincoln. This loss, coupled with his failure in the political arena, finally caused Lincoln to reopen communication with God. Certainly God had been there all the time, but Lincoln had put Him on "hold" for twenty-some years.

During this time Lincoln probably thought back to four years previously, to a political campaign in which he'd been forced to respond to an accusation that he was an infidel (an unbeliever). He had answered with these words printed on handbills:

> I have never denied the truth of the Scripture; and I have never spoken with intentional disrespect of religion in general, or of any denomination of Christians in particular. . . . I do not think I could myself, be brought to support a man for office whom I knew to be an open enemy of, and scoffer at, religion.[1]

Now, looking back, he must have thought, "True, I said I had never denied that truth . . . but neither did I say I *affirmed* that truth. Come to think of it, what *do* I believe?"

As we will see, it was at this time, the lowest ebb of Lincoln's relationship with God, that Dr. James Smith came into his life. Smith was pastor of the Springfield First Presbyterian Church. He had written a ponderous defense of God and Christianity, called *The Christian's Defence* [sic]. Lincoln engaged that book fiercely and, with the help of its author, clawed his way back to God—not through emotion or blind faith but through his *mind*.

Witness what Abe wrote to his stepbrother, John D. Johnston, on January 12, 1851, less than twelve months after Eddie's death:

> I sincerely hope father may recover his health, but tell him to remember to call upon and confide in our great and good and merciful Maker, who will not turn away from him in any extremity. He notes the fall of a sparrow, and numbers the hairs of our head, and He will not forget the dying man who puts his trust in Him. Say to him . . . that if it be his lot to go now, he will soon have a joyous meeting with many loved ones gone before, and where the rest of us, through the help of God, hope ere long to join them.[2]

Five days later, Thomas Lincoln died. But his son was once more walking according to the Bible Thomas had endeavored to keep at the center of Abe's early life.

The Thinker (1854–1860)

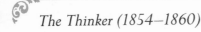

> *Lincoln was the most original of American religious thinkers.*[3]
> —REINHOLD NIEBUHR *(Union Theological Seminary)*

One day during these years, Lincoln experienced an epiphany. The Bible, he realized, was far more than just a religious book—it was a book about *nations*. He discovered that God was not only a personal God but that He cared just as much about the fate of nations as He did about individuals. Once Lincoln realized this, the Bible became immensely relevant to him as he interpreted day-to-day political news.

> Lincoln was drawn to the Bible partly because it deals so largely with events. The divine Ruler is seen throughout both the Old and New Testaments as the God of history. The chief way, Lincoln saw, in which God's will is revealed is not in abstract ideas, but in the development of the story of man's struggles, particularly his struggle to be free. The Israelites *did* become liberated from Egyptian bondage; they *did* occupy the promised land; they *did* prepare the way for the coming of Christ; the infant Christian fellowship *did* survive.[4]

Lincoln couldn't help wondering how it was that Americans could tolerate something as terrible and inhuman as slavery for almost 250 years without taking a moral stand on the issue. As he began to study slavery from a biblical perspective, noting as he did that both abolitionists and slavery advocates supported their positions by referring to the Bible, he discovered to his dismay that nowhere in the Bible is slavery condemned. Yet the very notion that the God he so revered could condone slavery struck him as preposterous. After a great deal of study, he found the answer in the most unexpected of places—in Genesis 1:27: "So God created man in his *own* image, in the image of God created he him; male and female created he them."

Lincoln's logical mind seized on this truth, and then the ramifications became clear. If each of us—no matter what race, color, or sex we might be—is created in the image of God, how then can we legally categorize Negro men, women, and children as mere things? The U.S. Constitution itself referred to slaves at *chattels* and considered a slave as only three-fifths of a person.

Eventually, these thoughts began percolating into Lincoln's speeches.

More and more, he reached back to Independence Hall, when we as a nation articulated to the world for the first time:

> We hold these truths to be self evident: that all men are created equal; that they are endowed by their creator with certain unalienable rights; that among these are life, liberty and the pursuit of happiness.

In an address given at Lewistown, Illinois, on August 17, 1858, Lincoln referred to this great truth when he said that the dignity of man is *derivative*. One writer said: "Man's glory lies not, Lincoln thought, in 'his goodness,' for this is often nonexistent. He derives glory, instead, from his being made in the image of the Living God."[5]

And here Lincoln separated himself from deistic thinkers, such as Thomas Jefferson, who refer to God abstractly as the Creator who simply watches what man does. To Lincoln, God was the "Living God," someone actively involved in all that takes place in the lives of His children.

Lincoln perceived that slavery, at that time existing only in certain states, was on its way to being expanded into all the territories and even into heretofore free states, indeed, into the entire nation; the die was cast. Slavery, Lincoln realized, was a *moral* issue and must be dealt with head-on.

And head-on he would hit it, most noticeably in the definitive speech of his lifetime: the House Divided speech. In this speech, given on June 16, 1858, Lincoln took Christ's words found in Matthew 12:25, Mark 3:25, and Luke 11:17 and thundered, "A house divided against itself cannot stand!" Then he applied Christ's statement to America: "I believe this government cannot endure permanently half *slave* and half *free*."

That one speech would separate him from the pack of political figures. It revealed him to the American people as perhaps the only visionary who had a full grasp of the long-term impact of slavery on the nation and its people.

The Prophet (1861–1865)

He is one of the few men in history, our own history and all history, whose religion was great enough to bridge the gulfs between the sects, and to encompass us all.

—WILLARD L. SPERRY *(Dean, Harvard Divinity School)*

In 1861, admiration for Abraham Lincoln swelled and he was elected president. What is amazing is this: Had Lincoln died in 1857, no one would remember him today. Even had he died three years later, in 1860, he'd merely be the stuff of a Trivial Pursuit game. Thanks to the steepest learning curve in recorded history, the four-year crucible of the Civil War transformed a merely articulate plainsman into "the greatest American of them all."

These four years were also a journey of discovery in terms of Lincoln's personal relationship with God. The very magnitude of the problems facing him drove him to his knees. Humanly speaking, he was facing an impossible task. Emerson, later looking back through the war years, likened Lincoln's role to someone climbing aboard and taking control of a tornado—and not being able to get off for four years!

Without question, Lincoln's real moment of truth occurred on February 11, 1861, at the Springfield railway station. It was a cloudy, stormy morning, mirroring the mood of both the president-elect and the crowd of over a thousand townspeople who had come to see him off. The news from the South had all been bad: Jefferson Davis was laying claim to half of the republic; rumors had it that secessionists planned to take over the capital, keep Lincoln's votes from being validated, and throw the nation into chaos. No known guidebook or map book could help him, for nothing like this had ever happened in America before. He would have been superhuman had he not felt a trembling in his knees.

Suddenly, there came the sounds of ringing bells and a rushing train. As the conductor reached for the starting bell, Lincoln raised his hand to command everyone's attention. Startled, the conductor's hand froze in midair. And the people of Springfield heard for the last time the voice of the man who had dwelt with them for the last twenty-four years. As he spoke, they came to share the ominous conviction of the nation's new leader: That terrible things awaited him on his eastward journey—and in all likelihood they would never meet again:

> My friends, no one, not in my situation, can appreciate my feeling of sadness at this parting. To this place, and the kindness of these people, I owe everything. Here I have lived a quarter of a century,

and have passed from a young to an old man. Here my children have been born, and one is buried. I now leave, not knowing when or whether ever I may return, with a task before me greater than that which rested upon Washington. Without the assistance of that Divine Being who ever attended him, I cannot succeed. With that assistance, I cannot fail. Trusting in Him, who can go with me, and remain with you, and be everywhere for good, let us confidently hope that all will yet be well. To His care commending you, as I hope in your prayers you will commend me, I beg you an affectionate farewell.[6]

Then the conductor rang the bell, and the train disappeared into the falling rain. At every place the train stopped in the long, circuitous twelve-day trip to Washington, throngs awaited him, each person eager to see and hear him and be reassured by him. Each stop lowered an additional weight of responsibility and accountability onto his shoulders.

Looking out the window, as town after town receded into the distance, he had to have prayed, "God, You are all I have to see us through."

INAUGURATION DAY, MARCH 4, 1861

You have no oath registered in Heaven to destroy the government, while I have the most solemn one to "preserve, protect, and defend it."

—ABRAHAM LINCOLN

According to Lincoln's wife, Mary, her husband finished composing the conclusion to the first inaugural speech the morning it was delivered. "The family being present, he read it to them," she wrote. "The family retired to an adjoining room, but not so far distant but that the voice of prayer could be distinctly heard."[7]

Before Lincoln, a long series of presidents had been reluctant to express their hopes and fears in religious terms. In contrast, Lincoln spoke openly about his dependence and the nation's dependence on God. This precedent made it possible for future presidents to refer to prayer, divine guidance, and God without embarrassment or fear of ridicule. Abraham Lincoln was the first openly Christian American president.

By this time, war clouds were hovering over the land. To Lincoln, the oath of office became a very serious thing. As he repeated the following words after the chief justice, a conviction came over him: "I, Abraham Lincoln, do solemnly swear that I will faithfully execute the office of President of the United States, and will, to the best of my ability, preserve, protect, and defend the Constitution of the United States." It was the conviction that these were not mere political words—they were *holy* words, for he had uttered them as a promise to God.[8]

NATIONAL DAYS OF PRAYER

Things did not go well for Lincoln in 1861. On April 14, Fort Sumter capitulated to secessionist forces—the rebels. On July 21, Lincoln and the North were humiliated by the retreat of the Northern army at the Battle of Bull Run. Six days later, Lincoln asked General George B. McClellan to take command of all the Union armies.

In this sober mood, Lincoln, upon the suggestion of Congress, called for a Day of National Prayer. He set it for the last Thursday in November. He chose Thursday because it would not tread on any existing holy days observed by American churches. From this time on, having such events on Thursdays became the norm.

Part of Lincoln's announcement of the Day of National Prayer reads:

> And whereas when our beloved country, once, by the blessing of God, united, prosperous, and happy, is now afflicted with factions and civil war, it is peculiarly fit for us to recognize the hand of God in this terrible visitation, and in sorrowful remembrance of our own faults and crimes as a nation and as individuals, to humble ourselves before Him, and to pray for His mercy.[9]

Lincoln called for national prayer more than once—indeed, he did so whenever he felt the overwhelming need for the country to beseech the Lord God for aid or guidance or to thank Him for providing them. These calls to prayer, fasting, and humiliation—and later to gratitude and thanksgiving—became central acts of Lincoln's presidency. There were nine in all: two in 1861, one in 1862, three in 1863, and three in 1864. He was getting ready to call for a tenth in 1865 when his life was cut short.

As Lincoln continued to study God in the Bible, he became increasingly convicted that nations are just as morally responsible for their actions as are individuals. He believed that Americans would stand before God in judgment *as a people.* Lincoln was convinced that, for its almost 250 years of complicity in human slavery, America would receive a proportionate accounting and penance from God. Lincoln's greatest statement on this subject would appear in his Second Inaugural Address.

1862—A Solemn Vow

On February 20, 1862, eleven-year-old Willie, the pride and joy of both his father, Lincoln, and mother, died of typhoid. This loss, reminding him so painfully of the loss of Eddie twelve years before, plunged Lincoln into the deepest valley of his life. Compounding his anguish, his wife, Mary, withdrew from Abe and their youngest son, Tad. Indeed, Mary would never fully recover from the shock of this second loss. Thus Lincoln was forced to carry on alone. In his heartbreak, Lincoln found solace and comfort only in God and in the faith that he would be reunited with both sons in the hereafter.

The year 1861 had been bad for Lincoln, and 1862 provided more of the same. With war now declared, the rookie president underwent a baptism of fire like no other. A political group composed of aggressive "hawks" castigated Lincoln for not marching armies to Richmond, the capital of the Confederacy, and ending the war. The opposite group, the peace-at-any-price party, declared that it was impossible to defeat the Confederacy and that the thing to do was to make terms with them and let them secede. The Senate Committee on the Conduct of the War told the president in no uncertain terms how the war should be fought. When McClellan retreated after the Seven Days' Battle in Richmond, the vitriol became almost more than flesh and blood could bear. Lincoln said:

> If I were to try to read, much less answer, all the attacks made on me, this shop might as well be closed for any other business. I do the very best I know how—the very best I can; and I mean to keep doing so until the end. If the end brings me out all right, what is said against me won't amount to anything. If the end brings me out wrong, ten angels swearing I was right would make no difference.

On June 24, Lincoln visited his friend and mentor, Winfield Scott. Apparently the president unburdened his heart to the wise old general. Neither man ever divulged what was said there that day, but the counsel must have been clear and to the point, because when Lincoln returned to Washington, he seized control. In quick succession, the president removed McClellan from command, sacked General John Fremont for insubordination, and issued a call for 300,000 three-year troops. Lincoln realized that if he failed to dominate the war effort, others would. And so he used the wartime powers given him in the Constitution to rule with a firm hand for the next two and a half years.

For a long time Lincoln had been wrestling in his mind and with God about the issue of slavery. He had initially been convinced that since the North held the high moral ground on the issue, God would give the Union His blessing. But after a number of military reversals, he was forced to reconsider his opinion. God appeared to be blessing the South with victory after victory. He finally concluded that as long as the North failed to emancipate the slaves, God would not bless its war efforts. If the war were fought just to preserve the status quo—which included slavery—then there was no moral high ground for the North at all!

On Sunday, July 13, riding in a carriage to a funeral in the countryside with Secretaries Seward and Wells, Lincoln confided in them his determination to issue an emancipation proclamation. He had wrestled with the thorny issue of how it could be constitutionally done for a long time, he told them, and had concluded that he already had the power to do it as commander in chief on the grounds of "military necessity"—but only in those areas in open rebellion.

In those states that were not joining the Confederacy, most notably the border states, he currently had no authority to emancipate the slaves. To do so would be unconstitutional because such action could not be covered by "war powers." However, he could do so if Congress would pass an amendment to the Constitution in order to make it permanent. This, he told them, was his strategy.

Lincoln brought his plan to the Cabinet on July 22. Secretary of State Frederick Seward objected. He said that issuing such a document without an amendment or even a recent military victory to give it strength would make the United States a laughingstock. So it was put on hold.

On August 30, as the Second Battle of Bull Run was being fought, Lincoln sat with Dr. Phineas D. Gurley on the back porch of the White House, worrying about the battle outcome. When the strain became so great it was almost unbearable, Dr. Gurley knelt in prayer, and "Lincoln knelt beside him and joined reverently in the petition."[10]

The result of the battle, however, was the same as the First Battle of Bull Run: another defeat, this time with General John Pope in command of the Union forces.

It was shortly after this that John Hay, Lincoln's assistant, went into Lincoln's office when Lincoln was elsewhere and noticed a piece of paper with Lincoln's writing on it on the desk. Lincoln had never intended any other eyes but his own to see it. Yet when Hay read it, he was so moved that he wrote out a copy for himself and kept it secret until long after Lincoln's death. It has since become known as "Meditation on the Divine Will," and is considered to be one of the most profound spiritual documents ever written:

> The will of God prevails. In great contests each party claims to act in accordance with the will of God. Both may be, and one must be wrong. God can not be for, and against, the same thing at the same time. In the present civil war it is quite possible that God's purpose is something different from the purpose of either party—and yet the human instrumentalities, working just as they do, are of the best adaptation to effect His purpose. I am almost ready to say this is probably true—that God wills this contest, and wills that it shall not end yet. By His mere quiet power, on the minds of the now contestants, He could have either saved or destroyed the Union without a human contest. Yet the contest began. And having begun He could give the final victory to either side any day. Yet the contest proceeds.[11]

There is in "Meditation on the Divine Will" no arrogance, no claims that God was on the Union side. But rather we see the articulation of a gut feeling that God—the God to whom both North and South prayed every day—had to have a great purpose in mind, a valid reason for permitting the bloodbath to continue. When Lincoln was asked if God was on the Union's side, Lincoln's unvarying response was that what was *really* important was whether they were on God's side.

Of "Meditation on the Divine Will" Hay maintained that "It was penned in the awful sincerity of a perfectly honest soul trying to bring itself into closer communion with its Maker."

After Pope's debacle at the Second Battle of Bull Run, Lincoln reinstated McClellan as head of the Union army. At about this time, General Robert E. Lee, in command of the army of the South, concluded that the Confederacy's best opportunity to win the war would be to cross the border and attack the North. So this is what he did, and thus began the most desperate hour in the war.

By September 16, Lee and Thomas "Stonewall" Jackson had combined their forces along Antietam Creek, Maryland, and were near enough to Washington, D.C., to make a Confederate victory in the war seem possible and even likely. General McClellan, although having almost twice as many men as Lee, managed only a standoff in this battle. He was content merely to see Lee retreat back across the border into Confederate lands. Over 26,000 men fell at Antietam.

Nevertheless, the Union forces had fought the Confederate invasion to a standstill and had turned the army away. Five days later, Lincoln called his Cabinet together and announced that after wrestling with God over the issue of slavery and the continued casualties in battle after battle, he had come to a conclusion. "I made a solemn vow before God," he said, "that if General Lee were driven back from Pennsylvania, I would crown the result with the declaration of freedom for the slaves." Since he already knew of the division in the Cabinet, he did not even take a vote, as had been his custom.

On January 1, 1863, Lincoln signed the Emancipation Proclamation—as he had vowed to God he would. Hudson Strode, biographer of Jefferson Davis, declared that:

> When Lee crossed the Potomac back into Virginia on that September 19, 1862, the curve of the Confederate fortunes turned decisively downward. Never again was President Davis to know such golden prospects for independence. . . . And if Lee had been victorious the Emancipation Proclamation would have been postponed and probably never have been issued.[12]

The Guiding Hand—1863

It is fortunate that the leader of the nation in its time of greatest internal division was a thinker as well as a politician. . . . The way in which the Emancipa-

tion Proclamation was originated, developed, and superbly timed, far from being accidental, was the product of reasoning concerning both order and justice.

—Reinhold Niebuhr

Students of human nature are often staggered by Lincoln's story. While most people begin to plateau and even decline intellectually as they enter their fifties, this is when Lincoln experienced the greatest growth of his lifetime. Lincoln scholar Nathaniel Stephenson said:

> Lincoln's final emergence was a deeper thing than merely the consolidation of a character, the transformation of a dreamer into a man of action. The fusion of the outer and inner person was the result of a profound inner change. . . . Lincoln grew immeasurably as he came to think of himself as an "instrument of God's will.". . . The sense that there really is a Guiding Hand, which makes possible a genuine calling for both individuals and nations, gave a tremendous new sense of moral strength. It was not enough to watch events and to muddle along day by day. What was more important, Lincoln came to believe, was the effort to discern a pattern beneath the seeming irrationality of events. He had come to really believe that God molds history and that He employs erring mortals to effect His purpose."[13]

On May 4, a Union force led by Joseph Hooker experienced a devastating defeat at Chancellorsville, Virginia. But for the South it proved to be a Pyrrhic victory, for in that battle Stonewall Jackson was killed by friendly fire. That catastrophic loss proved to be the real turning point of the war.

On July 1, 1863, Lee had once again invaded the North, bringing his army to the obscure hamlet of Gettysburg, Pennsylvania. If he had defeated the Union army there, then Harrisburg, Philadelphia, Baltimore, and Washington would all have been in range of his forces. At the very last minute, Lincoln gave the responsibility of stopping Lee to George G. Meade. Everyone sensed this would be "the big one."

For the first time in the war, nothing would go right for Lee. The battle was a major defeat for the South. Two days later Lee retreated, never again to take his army across the Potomac. So pivotal was Gettysburg that military historians consider it to be one of the most decisive battles ever fought.

There is a little-known story from this battle, a story that further illustrates Lincoln's faith. During the Battle of Gettysburg, one of the Union commanders, General Sickles, was wounded. He was brought to Washington, where one of his legs was amputated. President Lincoln visited him. As the two men discussed the battle, Sickles asked the president what his thoughts had been when word had reached him about the two great armies closing in on each other.

Lincoln responded that when so many around him were panic-stricken, he went into his room, locked the door, knelt down, and prayed. "I told Him that this was His war," Lincoln said, "and our cause His cause, but we couldn't stand another Fredericksburg and Chancellorsville." The Union had suffered 12,653 casualties in the former battle and 17,287 in the latter. After his prayer, Lincoln declared that he sensed all would go well. All *did* go well, in that the Union won the key battle of the war—but still 43,449 men died, making it the bloodiest battle of the Civil War.[14]

Though the war would not end until 1865, the tide had turned for the North, and the president could begin tending to other matters. On September 28, Sara Josepha Hale, the editor of *Lady's Book*, wrote the president asking for an appointment. She proposed that the president set up a national celebration of Thanksgiving. Thanksgiving, though originating in colonial days, had been only sporadically observed in the decades since—and never at a set time. After the victories at Gettysburg and Vicksburg, Lincoln was convinced that there was much to be thankful for, and he agreed to her proposal. Thus the annual holiday of Thanksgiving came to be an integral part of American life.

That first Thanksgiving Proclamation neither asked people to assemble in their customary places of worship nor called them to prayer as Protestants, Catholics, or Jews. Rather it called all Americans to gather as members of one common family to give thanks. They were to assemble on the third Thursday of November in any secular building they should choose. According to Lincoln biographer Elton Trueblood:

> Lincoln was taking seriously the idea which had grown upon him for a long time, that God is able to call a *nation*. God, he believed, calls a nation to service, especially that of liberation from bondage of all kinds, but He also calls the nation to prayer. . . . After years

of mental struggle, Abraham Lincoln was at last performing a prophetic role. With characteristic honesty, he did not ask the people to engage in practices in which he did not, himself, engage.[15]

Speaking of Lincoln's nine public Proclamations, Trueblood declared that:

What is increasingly obvious is that he attempted to express a faith for the entire people, regardless of denominational affiliation. His appeal was directed to Jews as well as Christians. He did not hesitate, on some occasions, to refer to Christ as the "Savior." But as president of the whole people he sought to point primarily to the One whom Christ revealed, and who, he believed, is the Father of all.[16]

Just days before Thanksgiving, on November 19, on the battlefield of Gettysburg, Lincoln joined tens of thousands in dedicating that battlefield's cemetery. Edward Everett's main speech took two hours—Lincoln's Gettysburg Address was only 272 words long. There was nothing in the Gettysburg Address that refers to either the town or the battle. Allan Nevins noted that Lincoln:

chose to speak not to his country alone but to aspirants for freedom in all countries, and not to his own moment in history but to the centuries. The proposition that all men are created equal was a truth for the ages, and if America, under God, achieved a new birth of freedom, it would stand as an object lesson to all nations.[17]

The Gettysburg Address ends with these words:

[W]e here highly resolve that these dead shall not have died in vain—that this nation, under God, shall have a new birth of freedom—and that government of the people, by the people, for the people, shall not perish from the earth.

Interestingly enough, Trueblood points out that the words "under God" do not appear in Lincoln's speech notes. Evidently, Lincoln added them extemporaneously. In Lincoln's day, those two words were not in general use.

Today, we honor those two words of Lincoln every time we recite the Pledge of Allegiance to the Flag.

We may also think of Lincoln every time we look at one of our coins or paper bills. The words "In God we trust" were first used during Lincoln's administration.

WITH MALICE TOWARD NONE

Mr. Lincoln, that was a sacred effort.
—FREDERICK DOUGLASS

The city of Washington had never seen so many people as those who thronged it during that first week of March. Lincoln had been reelected president, and people were coming in droves to hear his second inaugural speech. By March 2 there were so many that no one knew where to put them. Compounding the problem was the fact that Washington had become a vast hospital for those wounded in the war. In the Capitol building alone, 2,000 cots lined its halls and filled the great rotunda.

It had been raining for days. The tens of thousands of people who slogged toward the Capitol in ten inches of mud that memorable morning were worried they wouldn't even get to hear the president. The rain was coming down in torrents, and if it didn't stop, Lincoln would be forced to speak inside. And, remarkably, fully half the crowd was black. For the first time in 246 years they could be there to hear *their* president.

Everyone wondered what the president would say. Historian Ronald C. White, Jr., in his splendid book, *Lincoln's Greatest Speech, The Second Inaugural*, noted that many wondered if the speech would at least be thirty-five minutes long, as the First Inaugural Address had been.

There were so many questions to be answered. Would the president take this opportunity to castigate those who'd made his life hell by the terrible things they'd said and written about him? Would he gloat over his accomplishments now that the South was in shambles and the war all but over? Would this be the time he would articulate revenge for all the suffering the South had inflicted on the nation? After all, the South was now all but a conquered nation, its economy in ruins, and the cream of its young men dead or disabled. Would he speak about the freed slaves? Would they be given suffrage?

Then the great moment came. In author Ronald C. White's words:

As Lincoln rose, he put on and adjusted his steel-rimmed glasses. He held in his left hand his Second Inaugural Address, printed in two columns. . . . Precisely as Lincoln began to speak, . . . a star made its appearance . . . over the Capitol and it shined just as bright as it could be. Just at that moment the sun, which had been obscured all day, burst forth in its unclouded meridian splendor, and flooded the spectacle with glory and with light.[18]

Lincoln then began to speak. Here is the core of his Second Inaugural Address:

Both parties deprecated war; but one of them would *make* war rather than let the nation survive; and the other would *accept* war rather than let it perish. And the war came. . . .

Both read the same Bible, and pray to the same God; and each invokes His aid against the other. . . . The prayers of both could not be answered; that of neither has been answered fully. The Almighty has His own purposes. . . . If we shall suppose that American Slavery is one of those offences which, in the providence of God, must needs come, but which having continued through His appointed time, He now wills to remove, and that He gives to both North and South, this terrible war, as the woe due to those by whom the offence came, shall we discern therein any departure from those divine attributes which the believers in a Living God always ascribe to Him? Fondly do we hope—fervently do we pray—that this mighty scourge of war may speedily pass away. Yet, if God wills that it continue, until all the wealth piled by the bondsman's two hundred and fifty years of unrequited toil shall be sunk, and until every drop of blood drawn with the lash, shall be paid by another drawn with the sword, as was said three thousand years ago, so still it must be said "the judgments of the Lord are true and righteous altogether."

With malice toward none, with charity for all; with firmness in the right, as God gives us to see the right, let us strive on to finish the work we are in; to bind up the nation's wounds; to care for him who shall have borne the battle, and for his widow, and his orphan—to do all which may achieve and cherish a just, and a lasting peace, among ourselves, and with all nations.[19]

The second inaugural speech is not only the greatest state paper of the nineteenth century and one of the greatest speeches in world history, it has also become a theological classic. Though only one-fifth as long as the first inaugural speech, it is far more memorable. There is a grandeur in Lincoln's prose that had not existed four years before.

As Lincoln looked back to Gettysburg, the battle that so easily could have gone the other way, he had to have thought, *What if?* That it did not go the other way, Trueblood maintained, was because:

> of the Guiding Hand of God. The occasion on March 4, 1865, gave Lincoln his best opportunity to state the Biblical faith which, by this time, had come to form the center of his conviction. It included fourteen references to God, many scriptural allusions, and four direct quotations from the Bible. It is difficult to think of another state paper so steeped in Scripture and so devoted to theological reflection.[20]

Readers around the world were quick to realize its greatness. Even the London *Spectator*, so often negative about Lincoln and the war, remarked:

> We cannot read it without a renewed conviction that it is the noblest political document known to history, and should have for the nation . . . something of a sacred and almost prophetic character. Surely, none was ever written under a stronger sense of the reality of God's government, and certainly none written in a period of passionate conflict ever so completely excluded the partiality of victorious faction, and breathed so pure of a strain of mingled justice and mercy.[21]

The key sentence is this: "The Almighty has His own purposes"—a direct outgrowth of what he had written in "Meditation on the Divine Will" two and a half years before. In essence, Lincoln was saying that "though with our limited understandings we may not be able to comprehend it, yet we cannot but believe that He who made the world still governs it." The God of the second inaugural speech is not only a Living God, He is also personal and fully involved in contemporary history.

Lincoln was assassinated forty-one days later.

Trueblood pointed out that though the assassination of Lincoln was tragic, how much more so it would have been had it taken place two months earlier and the nation and the world had been deprived of the full flowering of Lincoln's mind, heart, and soul.

The speech is significant in that in it the president articulated how he would have treated the Southerners had he lived. In short, he would have treated them as though they had never left the Union at all—as though they had, like Christ's Prodigal Son, simply come home.

Winston Churchill declared that "the death of Lincoln deprived the Union of the guiding hand which alone could have solved the problems of reconstruction and added to the triumph of armies those lasting victories which are gained over the hearts of men."[22]

THE PROPHET PRESIDENT

In the generations since Abraham Lincoln's death, people have come to perceive him as our only prophet president. He was, in a sense, a Moses—an executive and legislative genius who led his people through unbelievable perils. He was also a Samuel, first prophet of the Old Testament, in that he served as military advisor and father figure and even as a prophet-king. He was a Daniel, prophesier and imperial executive. And he was a Jeremiah because, like the "weeping prophet" of the Bible, Lincoln was a prophet of anguish.
So much more could be said about the life of Abraham Lincoln, the first president to speak openly of his Christian faith. Of the untold thousands of summations of Abraham Lincoln's life, it would be difficult indeed to match that of Joseph Fort Newton's:

> Events marched rapidly; the slaves were freed; the armies of the
> South melted away; and the hand that guided the war was held out
> in brotherly forgiveness. Perhaps the men of the future, looking back
> from afar, unbiased and clear-eyed, will say that the noblest feat of
> the genius of Lincoln was the policy he outlined for dealing with the

South after the war. There was no rancor in it, no gleam of selfish pride in power, but a magnanimity in triumph that led Tolstoi to say that he was "A Christ in miniature." His words had in them, towards the end, a tenderly solemn, seer-like quality of blending prophecy and pity. There was in him, then, something of that touch of gentleness in sadness, as if presaging doom; and this is what men felt when they caught his eye, which so many said they could never forget. His death, coming at such an hour, filled the nation with an awe akin to that evoked by the great tragedies—something of inevitability, much of mystery, as impossible to account for as it is to measure the heavens or to interpret the voices of the winds.[23]

Now we come to the part of the book where we explore Lincoln's life in a chronological, biographical fashion. It is my hope that this brief survey of his faith will allow you to spot its impact and trajectory amid the noise and fury of the details of his life.

PART TWO

THE MAKING OF

Abraham Lincoln

Abraham Lincoln, Monmouth, Illinois, October 11, 1858

*Cabin in which Lincoln was born, near Hodgensville, Kentucky
(February 12, 1809)*

CHILD OF THE
Frontier

All that I am or hope to be, I owe to my angel mother.

—ABRAHAM LINCOLN

It had been a tough voyage—two long months cooped up in a little box of a ship with more passengers than it was built to accommodate. Some had become violently seasick during periodic storms or turbulent waters. Seventeen-year-old Samuel Lincoln leaned over the railing and thought back over the last year.

Trouble, trouble, and nothing but trouble. For eight years King Charles had refused to let Parliament meet, and life for Puritans had so deteriorated that the exodus to the New World had never slowed. Seventeen years ago it was, the year I was born, when the Mayflower first landed on these shores. Never thought I'd ever join them. When Father apprenticed me to the Hingham weaving-master, Frances Lawes, I hadn't even an inkling he'd already caught New World fever. But once he started working on me, I could hardly control my excitement. After all, with two brothers and a cousin—Thomas, Daniel, and Nicholas Jacob—already over there, I wouldn't be lonely. New Hingham—even the name of their little settlement would be the same. But even so, it was hard to leave home; after all, five generations of Lincolns have lived in dear old Hingham.

Suddenly, someone broke into his thoughts: "Land Ho!" Sure enough, far ahead he saw the dim outline of the misty coast of the Puritan's Promised Land—Massachusetts.

Young Samuel would soon marry Martha, a fellow colonist, and build a home large enough to house all thirteen of their family. Eight of their children (four boys and four girls) would survive to adulthood. Three of their descendants would become Commonwealth governors.

One of Samuel's grandsons, Mordecai Lincoln, moved to Berks County, Pennsylvania, around 1730, right next door to the Boones (a Quaker family): the squire, George, and Daniel. The Lincoln and Boone children grew up together. Thus it was not surprising that two of Mordecai's children, Sarah and Abraham (not the Abraham Lincoln who became president), married Boones. In time, Mordecai's son John and John's wife, Rebecca, along with a number of the Boones, moved south into Virginia's Shenandoah Valley.

One of their sons, Abraham, grew up and fell in love with the high-spirited Bathsheba Henning. Her aristocratic father threatened to disinherit her if she married Abraham, but she followed her heart and married him anyway. In 1782 she followed him into the Kentucky wilderness on the other side of the mountains, at the suggestion of their kinsman, the soon-to-be famous Daniel Boone. They came with means enough to purchase around 3,000 acres.[1]

Abraham and Bathsheba had known the risks involved in such a move. They knew that Kentucky was called "that dark and bloody ground" for a good reason: the Indians were anything but happy with the steady migration of white settlers into the Ohio River Valley. Certainly Abraham and Bathsheba could not say they hadn't been repeatedly warned about the ever-present danger of Indian attacks.

As time passed, Abraham and his three sons were able to clear considerable land and construct a small log cabin. Since the Indian menace continued, they'd return to the settlement each evening. Even so, never did he leave in a morning without fearing he'd return to find his cabin in ashes and his wife and daughters Mary and Nancy murdered or carried off to a captivity almost worse than death. Bathsheba was just as fearful. What if something happened to her man and she and the children were left defenseless on that wild frontier? The very worst fate that could befall a frontier family.

Indeed, her worst fears were realized. Arriving at his property one fateful day, Abraham sent his two oldest sons, Mordecai and Josiah, to work some distance away, while Thomas, only seven, stayed with him. Suddenly, the stillness of the morning was shattered by a gunshot. Having been drilled by their father many times, the boys wasted not a second.

While the middle brother, Josiah, raced off to the fort to get help, fourteen-year-old Mordecai ran to the cabin. Inside, he seized the rifle and peered out through a loophole. He saw a war-painted Indian standing over his father's body and reaching down to pick up little Thomas. Mordecai took aim at the white ornament on the Indian's chest and brought him down with one shot. Then he retrieved little Thomas and climbed up the pegs in the wall to the loft. Through an aperture he opened fire on the Indians creeping toward the cabin. He was able to hold his own until help came from the fort.

Though the children were saved, Abraham was dead. To Bathsheba, it must have seemed like the end of her dreams. She and Abraham had left the security of the settled East for the frontier West of the mountains, knowing what the price of courage might be. But that was small comfort to her now. The partner who gave meaning to her life and daily shored up her courage was gone. What should she do? Go back home to family and friends? Or risk more tragedy by remaining in the wilderness?

She chose as she knew Abraham would have wanted. She stayed, moving to a more settled region that later became known as Washington County, Kentucky. It was brutally hard for a widow to raise five children alone on the frontier. It was hard, too, for the children. But out of that anguish, out of that sacrifice, came strength and courage in those children.

Bathsheba had no way of knowing—nor did Mordecai—that by saving the life of his seven-year-old brother Thomas, he had made possible the life of the sixteenth president of the United States.[2]

THOMAS'S DREAM WOMAN

I do love an open fireplace; I always had one at home.
—ABRAHAM LINCOLN

Little Thomas would never fully recover from the untimely death of his father. With four other children to care for and no husband to earn a living, it was all Bathsheba could do just to survive. Not surprisingly, Thomas was set adrift. He grew up without much education, surviving by working for whoever would hire him. But Thomas had always been deeply spiritual, convicted that God had a plan for his life.

He was also convinced that God had a wife for him. On the frontier, the norm was to marry young (fourteen to sixteen for girls and fifteen to eighteen for boys). Yet those years came and went for Thomas. But when, in his midtwenties, he came into a portion of his father's estate, at long last he had something to offer.

At first he thought Sarah Bush might be the one. He'd even proposed to her, but she chose to marry another. Finally, he began to wonder if he'd ever find the woman God intended for him. Then, according to Carl Sandburg, there came a strange dream of a path that led to a house he'd never seen before. Inside that house the chairs, the table, the fireplace were as real as though he were awake. At the fireside sat a young woman. As he came closer, he could see clear as crystal her face, eyes, and lips. She was paring an apple.[3]

The next morning, he vainly tried to figure out what the dream meant. Was God trying to tell him something? It so haunted him that he left his brother Mordecai's cabin and took a walk. It wasn't long until the path ahead of him began to look familiar. So did the house at the end of it. The door was open, just as was true in the dream. As he peered in, chills went up his spine: there, by the very same fireplace, the exact woman in the dream sat—her face, eyes, and lips the same. *And she was paring an apple!*

Years later, Thomas told this experience to his son. His son would never forget it.

From that moment on, there was never a doubt concerning the woman God had chosen for his wife. And so the courtship began. It was said Nancy Hanks was beautiful. Though bordering on illiterate, she was extremely intelligent, perceptive, affectionate, and deeply spiritual.

She'd been looking for a man like Thomas: one with staying power, adventuresome, a hard worker (perhaps a carpenter craftsman like her brother Joseph) with absolute integrity who would make God the center of their home. And as an orphan, she longed for a home of her own. So it was that on June 12, 1806, in Beechland they were married. He was twenty-eight and she was twenty-three.[4]

It wasn't much, that first cabin, only fourteen feet square, just off the main street of Elizabethtown. When her work was done, Nancy would sit down under the big tree near the cabin and think about the future. Frail as she'd always been, she knew she wouldn't be able to survive very many children—and the usual family size in Hardin County was fourteen (of the average twelve children, at least half would die in childbirth or from childhood or teenage diseases). Why, within 300 feet from their cabin lived a family of fourteen, including two dogs, a cat, and the village teacher—all in a 14-by-14-foot cabin just like theirs!

It wasn't long before Nancy realized she was pregnant. And thank the good Lord, she survived the delivery of a little girl on February 10, 1807. They named her Sarah. They moved then to a cabin by Sinking Spring, near Hodgenville. It had but one window and one door, swinging on leather hinges, and the floor was dirt.

Then, in the early morning of February 12, 1809, Peggy Walters, the so-called "granny woman," was summoned by Thomas, arriving just in time to help the moaning mother through the ordeal of her second childbirth. What happened next was chronicled by Carl Sandburg:

> A little later that morning, Tom Lincoln threw some extra wood on the fire, and an extra bearskin over the mother, went out of the cabin, and walked two miles up the road to where the Sparrows, Tom and Betsy, lived. Dennis Hanks, the nine-year-old boy adopted by the Sparrows, met Tom at the door.
>
> In his slow way of talking—he was a slow and quiet man—Tom told them, "Nancy's got a boy baby." A half sheepish look was in his eyes, as though maybe more babies were not wanted in Kentucky just then.
>
> The boy, Dennis Hanks, took to his feet, down the road to the Lincoln cabin. There he saw Nancy Hanks on a bed of poles cleated to a corner of the cabin, under warm bearskins.
>
> She turned her dark head from looking at the baby to look at Dennis and threw him a tired, white smile from her mouth and gray eyes. He stood by the bed, his eyes wide open, watching the even, quiet breaths of this fresh, soft red baby.
>
> "What you goin' to name him, Nancy?" the boy asked.
>
> "Abraham," was the answer, "after his grandfather."[5]

The boy, Abraham Lincoln, would have no memories of the Sinking Spring farm. When he was only two the family moved and then moved again, more than once, always to a place much like the next, places not very different from the cabin built by the first American Lincoln, Samuel, for his wife Martha, back in 1637. It would be in cabins like this in which the boy would grow up and become whatever he willed himself to be.

According to Ida Tarbell, the fireplace would be the very heart of the home. The "cat and clay" chimney was made by mixing straw or grass with stiff clay and laying it in alternate layers with split lathes of hard wood. As Abe grew, he'd learn that feeding that fireplace was one of the essential tasks of a pioneer home, and it would be his personal responsibility to gather enough wood to keep the fireplace going all winter. There had always to be logs of at least half a dozen different sizes, green and dry, hard and soft. There had to be chips to kindle a fire and brush to make it blaze. And once cold weather set in, *the fire must never go out,* day or night, since matches had not been invented yet. He'd have to get used to catnaps during the night.

As for cooking, that would take place in a Dutch oven: a big iron pot with a cover, standing on long legs and kept continuously on the coals. Second only to it was a long-handled frying pan. Pretty much everything—salt pork, bacon, venison, rabbit, wild turkey, hot bread, and cakes—ended up in this pan at one time or another. In the summer, Nancy would escape the heat by cooking in the outside fireplace.

It was a self-contained world. Most everything they used, Nancy would make, whether it be lard, soap, or tallow for the candles. She was skilled at spinning and weaving. Rare indeed would be the day when she'd not be found at her loom or wheel, or making garments for Sarah, Abe, Thomas, or herself. She'd spin her own linsey-woolsey. In her "spare" time, over a long period, she'd patch together badly needed quilts.[6]

The third child born to Thomas and Nancy Lincoln died in infancy.

Heaven on Knob Creek

When I read aloud two senses catch the idea: first I see what I read; second, I hear it, and therefore I can remember it better.

—Abraham Lincoln

In 1811, Thomas Lincoln moved again. He was, it seemed, always moving on. But no place was in as beautiful a setting as the place they moved to when Abe was two years old. Only ten miles from Elizabethtown, the deep valley watered by Knob Creek was another world compared with what came before and after.

The boy would follow his father as he tilled his three little fields, the largest being only seven acres, using a wooden plow shod with iron. Even when very small, Abe was taught how to plant corn in evenly separated holes. When little Sarah got old enough, she had to help her mother and learn to milk the cow—more or less on the run. The Lincolns didn't even have a milking stool, but milked into a gourd while walking.

In all his life, Abe would spend less than twelve months in schoolrooms. The "teachers" were normally untrained and at best could help students learn how to spell, read, write a little, and cipher to the Rule of Three. The little log schoolhouse in this new place had a dirt floor, no window, and one door. Since they had no paper on which to write, they could use only chalk on slate. Their only textbook was a Bible. They learned their lessons by saying them out loud until it was time to recite: alphabets, multiplication tables, spelling, all speaking at once. It was bedlam. Such a school was called, with good reason, a "blab school." In later years, Lincoln declared that even so, it was here he learned to write and sign his name.

There was, during this period, one very close call Abe's parents never learned about. According to Abe's classmate, Austin Gollaher, on a Sunday when he and his mother visited the Lincolns:

> "Abe" and I played all day. Finally, we concluded to cross the creek and hunt for some partridges young Lincoln had seen the day before. The creek was swollen by a recent rain, and in crossing on the narrow footlog, "Abe" fell in. Neither of us could swim. I got a long pole and held it out to "Abe," who grabbed it. Then I pulled him ashore.
>
> He was almost dead, and I was badly scared. I rolled and pounded him in good earnest. Then I got him by the arms and shook him, the water meanwhile pouring out of his mouth. By this means I succeeded in bringing him to, and he was soon all right.
>
> Then a new difficulty confronted us. If our mothers discovered our wet clothes they would whip us. This we dreaded from experience, and determined to avoid. It was June, the sun was very warm, and we soon dried our clothing by spreading it on the rocks about us. We promised never to tell the story, and I never did until after Lincoln's tragic end.[7]

But it was the majestic cedar trees of this virgin forest, the rocky heights he loved to explore, and the crystal-clear waters of Knob Creek that so etched themselves into his memories that he carried these years with him always, no matter where he removed to.

Indiana Calls

None are more worthy of being trusted than those who toil up through poverty.

—Abraham Lincoln

Nancy knew the signs. Her husband was restless again.

She was right. Indiana was calling to Thomas Lincoln—for several reasons. First, both of them hated slavery. Kentucky, where they were, was a slave state, but Indiana was free. Then there was that not-so-small problem with Kentucky property: so many layers of overlapping ownership existed that hardly a title in the state would hold up in court. Even Daniel Boone had lost almost everything he owned in Kentucky.

Abe was seven that autumn of 1816 when moving day arrived. No humbler cavalcade ever invaded the Indiana wilderness. Besides the two children, their earthly possessions consisted of insufficient bedding, some clothing, a few pots and pans, and Thomas's rifle and tools. Two borrowed horses represented the transportation. The 100-mile trip would take them a week.

A thick and mighty virgin forest covered the land. Some of the trees were between twenty-five and fifty feet in circumference, towering a hundred feet high, so dense that sunlight rarely reached the ground. The Lincolns were likely to see, at any turn of the path, raccoon, squirrel, opossum, skunk, deer, bear, wolf, wildcat, or panther. Incredible numbers of passenger pigeons filled the skies; one flock was estimated at 250 miles across, taking three days to pass. Swarms of mosquitoes rose from dank, stagnant pools and misty swamps. It was a journey Abe and Sarah would never forget.

After they had crossed the Ohio River, the real work began. Thomas set about felling trees and cutting underbrush and vines through which the oxen would be able to drag sleds or wagons. Over stumps and rocks and across gullies, bogs, mounds, and soggy ground they crept onward until they reached the spot where Abe would spend the next fourteen years of his life.

Pigeon Creek

The best thing about the future is that it comes only one day at a time.

—Abraham Lincoln

Neighbors shook their heads. Why in the world would that new neighbor from Kentucky choose a cabin site so far from water? The nearest spring or creek was over a mile away! Especially did the women empathize with Nancy.

Too late Thomas realized his mistake. And though he poked more holes into the ground than a badger, it was to no avail. Abe would pay the biggest price: he'd spend the rest of his growing-up years lugging buckets of water—several miles each time. Most men would have moved to another place near water once they realized they'd made such a disastrous mistake. But not Thomas. Stubbornly he refused to admit he'd been wrong.

Neither did Thomas start building a cabin anytime soon. He was content with that contraption pioneers called "a half-faced camp"—a shed of poles enclosed on three sides, but wide open on the fourth. Never could the fire be permitted to go out, otherwise wild animals might attack them at night. And how everyone dreaded it when the wind would shift—impossible to breathe inside! This condition lasted an entire year.

What joy it was to see Uncle Thomas and Aunt Elizabeth Sparrow, with Dennis Hanks, pull into the clearing that fall! Now Thomas completed his doorless, windowless, floorless cabin so the Sparrows could take over the half-faced camp. Abe helped. Almost never, it seemed, was he without an axe in his hands.

It was a struggle just to survive, but they made do. Thomas raised enough corn on the land to support life, and the dense forest was teeming with game. The deer he shot provided them not only with food but also material for breeches and shoes (shoes the children rarely bothered to wear, not even in the dead of winter). Not surprisingly, malnutrition resulted from such a diet.

As for furniture, Thomas made a few three-legged stools, and their bedstead consisted of poles stuck between logs in a corner. At night, Abe and Sarah would climb a ladder of wooded pegs in the wall to the loft.

In the cabin were only three books: the Bible, the catechism, and a spelling book. Abe soon knew the catechism and spelling book by heart—and much of the Bible. He wondered sometimes if any other books than these existed somewhere.[8]

Then came the summer of 1818, a date burned into Abe's mind forever. Word drifted through the settlement that the dreaded "milk disease" was moving their way. The disease, caused by cattle eating white snakeroot or rayless goldenrod, poisoned both the cow and those who drank its milk.

One day soon thereafter, the mysterious disease drifted into their clearing. Thomas and Betsy Sparrow (Nancy's surrogate parents) were stricken with it almost simultaneously. Nancy and Thomas ministered to their needs night and day. Alas, it wasn't enough. In late September, both of them died. A spot was suggested for burial, a beautiful nearby knoll. Thomas sorrowfully constructed coffins out of green lumber. Neighbors gathered to say their good-byes, but no preacher could be found to perform the funeral.

A few days later, at about three o'clock in the morning, Abraham and Dennis were asleep in the loft when they were awakened by a sound they'd hoped never to hear again: milk sickness attacking Nancy Lincoln. The boys hurried over to a neighbor's cabin to get help. But this case proved much more virulent than that of the Sparrows. Abe and Sarah saw the white coating on their mother's tongue gradually turn brown, they saw her body consumed with raging fever, her hands grow colder, and her pulse grow slow. They knew there was no hope.

Remembering those tragic days, Dennis Hanks said of Nancy:

She knew she was going to die and called the children to her dying side and told them to be good and kind to their father—to one another and to the world, expressing the hope that they might live as they had been taught by her to live.

At the end, the desperately ill woman spoke directly to her son:

I am going away from you, Abraham, and I shall not return. I know that you will be a good boy, that you will be kind to Sarah and to your father. I want you to live as I have taught you, and to love your Heavenly Father.[9]

And then, on October 5, she, too, was gone. Those parting words would never be erased from Abe's memory.

Only now that the breath had left her did Thomas really *see* her. Their day-to-day struggle to survive had been so demanding he'd failed to comprehend how hard it had been on the frail beauty he'd married. She was only thirty-six years old, and yet in those thirteen years of marriage and three childbirths she'd been battered into old age.

His mind couldn't help but wander back through the years to that prophetic dream he'd had so long ago. She'd come into his life—and gone. For what reason? Why had God sent him to that cabin, to the woman paring apples by the fireplace? But, not being a reflective man, he pushed those memories aside, for now awaited the saddest task of his life: constructing yet another coffin, the third in only days, and burying his wife with the others. Already the cabin seemed cold and empty. *She was not there anymore.* Dimly, he began to value what he'd so long taken for granted.

So once again, Thomas constructed a coffin made of green wood. Once again the neighbors gathered for the sad procession up to the knoll, and once again the earth received its own.

Abe was nine. He'd always been very close to his mother. Now she was gone, and he was devastated. He was numb almost beyond tears. Both adoptive grandparents gone—and now his mother, too. The cabin and the half-faced camp seemed desolate without the singing, Bible-quoting mother all of them had taken for granted. Eventually, Thomas dictated words to his son, who laboriously wrote out a letter to Pastor Elkins of Kentucky to come visit them and preach a funeral service.

Three long months later a stranger on horseback rode into the Pigeon Creek area, asking directions to the Thomas Lincoln cabin. It was Pastor Elkins.

The following Sunday people streamed in from all over the region—in carts, wagons, on foot, and on horseback. The pastor's tribute to Abe's mother finally brought a semblance of peace and closure to the boy.[10]

It was a terrible year for all concerned. Thomas had been struggling to make it here with a wife's assistance; without her, it was almost impossible. Poor little eleven-year-old Sarah was being crushed by the responsibility of running a household for three males. There was no longer anyone to make their clothes, either. Each month that went by found the cabin looking more and more like a pigsty.

It desperately needed a woman.

Thomas decided it was high time he journeyed back to Kentucky.

Indiana cabin in which Abraham Lincoln grew up (windows were added after Sally Bush Johnston came)

A NEW

Beginning

*I had a good Christian mother, and her prayers
have followed me thus far through life.*

—ABRAHAM LINCOLN

A NEW MOTHER

The hundred-mile walk back to Elizabethtown, Kentucky, took a while, but Thomas relished it. It was good to get away from challenges too daunting to face alone. He knew Abe and Sarah would be all right with the neighbors checking in on them. As he went along, he kept mulling over the words he would say to Sally Bush Johnston, his first love. Her husband had died of the "cold plague" in 1814, five years previously, leaving three children behind.

Upon arriving at Elizabethtown, he wasted not a second. He walked straight to the widow's home and dispensed with the preliminaries: "Miss Johnston, I have no wife and you no husband. I came a-purpose to marry you. I knowed you from a gal and you knowed me from a boy. I've no time to lose, and if you're willin' let it be done straight off." [1]

Neither did she romanticize the situation, merely answering him with three stark words: "I got debts."

She gave him a list of those debts. Thomas paid them, a license was issued, and they were married the very next day: December 2, 1819. He was forty-one, she thirty-one.

Trying to explain why the agreement with each other was reached so quickly, many years later, Dennis Hanks observed, "Tom had a kind o' way with women, an' maybe it was somethin' she took comfort in to have a man that didn't drink an' cuss none."

Sally Bush Lincoln, the new bride, must have wondered, as she rode with her new husband on the high front seat of the jolting wagon, *Just what have I gotten myself into? I don't really know this man. True, I knew him years ago, but that was then. Wonder what he's really like now?*

Then, looking back at the three children nearly buried in the stuff brought from home and catching a wistful smile from Tilda: *And what about them? Granted, they need a father, but how will Thomas relate to them? I can just imagine the thoughts running through their heads: Two days ago they hardly knew who Thomas Lincoln was—now he's their father!*

And I can't help wondering too about what it is we're riding toward. The way Thomas described the place, it sounded wonderful—but what if it's not? Well, it's too late now. I'll just have to make the most of whatever comes. God will surely see us through.

But what about Sarah and Abe? Two more children to take care of. . . . And Dennis Hanks—he ought to be about eighteen now—almost a grown man. What a shock it will be to Sarah and Abe to see us! Thomas said he didn't tell them about me because he didn't know if I'd marry him—after all, I'd already turned him down once. Oh my. Oh my!

All this time, Thomas, from his side of the seat, had probably been surreptitiously taking her in. *Sally's a good-looking woman. Only eight years older than Nancy when we married. I'll be surprised if she doesn't have a lot more energy than Nancy ever had. I won't be able to loaf around much. And, goodness me: three more children! Just what I need at my age. Oh, well, like I always say, "If ever you make a bad bargain, just hug it all the tighter."*

A raft ferried them across the half-frozen Ohio River. The air became colder, and the wheels sank deeper into the snow, making it harder for the four straining horses to pull their heavy load.

Five days after leaving home, there ahead of them was a clearing and the cabin Thomas had told her about—but it had no windows, only a deer-skin-covered opening instead of a solid door, and the roof looked like it was unfinished. *Oh my.*

And here they came: her new daughter, her new son. Absolutely silent. As well they should be! *What must the thoughts be that are running through their heads!*

Inside the cabin, her heart sank further: *Not even a floor! How dare Thomas not tell me! Only one room. A crude bedstead—mattress made of moldy-looking*

cornhusks; bedcovers merely animal skins and what looks like rags or unusable clothing. All this time, Thomas saying nothing. Good! I hope he's ashamed of himself for leading me on so! Clambering up the pegs in the wall like a monkey, she reached the loft, filthy like everything else about the place. Just matted leaves, leaves that had been there a long time, she strongly suspected by the odor.

Back on the dirt floor again, she felt like crying. Instead, she made her voice as stern as she could make it. "Tom, fetch me a load of firewood. I aim to heat some water."

The fire blazing, the water heated, Sally tackled first things first. "Sarah, Abe, please come here by the fire." She took in her own brood: John, another Sarah, and her mischievous Matilda. They weren't saying anything, just standing there. *Can't deal with them now, I've got work to do.* Work indeed! Abe and Sarah were in dreadful condition. Their pitiful lack of *everything* did something to her mothering heart.

"Come closer, dears," she said. As she took in the accumulated grime on their faces, hands, and feet and their matted, tangled hair, the very desperateness of their need for her did something totally unexpected in her heart. There would not be, after all, a prolonged period of gradually beginning to care for them and then hopefully loving them over time. Instead, overwhelmed by a rush of love and belonging, she gathered them into her arms—grime, matted hair, and all—and kissed them.

She washed them and untangled their hair. She addressed their bare, frost-cracked feet and their tattered clothing. She made full use of a gourd of home-made soap she'd brought along. *Poor dears! I'll make them look a little more human. And isn't life strange? Many years ago I turned this man down in order to choose another. From that "another" came three children. Thomas later found a woman whom he could love as much as he loved me, and had two children with her. And now, . . . by some strange process only God can understand, Tom and I are together after all, with five children! Dear Lord, you must have a strange sense of humor to do this to me.*

Young Abe couldn't get over it all. When the wagon was unloaded, he ran his thin fingers over such wonderful things as a walnut bureau that cost an unbelievable forty dollars, a clothes chest, a loom, and six *real chairs*! And besides there was a quantity of bedding, crockery, tinware, and ironware. That night, when he and his sister climbed to the loft, they discovered their new mother had tossed out the matted leaves. In their place was a feather mattress, a feather pillow, and a warm blanket.

They almost wondered if they were dreaming.

The next morning they woke to a new life. A force had arrived yesterday that from now on would have to be reckoned with. The word "stepmother" didn't last even a day: by the time they stretched out luxuriously in their feather bed again, that loving woman with rosy cheeks and bright curly hair was . . . well . . . just Mother.

For Sally's part, when she awoke the next morning, everything had changed, too. It would be a beautiful day, for Thomas still loved her. And she remembered from long ago how to manage him. The trick: to keep him from knowing he was being managed. She smiled. The onetime belle of Elizabethtown now rose, dressed, and walked outside to study her new wilderness world. *Let's see, after breakfast, which project should come first?*

That wasn't a hard decision to make. It had to be a puncheon floor! Soon the sounds of axes biting into trees and the sawing that followed seemed to never stop. Next project: completing and strengthening the roof. She even got Thomas to ride off to a town some thirty miles away to purchase window sashes and a solid door. He then filled the cracks between the logs and whitewashed the inside walls.

Meanwhile, Sally began making homespun clothing for her two new children: deerskin britches, moccasins, and a coonskin cap for Abe. When he put on his new clothes, she held up a mirror so that for the first time in his life he could see himself. "Land o' Goshen," he said, "is that *me?*"

Only then did Sally tackle the biggest problem of all: taking two sets of children and an eighteen-year-old nephew and somehow making a family of them. First, their names. There were now three Sarahs in the 18-by-18-foot cabin. Wouldn't do for all three to come running every time someone called for "Sarah." She settled the matter by deciding to go by her earlier nickname, "Sally." Thomas's daughter, Sarah, could keep that name. And her own daughter could go by her other name, Elizabeth. John was just John, and Matilda they'd called Tilda ever since she'd been a baby. As for making them into a family, if she just loved each one equally, as though all five had always been hers, how could they help but become a family?[2] It worked. Like yeast, her mothering love changed everything.

Well, almost everything. Thomas would always remain Thomas, doing enough to get by but never enough to have a surplus of anything. As a result, the family larder was permitted to get very low sometimes. Once, when all they had to eat was potatoes, and Thomas had said the blessing, Abe added, not quite under his breath, "very *poor* blessings."[3]

To Abe, either something was true or it wasn't, and either you were honest or you were not. This was a lesson he taught Tilda one morning. Abe had left early, a sharpened axe on one shoulder and his lunch in his hand, planning on spending the entire day felling trees. Tilda, who loved her new brother dearly, was always begging to come along, but her mother refused to let her go. But on that particular morning, Tilda, being "young and frolicsome," sneaked out on mouse-quiet feet and followed Abe down the deer-path.

He, little dreaming that a little girl was sneaking up on him, went singing along his way. When Tilda got within a couple feet of him, impishly she decided to surprise him. So she darted forward and, with a catlike leap, landed squarely on his back. With one hand on each shoulder, she planted her knees in the middle of his back and dexterously brought the powerful rail-splitter to the ground. It was a trick familiar to every schoolboy.

But in the fall to the ground, the sharp edge of Abe's axe embedded itself in Tilda's ankle, inflicting a bloody wound. Abe quickly tore off pieces of cloth from his shirt and from her dress to staunch the flow of blood.

When her weeping finally subsided, Abe looked sorrowfully down on her with blank astonishment. He knew that his sister's disobedience would cause a real disturbance when she got home. "Tilda, what are you going to tell your mother about how you got hurt?"

"Tell her I did it with the axe," she sobbed. "That will be the truth, won't it?"

"Yes, that would be the truth, but not *all* the truth. Tell the whole truth, Tilda, and trust your good mother for the rest."[4]

Of her brother, Tilda would later say, "He was good to me, good to all. . . . Abe seemed to love Everybody and Everything; he loved us all, and especially Mother."

It was true. Years later, Abe would say, of the encouragement he'd always received from his mother, "She was my best friend in the world, and no son could love a mother more than I loved her."[5]

Dennis Hanks said of his new mother:

In a few weeks all had changed; and where everything was wanting, now all was snug and comfortable. She was a woman of great energy, of remarkable good sense, very industrious and saving, and very neat and tidy in her habits, and knew exactly how to manage children. She took an especial liking to young Abe. Her love for him was warmly returned, and continued to the day of his death. But few children loved their parents as he loved his stepmother. He was encouraged by her to study, and any wish on his part was gratified when it could be done. The two sets of children got along finely together, as if they had been children of the same parents. Mrs. Lincoln soon discovered that Abraham was a boy of uncommon natural talents and that, if rightly trained, a bright future was before him, and she did all in her power to develop those talents.[6]

Years later Dennis married Elizabeth, who would have been about fifteen at the time, making Sally Lincoln his adoptive mother *and* his mother-in-law.

Without question, the coming of Sally Bush Lincoln dramatically changed the course of Abraham Lincoln's life. She gave him a future.

Indiana School Days

I feel the need of reading. It is a loss to a man not to have grown up among books. . . . Books serve to show a man that those original thoughts of his aren't very new after all.

—Abraham Lincoln

Abe's schooling was always in such short segments so agonizingly far apart. With a Mr. Dorsey, Abe learned arithmetic and "spelling for places" (his classmates called it "trapping," as they trapped up or down the line depending on how well they spelled). Abe always "trapped up," for he never misspelled a word.

Four years later, Abe was able to study again for a brief period, this time with Andrew Crawford. Crawford was the first teacher to break through to the boy, motivate him, get him to stretch his wings. He was most impressed with Abe's honesty. Nothing could induce him to tell even a partial lie.

As Crawford spoke with Abe's parents about the boy's future, he quickly discovered that while he had an ally in Sally, in Thomas he had only a father determined to keep his son uneducated and on the farm. From this time on,

Abe and his mother drew ever closer, and the gap between father and son continued to widen.

Abe's favorite books early on were the Bible, *Aesop's Fables*, *Robinson Crusoe*, *The Pilgrim's Progress*, a *History of the United States*, and Parson Weems's *Life of Washington*. To Abe, books were windows to a vast unknown he yearned feverishly to know.

Sally Lincoln observed this hunger:

He read diligently. He read everything he could lay his hands on, and when he came across a passage that struck him, he would write it down on boards, if he had no paper, and keep at it until he had got paper. Then he would copy it, look at it, commit it to memory, and repeat it. He kept a scrapbook, into which he copied everything which particularly pleased him.[7]

Of this trait, Lincoln later observed, "I am slow to learn and slow to forget that which I have learned. My mind is like a piece of steel—very hard to scratch anything on it, and almost impossible after you get it there to rub it out."

Not surprisingly in a virtually illiterate society such as the Indiana frontier, books were in extremely short supply. Consequently, if Abe heard about the existence in the region of a book he'd never read, he'd walk many miles just to borrow it.

One such book, Parson Weems's *Life of Washington*, got him into trouble. After borrowing it from Josiah Crawford, who lived a number of miles away, he read it with such eagerness that when he climbed the pegs to the loft, he took the book with him and read far into the night until the nubbin of the tallow candle sputtered out. Then he placed the book between two of the logs of the cabin so that he could continue reading it at dawn. Unfortunately, in the middle of the night, a violent rainstorm came up. When he awoke in the morning, he discovered to his dismay that the book was sopping wet.

After drying it as best he could, he walked out to Crawford's farm and with great trepidation told his story. Since he didn't have any money, he offered to work off the value of the wrecked book. Crawford fixed the price. Abe pulled corn for three days and became owner of the fascinating book. Over and over he read the story of the greatest American of them all—his exploits, adventures, and virtues.[8]

Following the plow in breaking the prairie sod, he pondered Washington's story and longed to imitate him. It was while reading—indeed, memorizing—the book that Abraham Lincoln first began to dream of himself becoming a doer of great deeds. Why could he not also become a soldier and a patriot? Bred in solitude as he was, brooding and thoughtful, he began turning over in his mind how such a dream might someday come true.

He had no illusions as to the odds stacked against him, poor and uneducated as he was. Eventually, having wrestled with the subject for many months, he came to a solid conclusion: the only way for him to achieve such an unlikely dream would be to build a foundation under that dream. To take advantage of every moment, reading every book that came his way—not merely read but internalize it, so it became part of him. Going to school "by littles," as he put it, he also realized he would be forced to be his own educator. If he was to become the success he envisioned, it would not happen by chance but rather because he'd so prepared himself that when the great do-or-die moment came, he would be ready to seize it.

Many years later, after he'd learned that even Washington had flaws, Lincoln observed rather wistfully, "Let us believe, as in the days of our youth, that Washington was spotless; it makes human nature better to believe that one human being was perfect: that human perfection is possible."

Spelling, Manners, and Moonrise

I could not have slept if I had not restored those little birds to their mother.
—Abraham Lincoln (*after leaving a group of friends to pick up a*
fledgling, climb a tree, and tenderly return the bird to its nest)

Abe's classmates were quick to note that the tallest among them was absolutely intolerant of any mistreatment of animals. He would get especially angry when boys would catch terrapins (freshwater turtles) and put coals of fire on their backs. Once, when a cruel classmate threw a terrapin with such force at a tree that it all but crushed the animal, Abe fiercely turned on him, orating on the inhumanity of such treatment of defenseless creatures, holding up the boy to such scorn that none of those there that day ever forgot it.

One day, in a spelldown, Teacher Crawford spoke the word "defied." The girl to whom it was given, spelled it "d-e-f-i-d-e," the next one "d-e-f-y-d," the third, d-e-f-y-e-d." Crawford became angry. "What!" he bellowed, "these big boys and girls not able to spell the simple word 'defied'! There shan't one of you go home tonight if you don't spell it, you lazy, ignorant louts!"

Next in line was a pretty girl by the name of Katy Roby, upon whom Abe had a bit of a crush. Katy, not having the remotest idea of how to spell it and scared to death of bringing Crawford's accumulated wrath down on her head, in desperation turned to the best speller in the region. Describing the moment later, she remembered:

> I saw Abe at the window; and he had his finger in his *eye*, and a smile on his face. I immediately took the hint that I must change the letter 'Y' into an 'I.' Hence I spelled the word, and the class was let out.

Though Katy later declared she and Abe were never in love with each other, they greatly enjoyed strolling down to the river in the evenings. Here they liked to sit on the bank, dangle their feet in the water, and watch the moon come up:

> One evening, our discussion turned to planets. I didn't suppose that Abe, who had seen so little of the world, would know anything about them, but he proved to my satisfaction that the moon did not go down at all—that it only seemed to; that the earth, revolving from east to west, carried us under, as it were. "We do the sinking," he explained, "while the moon is comparably still. The moon's sinking is only an illusion." I at once dubbed him a fool, but later developments convinced me that I was the fool, not he. He was well acquainted with the general laws of astronomy and the movements of the heavenly bodies, but where he could have learned so much . . . I could never understand.

Some years later, Katy would marry another classmate, Allen Gentry.[9]

But school days were permitted to take all too little of Abe's growing-up years—his father made sure of that. In fact, at the very time when Abe was so desperate for learning, Thomas hired him out to whoever would buy his services in the community, in spite of his mother's expressed desire for him to continue his studies.

Of all the duties assigned him, Abe most enjoyed riding the horse to the mill. It was such a change from chopping down trees. Besides, he loved to watch the mill's primitive and cumbersome machinery and study how each piece of machinery worked.

One day, when he was around nine, he took a bag of corn, mounted the flea-bitten gray mare, and rode leisurely to Gordon's Mill. His turn didn't come until late afternoon. Since each man was expected to provide his own power, Abe hitched the mare to the arm. As the animal moved around, the machinery responded with proportional speed—or lack of it. Abe, mounted on the arm, found it necessary to frequently use his whip, otherwise, the horse would stop. Each time the whip action took place, Abe would say, "Get up, you old hussy." Finally, resenting Abe's whip, just as the words, "Get up" were said, the horse elevated a shoeless foot and kicked him in the forehead, sending him sprawling.

Mr. Gordon, the miller, hurried into the ring, picked up the senseless boy (whom he took for dead), and sent for his father. His father came, loaded the body in the wagon, and took him home. Abe lay unconscious all night, but toward day there were signs of life. The blood beginning to flow normally, his tongue struggled to loosen itself, his body jerked for an instant, and he awoke, blurting out the other three words interrupted at the mill, "you old hussy."[10]

Lincoln would talk about this strange phenomenon for the rest of his life, this memorable experience that so easily could have been his last. God must certainly have had a reason for sparing his life.

Abe Grows Up

It really hurts me very much to suppose that I have wronged anybody on earth.
—Abraham Lincoln

When Abe was eleven, his body began to change. From that time on, he grew so fast that it was almost impossible for his mother to keep him in clothes that fit. As plainsmen put it, he was "shooting up into the air like green corn in the summer of a good corn year." Others contented themselves with "Land o' Goshen, that boy air a'growin'!" In an age when most men grew to midway between five and six feet, Abe seemed to be a veritable giant, reaching nearly six feet four inches by the time he was seventeen.

His feats with the axe became legendary. The insides of his hands developed calluses as thick as leather. Over time he'd so mastered the art of woodcutting that it caused one neighbor to comment: "Abe can sink an axe deeper into wood than any man I ever saw." Another said, "If you heard him fellin' trees in a clearin', you'd say there was three men at work by the way the trees fell."

He developed prodigious strength, too. He would amaze people with his lifting power, once picking up a 600-pound chicken house and easily carrying it to where a farmer wanted it. Another time, it was said he lifted an unbelievable thousand pounds! Today we don't think of Lincoln as a strapping lumberjack renowned for his brute strength, but that was how he was thought of as a young man.

Paradoxically, this strength was matched by gentleness, consideration, and kindness. Going home late one cold frosty night with some of his friends, Lincoln and company almost stumbled over a large shape in a mud puddle. They stopped to see if it was a wallowing hog. Instead, it was a man—dead drunk. They shook him by the shoulders and doubled his knees to his stomach, but to no avail: he just kept on snoring. The wind getting colder by the minute, the other boys declared they were going home.

Abe refused to leave. He stepped into the muck, reached his arms around the drunk, raised all that dead weight to his shoulders, and carried him to Dennis Hanks's cabin. There he built a fire and rubbed the man's limbs until he was warm.

Afterward, the man told everyone, "Abe saved my life. As cold as it was, I'd have been dead before morning."[11]

THE CHRONICLES OF REUBEN

Abraham Lincoln,
His hand and pen,
He will be good,
But God knows when.

—ABRAHAM LINCOLN *(found in childhood notebook)*

Not all of Lincoln's early life is admirable. Perhaps least of all his early habit of writing uncomplimentary letters about individuals he disliked or had a grudge against, then releasing them to the public anonymously. The best-known of such early efforts was born in his animosity against the Griggs clan in Indiana.

The feud began when on January 20, 1828, Abe's sister, Sarah, died from childbirth complications. Abe blamed her husband, Aaron, and the Grigsby family for "neglect"—failing to call a doctor in time to save her life and the life of the baby. In mid-April of 1829, when two of Abe's in-laws—Reuben, Jr., and Charles Grigsby—were married, and Abe was conspicuously *not* invited, so angry was Abe that he determined on suitable revenge: Through a confederate, he implemented a confusion of brides and grooms after the festivities (the grooms entering the wrong bedrooms), to be corrected quickly as soon as the guests had been informed of the "joke." With this incident for a text, Abe wrote an account titled, "The Chronicles of Reuben." According to Beveridge, "This he dropped at a place on the road 'carelessly, lost as it were,' and it was found by one of the Grigsby family. It was anonymous, of course, but everybody knew who wrote it—nobody in the neighborhood but Lincoln could have written it. It was done in imitation of Old Testament narrative, and described the wedding and reception of the Grigsby boys, ending with a bold picture of the mix-up at the close of the merriment:

"'It came to pass when the sons of Reuben grew up that they were desirous of taking to themselves wives, and, being too well known as to honor in their own country, they took a journey into a far country and there procured for themselves wives . . .

"'And when they had made an end to feasting and rejoicing the multitude dispersed, each going to his own home.

"'The family then took seats with their waiters to converse while preparations were being made in two upper chambers for the brides and grooms.

"'This being done, the waiters took the two brides upstairs, placing one in a room at the right hand of the stairs and the other at the left.

"'The waiters then came down, and Nancy, the mother, then gave directions to the waiters of the bridegrooms, and they took them to the wrong rooms."

Needless to say, "The Chronicles" made a tremendous hit in the countryside and was even memorized by many.

Not content with this, Abe followed it up with a rhyme about another brother-in-law, William, who apparently was bald-headed and very ugly. Abe more than did these qualities justice. The result was a free-for-all frontier brawl.[12]

The brawl did nothing to cure Abe of anonymous letter writing. In fact it merely whetted his appetite for more of the same. This habit would bear bitter fruit down the line.

CALL OF THE RIVER

*When a boy I went to New Orleans on a flatboat and there I saw
slavery and slave markets as I had never seen them in Kentucky,
and I heard worse on the Red River plantations.*

—ABRAHAM LINCOLN

There is magic in rivers. When Lincoln was young, most inland commerce moved via river. Before the steam locomotive, towns that had access to rivers grew and towns that didn't have access to rivers died.

Abe had long been fascinated by rivers. So when given the opportunity in 1826 to run a ferryboat across the Ohio River from the mouth of Anderson's Creek, he jumped at the chance. As he piloted it across, the seventeen-year-old couldn't help but think back to the first time he'd seen the Ohio River ten years before. So much had happened since then!

Now there were strange stirrings within him. Even as his body reached full growth, so now his inner horizons began to stretch. People. He couldn't help but be transfixed, especially at night, when steamboats went by—lights from stem to stern, music wafting across the stillness, the sound of laughter. Here was a brave new world that woke a yearning in him, a yearning for he really knew not what.

Abe now became so restless that he hesitated hardly a second when in 1828, two years after his first float trip, James Gentry, the richest man in Gentryville and the town's founder, asked him if he'd be willing to accompany his son, Abe's classmate, Allen, and take a flatboat loaded with produce a thousand miles down to New Orleans.

Thus began the first great adventure of Abe's life. He and Allen soon discovered that controlling one of those unwieldy, sixty- to eighty-foot-long contraptions was anything but easy. They were at the mercy of storms, winds, sandbars, shoals, strange currents, turbulent water, and suddenly appearing islands.

Abe and Allen began learning the tough life of a riverman. Each day they'd float, pole, or steer. And each night they'd tie up to a tree or stump on the riverbank. The Ohio River followed the Indiana/Kentucky border all the way down to Cairo on the Missouri border, where the two great rivers meet. From here on, they'd be on the "father of waters," the Mississippi, floating down the border country of Kentucky/Missouri, Tennessee/Arkansas, Mississippi/Arkansas, and Mississippi/Louisiana to New Orleans on the Gulf.

On a good day, things would go well. The current would bear them Gulfward at a steady rate of four to six miles an hour. They would then relax a little, fry their pork or cornmeal cakes, wash their shirts, and wave as those new river wonders, steamboats, majestically moved past on their fourteen- to twenty-day passage between Pittsburgh and New Orleans. Here, on this main artery of American civilization, they never knew what they might see next.

On a bad day—or night—they might have to face river pirates. Just north of Baton Rouge, along the Sugar Coast, they tied up one evening and dropped off to sleep. They woke to find seven Negro river pirates on board. Their objective: steal the cargo and kill the crew.

Abe then really needed those great muscles of his, for, outnumbered seven to two, it was a life-or-death struggle, and the deck became spattered with blood. Abe wielded a great crabapple-tree club with fierce intensity, and one after another of the assailants was knocked off the flatboat. The ones who remained he and Allen chased into the woods. Abe ended up with a gash over his right eye that would scar him for the rest of his life.

No more rest that night! They quickly untied the flatboat and steered a course down the middle of the river, straining their eyes in the gloom to avoid disaster, for they dared not tie up again until they'd passed beyond that section of the river.

Not long after, they entered the fabled city of New Orleans.[13]

Here they encountered a life they'd never seen or experienced before. They saw mariners from all over the world: Dutchmen, Frenchmen, Swedes, Norwegians, Russians, Spaniards, and Italians—many carrying sharp knives they were quick to use in brawls. Oh, they were all here: sailors, teamsters, roustabouts, rivermen, timber cruisers, crapshooters, poker sharps, squatters, horse thieves, poor whites, prostitutes, and shackled slaves being lashed out of the city toward cotton plantations.

Three months after they'd left, the two young men returned home decorated with scars, armed with new stories, and filled with whirling thoughts of a hitherto-unknown world.

As mentioned earlier, Sarah Lincoln, Abe's only blood sibling, died in childbirth at the age of twenty-one. The next year Thomas decided to move the family again. In the autumn of 1829, with an epidemic of milk sickness approaching, Thomas packed up the Lincolns—including sons-in-law—and set off for Illinois. After he sold his land to James Gentry, by mid-February of 1830 the clan was ready to move.

Even though he was twenty-one and "of age," Abe helped them move one more time. After making one last pilgrimage to the graves of Nancy Hanks Lincoln and Sarah Lincoln Grigsby, he was ready to leave. Though they'd lived in Indiana for fourteen years, tangibly they were leaving with little to show for it. The four oxen, a horse, and wagon loaded with all their earthly goods represented all the thirteen of them had managed to salvage. Intangibly, they had one another—and sweet life.

They crossed the Wabash and Sangamon Rivers on the two-week trek. Since the ground froze at night and thawed during the day, the oxen were frequently slipping, the wagon axles groaning, and the pegs and cleats squeaking.

A dog was left behind one morning as the wagon crossed a stream. It ran back and forth frantically barking, imploring someone to come get it—but refused to enter the icy water. Abe, alone among the family in caring enough for the forlorn animal to do anything about it, took off his boots and socks, waded into the bitterly cold water, gathered the hound in his arms, and carried it across.

They were greeted in Illinois by the "Winter of the Deep Snow," with drifts fifteen feet high. By the next spring the land was one vast lake of melting snow. When Denton Offutt asked if Abe and two kinsmen (John Hanks and John Johnston) would like to take a flatboat down to New Orleans, he agreed. Indeed, he could hardly wait to get out on the river.

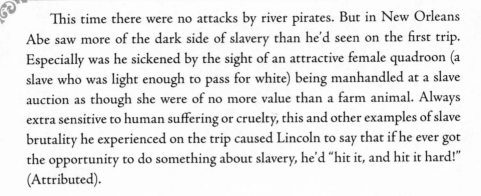

This time there were no attacks by river pirates. But in New Orleans Abe saw more of the dark side of slavery than he'd seen on the first trip. Especially was he sickened by the sight of an attractive female quadroon (a slave who was light enough to pass for white) being manhandled at a slave auction as though she were of no more value than a farm animal. Always extra sensitive to human suffering or cruelty, this and other examples of slave brutality he experienced on the trip caused Lincoln to say that if he ever got the opportunity to do something about slavery, he'd "hit it, and hit it hard!" (Attributed).

Joshua and Fanny Speed

THE VILLAGE OF
New Salem

Time, what an empty vapor tis
And days, how swift they are
Swift as an Indian arrow
Fly on like a shooting star.
The present moment just, is here
Then slides away in haste
That we can never say they're ours
But only say they're past.

—ABRAHAM LINCOLN *(written as a teenager, found later in his copybook)*[1]

BEGINNING A NEW LIFE

I am a slow walker, but I never walk back.
—ABRAHAM LINCOLN

Once the cargo had been disposed of in New Orleans, Lincoln, John Hanks, and John Johnston boarded a northbound steamboat. Sometime later, after disembarking in St. Louis, the trio walked more than a hundred miles clear across the state to the Goose Neck Prairie region of Coles County, which the family had moved to after the terrible winter.

After recounting the story of the voyage to the family, the twenty-two-year-old Lincoln realized his time had come. He was now a man. Whatever he'd accomplish in life would happen not by chance but by deliberate planning, so he began saying his adieus. His mother, Sally, tied up all his earthly possessions in a bundle, and Lincoln, running a stick through it where the knot was tied, was ready to go. It wasn't difficult to leave his father, but it was extremely difficult to leave his mother, the mainstay of his life ever since her coming in 1819.

Struggling to hold back the tears, he stepped out the door and headed for the town of New Salem, a number of walking days away. Across the prairies, his long legs ate up the miles, his head and shoulders showing above tall grass that hid horses, cattle, and men of average height.

Some time after his son left, Thomas remarked to a visitor:

> I s'pose Abe is still fooling hisself with eddication. I tried to stop it, but he has got that fool idea in his head, and it can't be got out. Now I hain't got no eddication, but I get along far better'n if I had.[2]

THE TESTING TIME

Towering genius disdains a beaten path. It seeks regions hitherto unexplored. It sees no distinction in adding story to story, upon the monuments of fame erected to the memory of others. It denies that it is glory enough to serve under any chief. It scorns to tread in the footsteps of any predecessor, however illustrious. It thirsts and burns for distinction, and, if possible, it will have it, whether at the expense of emancipating slaves, or enslaving freedom.

—ABRAHAM LINCOLN *(January 27, 1837, Lyceum Address)*

We have no record of Lincoln's thoughts as he made the hundred-mile-plus trek from Goose Neck Prairie to New Salem. The trip would have taken—depending on his route, pace, and distractions—a good portion of a week. Though we do not know what his ruminations were, we can assume his thoughts meandered in a pattern somewhat like this:

I am free at last! Free to do whatever I want, free to become whatever I will myself to accomplish. Mother—oh, how very much I owe to her! I shudder to think what I would be today had she not come into my life twelve years ago! At least I can thank Father for marrying her. But as for the dream in my heart, Mother shares it—always has, but Father never has. He has no apparent ambition beyond grubbing around in his corn patch and shooting game in the woods.

So, who am I? I don't really know—I've really never been alone before, for more than hours, that is. What do I really believe? Don't know that, either. The Bible? I've memorized so much of it—but how much of it is part of who I am? Again, I don't know. I'm sure, in time, though, I'll know the answer.

One thing I do know: those two trips downriver to New Orleans have changed me. Especially New Orleans. I'd been so isolated up 'til then—had no concept whatsoever of such a world! Everywhere we looked we saw brutality, prostitution, slavery as we'd never seen it before. We saw cheating, abuse of children, thievery, bullying, mistreatment of women, gambling, obscene language—oh, what didn't we see! My mind is still reeling. I felt completely out of place there . . . a lamb among vicious wolves. Dirty. Yes, dirty—I can feel it still.

I'm coming into a little town now. That's an interesting little church . . . I think I'll go over and get a closer look. . . .

It was well worth the stop. What memories it brought back. Good and bad. Some of the ministers I've really liked—even admired. Many of them, even as a child, I felt uncomfortable around. Trying desperately to so frighten us out of hell that we'd choose heaven out of fear instead of love. Even their reasoning made little sense—or rather lack of reasoning. Wondered if they even knew what logic was. And they attacked other churches with such hatred, it revolted me. Didn't we all worship the same God? . . .

Women. Saw a lot of the wrong kind in New Orleans. Some on the steamboat coming home, too. Was I attracted to them? Y-e-s, more than I like to admit. I was especially tempted by one on the steamboat. But not at all the kind of woman I'd want to marry and have children with. Wonder what I'll find in New Salem. Hope there are some pretty ones. . . .

Perhaps in New Salem I'll find out who I am. Perhaps I'll find out if, deep down, I'm a good man—or will I discover my feet are of very weak clay? I'm looking forward to finding out—or am I? I'm so confused. Can everyone my age be this mixed up and not know who they are or where they're going?

The role of Providence in Lincoln's story is so obvious that it almost boggles the mind. Take the village of New Salem, which, in six short years, would set Lincoln's sails for life. Why was the town born shortly before he first showed up here in 1831? Why did it flourish just long enough for Lincoln to get his priorities straightened out and for him to develop a lifelong political following? Why was the town important when Lincoln needed it to be but not before? Why was it that Ann Rutledge would come into his life and leave it in the paths and streets of New Salem? And, coincidence to end all coincidences, why did the town die as soon as Lincoln left it for Springfield?

Now returned from New Orleans, Lincoln once again entered New Salem, a hamlet of fifteen log cabins, in late July 1831. That very first day, an election was going on, and there was need for a clerk who could read and write. Lincoln was given the role. Since most people could neither read nor write, voting was by word of mouth. Each voter told the election judges which candidates he wanted to vote for, the judge loudly called out the voter's name and choice of candidates, and those names were written down by the clerks. Thus Clerk Lincoln, with a goose-quill pen, got acquainted with nearly all the men of the town on his very first day there.

When Lincoln moved into the little village of New Salem, his reservoir of frontier stories made him immediately popular. In fact, within twenty-four hours after his arrival, virtually everyone in town was either repeating or listening to his droll stories.

Denton Offutt, man of big dreams, was the first to see potential in the young man and hire him. When Offutt opened his store in New Salem, Lincoln became his new clerk. But since Offutt was talkative and boastful by nature, it wasn't long before he really put his muscular clerk on the spot. The "Clary's Grove Boys," led by Jack Armstrong (the toughest roughneck in the region), when in their cups periodically terrorized the town. They'd developed a well-deserved reputation as being able to drink more whiskey, swear more lustily, and fight harder than those of any other group that congregated in New Salem every Saturday to trade, gossip, wrestle, pitch horseshoes, run races, get drunk, or maul one another with their fists. New Salem was anything but a quiet, religious country town.

One Saturday, Offutt loudly proclaimed that his new clerk could throw anyone who'd dare wrestle him—and sweetened the pot with a five-dollar bet. Not surprisingly, Jack Armstrong, who'd thrown or whipped every man who'd ever dared wrestle him, accepted the challenge. Lincoln, objecting to being volunteered by someone else for a wrestling match, finally agreed, providing that the contest would be a friendly rather than a violent one.

All New Salem came to watch. For some time the evenly matched contestants wrestled without either one getting the edge. According to Rowan Herndon, an eyewitness:

> After striving a long time without either man prevailing, Lincoln said, "Jack, let's quit. I can't throw you—you can't throw me." Armstrong agreed and the matter was ended in fun. This, indeed, was but natural, for, as one of the band declared, Lincoln's good humor,

wit, and flashing but friendly repartee had already drawn "him into our notice."[3]

If Lincoln had questioned whether he could remain true to his inner convictions in New Salem, Albert Beveridge could have put those fears to rest. After prodigious research, Beveridge summed up his conclusions:

Most astonishing to his militant admirers, Lincoln could read, an accomplishment only of the elect beyond their world. Then, too, he was the best fun-maker they had ever met and kept them laughing at jokes and shouting over roaring tales, not too delicate or subtle for their understanding. Yet he was no "hail-fellow-well-met," never familiar, although not aloof, and always respected the opinions of others. Stranger still: while the Clary's Grove Boys drank prodigiously and swore crashingly, and while Lincoln neither swore nor drank, he did not rebuke his boisterous, rollicking, aggressive associates.

Above all, they found that Lincoln was scrupulously truthful, and honest to well-nigh painful exactitude. What he said could be depended upon absolutely; and Lincoln's name "Honest Abe" became a synonym for fair dealing. Indeed, precise truthfulness and meticulous honesty were his most striking characteristics. So just was he that, on the regular Saturday holidays, Lincoln always was agreed upon as judge of contests of every kind and his decision accepted without question. Finally, and not least in the eyes of the Clary's Grove Boys, he stood by his friends—and with force if force were necessary. Lincoln became their hero, as much beloved as he was admired.[4]

They were also in awe of his enormous strength: he was reputed to have lifted a box of stones weighing over half a ton at Rutledge's Mill.

It is intriguing to note that though many in later life commented on his prodigious strength, common perception was that he was merely a tall, spindly beanpole of a man. Indeed it was not until Lincoln was dying and had been stripped by his doctors that no less an intimate than Gideon Welles, secretary of the Navy, was suddenly struck by the president's muscular torso, especially his arms.[5]

But Doris Kearns Goodwin points out an incident three years earlier that revealed he had the strength of a giant. In May of 1862, aboard the *Miami*, a five-gun cutter ship, Lincoln picked up an axe—they were massive and heavy in those days—and:

> held it at arm's length at the extremity of the [handle] with his thumb and forefinger, continuing to hold it there for a number of minutes. The most powerful sailors on board tried in vain to imitate him.[6]

Lincoln soon discovered that Offutt promised more than he was capable of delivering. Not long thereafter, Offutt mysteriously disappeared, and the young clerk was out of work.

PREACHING AND POLITICS

*The fact is, I don't like to hear cut-and-dried sermons. When I hear
a man preach, I like to see him act as if he were fighting bees.*

—ABRAHAM LINCOLN

Ever since he was a child, Lincoln had been fascinated with oratory. He honed his memorization skills in church. Undoubtedly those frontier preachers had no idea the little boy sitting there so quietly with his parents was listening and watching so intently that he missed not a word, an inflection, a nuance, or a gesture. During the following week, Lincoln would jump up on a stump and repeat the performance word for word, complete with inflections and gestures for whoever was in listening range. This drove Thomas crazy as whenever his son began one of his performances, all work on the place stopped.

Indeed, the story Lincoln told during his first day in New Salem, the story of "The Preacher and the Lizard," made the newcomer a household name all over the community. Unfortunately, the version that has come down to us is merely an abridgment, completely lacking all the little details that must have convulsed Lincoln's audiences. In those wilderness days when churches tended to be floorless and open to weather and wandering varmints, such things could and did happen:

> One Sunday, a preacher was delivering a sermon. He was wearing old-fashioned baggy pantaloons fastened with one button and no

suspenders, while his shirt was fastened at the collar with one button. In a loud voice he announced his text for the day: "I am the Christ, whom I shall represent today." And about that time a little blue lizard ran up under one of the baggy pantaloons. The preacher went ahead with his sermon, slapping his legs. After a while the lizard came so high that the preacher was desperate, and, going on with his sermon, unbuttoned the one button that held his pantaloons; they dropped down and with a kick were off. By this time the lizard had changed his route and circled around under the shirt at the back, and the preacher, repeating his text, "I am the Christ, whom I shall represent today," loosened his one collar button and with one sweeping movement off came the shirt. The congregation sat in the pews dazed and dazzled; everything was still for a minute; then a dignified elderly lady stood up slowly and, pointing a finger toward the pulpit, called out at the top of her voice, "I just want to say that if you represent Jesus Christ, sir, then I'm done with the Bible."[7]

But the boy listened just as intently to political speeches. Not only listened but gave them. Lincoln made his first speech when he was a mere boy, going barefoot, his trousers held up by one suspender, and his shock of hair sticking through a hole in the crown of his cheap straw hat.

In the company of Dennis Hanks, Abe, as a boy, attended a political meeting that was addressed by a typical stump speaker—one of those loud-voiced fellows who shouted at the top of his voice and waved his arms wildly.

At the conclusion of the speech, which did not conform with the views either of Abe or Dennis, the latter declared that Abe could make a better speech than that—whereupon he got a dry-goods box and called on Abe to reply to the campaign orator.

Lincoln threw his old straw hat on the ground and, mounting the dry-goods box, delivered a speech that held the attention of the crowd and won him considerable applause. Even the campaign orator admitted that it was a fine speech and answered every point in his own "oration."[8]

On March 15, 1832, the *Sangamon Journal* carried the notice that Abraham Lincoln—then only twenty-three—had announced his candidacy for the state legislature. From that time on, he was giving speeches wherever he could gather a crowd.

But all speech-making stopped when news swept the town that Black Hawk and his Fox and Sac braves were on the warpath, murdering settlers, pillaging, setting fire to settlements, and spreading terror across the Rock River part of the state. All the militia were called up by Governor Reynolds. Lincoln and many friends and neighbors promptly responded. Since the Clary's Grove Boys were such a large portion of the contingent, Lincoln was elected captain by an overwhelming majority. Later on, Lincoln would say that no honor he ever received meant more to him than this. A soldier from another command described Lincoln's company as "the hardest set of men I ever saw."

Interestingly enough, the officer who inducted Lincoln when he reenlisted was none other than Robert Anderson, the future commander of Fort Sumter. One day, Lincoln was leading his company across a field twenty abreast when they came to a fence with a narrow gate. Unable to think of a command that could address such a dilemma, Lincoln resourcefully shouted "Halt! This company will break ranks for two minutes and form on the other side of that gate!"

Later on, after reenlisting yet again, Lincoln helped bury five men who had been killed and scalped the day before. Years later, he recalled that awful moment:

> The red light of the morning sun was streaming upon them as they lay heads toward us on the ground. And every man had a round, red spot on the top of his head, about as big as a dollar, where the redskins had taken his scalp. It was frightful, it was grotesque, and the red sunlight seemed to paint everything all over.[9]

Paradoxically, though Lincoln never himself saw action in the short Black Hawk War, his closest contact with a live American Indian was when he saved the life of one, who, though he'd surrendered, was in the process of being killed by the vengeance-minded soldiers. About the only warlike skill Lincoln developed during the short conflict was broadsword fighting.

When he returned to New Salem after being mustered out, he resumed his campaigning for the legislature. But his campaign had lost too much momentum, and his first bid for office ended in failure.

LINCOLN THE STORE OWNER

Some things legally right are morally wrong.
—ABRAHAM LINCOLN

Since Lincoln still didn't know what occupation he would choose, he next blundered into the mercantile business. Having learned the ropes with Offutt, it was at least something he felt comfortable with.

It all began and ended so fast that he was left shaking his head. James and Rowan Herndon decided to sell the store they owned in New Salem. William F. Berry, who'd served as a corporal under Lincoln during the short-lived Black Hawk War, arranged to buy a half-interest in the store and offered the other half to Lincoln, who was boarding with him. Lincoln accepted, and they both signed notes since they didn't have cash. They were now one of three mercantile businesses in the little town. Their chief competition was the well-established partnership of Samuel Hill and John McNiel, and Reuben Radford, who was new in town, ran the third business.

One day, when Radford was out of town, he left his younger brother in charge with clear directions not to permit the Clary's Grove Boys to drink more than two drinks of liquor each. They came, each drank two, and, being denied more, they shoved the young storekeeper aside, drank until they were "rip-roaring" drunk, then trashed the store, leaving windows broken and the inventory in shambles. When Radford returned, he'd had enough, and offered to sell out at desperation prices.

Berry offered him $400, and the offer was accepted (Berry paid $23 cash along with two notes of $188.50 each, totaling $400). Berry then offered the inventory to Lincoln for $650. Lincoln accepted but insisted on doing an inventory himself. When complete, it was clear that the damaged inventory was worth $900, not $650. Lincoln insisted on signing a note for the higher figure.

So now Lincoln and Berry had only one competitor instead of two. All should have been well with them, but it turned out that a disproportionate percentage of their total inventory was liquor, and Lincoln was not at all interested in selling it. Berry *was* and, apparently on the sly, finagled a license to sell liquor by the drink. That was enough for Lincoln: he sold out to Berry, accepting his note.

Afterward Berry sold the business to the Trent Brothers, accepting their note. They subsequently skipped town in the middle of the night, leaving poor Berry with *all* the notes. At the worst possible time, too. New Salem was dying; in that barter economy, townspeople had no money to pay with, and with no road, no deep river, and no railroad connection, getting products in and out was extremely difficult. Finally, the business, in Lincoln's words, just "winked out." It was too much for Berry: on January 10, 1835, he died.

So who would repay all those notes? Lincoln was told that legally he was off the hook. But Lincoln wasn't called Honest Abe for nothing. Manfully, he shouldered the responsibility of paying back *all* the notes. He would spend the next twenty years of his life living on an extremely limited budget, repaying every last penny.[10]

Lincoln was like that. One day, when counting the money a woman had paid for dry goods, he discovered she'd paid him 6¼ cents too much. That night he walked six miles in order to pay her back. Another time, finding he'd mistakenly weighed tea with a four-ounce weight instead of an eight, he wrapped up another quarter pound and walked a considerable distance to deliver the rest of what the customer had paid for.

POSTMASTER OF NEW SALEM

No one ever got lost on a straight road.

—ABRAHAM LINCOLN

At this juncture, friends (of whom Lincoln always had many) stepped in to secure the office of postmaster of New Salem for him. The appointment was duly signed by President Andrew Jackson.

New Salem was on a 125-mile-long mail route that ran from Springfield to Monmouth. It took two days to get from one end to the other, with only one mail delivery a week. Initially it was carried on horseback, later by stagecoach.

Postal rates varied according to distance and number of pages in a letter. A single sheet cost 6 cents for the first thirty miles, 25 cents for more than four hundred miles. Two sheets were twice as much; three, three times as much. Neither stamps nor envelopes were used, letters being simply folded and sealed, with the postage charge was written on the outside. The addressee was stuck with having to pay the postage. Not surprisingly, rather than pay for extra sheets, many people, after writing on both sides of a sheet, would turn the paper over and write upside down between the lines.

Postmaster Lincoln was always keen to serve everyone's postal needs. When he thought someone was especially anxious to get a letter, he'd walk several miles, if necessary, in order to deliver it. If he was on an errand that took him into outlying areas, he'd usually carry (in his top hat) all the letters belonging to the people in that neighborhood and distribute them as he went along. His remuneration was meager: about $35 a year.

In 1836, when the postmastership was discontinued, the balance of income in his hands was $16 to $18. The Post Office Department was so little concerned with such an amount that it didn't ask about it until some years later.

Knowing how desperately poor he'd been during those years, a friend offered to lend him the money. Instead, Lincoln asked the agent to remain in his law office until he went over to his boardinghouse. He returned with an old blue sock with a quantity of silver and copper coins tied up in it. Once counted up, it was said to match the receipts to the penny. In all those years of great need, he'd refused to touch a penny of money he didn't consider his.

MENTOR GRAHAM

If you falter, and give up, you will lose the power of keeping any resolution.

—ABRAHAM LINCOLN

At every stage of life, when Abe most needed a mentor, that mentor was there for him. Such a mentor was the New Salem schoolmaster, who was appropriately named Mentor Graham.

Since the postmastership paid so little, Lincoln decided to learn the surveying profession, just as his hero George Washington had. There was a great need for qualified surveyors since so many speculators were buying large tracts of land and laying out new towns. Lincoln now borrowed the county surveyor's books, studying them night and day. Often he and Mentor Graham were up until midnight, interrupting their calculations only to go outside for more wood to keep the fire going.

With this help, Lincoln mastered both books, obtained a $50 horse on credit, procured a compass and a "chain," and by the end of 1833 began his surveying career, continuing until 1836. Old-timers maintained that, initially, unable to afford a metal chain, he used a wild grapevine.

An interesting story has come down to us that gives evidence of Lincoln's kindness of heart even in an exact profession such as surveying. When a surveyor, Mr. Lincoln first platted the town of Petersburg. Some twenty or thirty years afterward, the property owners along one of the outlying streets had trouble fixing their boundaries. They consulted the official plat and got no relief. A committee was sent to Springfield to consult the distinguished surveyor, but he failed to recall anything that would give them aid and could only refer them to the record. The dispute therefore went into the courts.

While the trial was pending, an old Irishman named McGuire, who had worked for some farmer during the summer, returned to town for the winter. The case being mentioned in his presence, he promptly said:

> I can tell you all about it. I helped carry the chain when Abe Lincoln laid out this town. Over there where they are quarreling about the lines, when he was locating the street, he straightened up from his instrument and said, "If I run that street right through, it will cut three or four feet off the end of _____'s house. It's all he's got in the world and he never could get another. Reckon it won't hurt anything out here if I skew the line a little and miss him."

The line was "skewed," and hence the trouble—and more testimony furnished as to Lincoln's abounding kindness of heart that would not willingly harm any human being.[11]

As for New Salem, it was, for Lincoln, his university of the world, his *Pilgrim's Progress*'s Vanity Fair: all the temptations of the world could be found in those fifteen or so log cabins. Indeed, for the time, the town would have been considered "fast," and it is an absolute miracle Lincoln was able during the steep learning curve of his six years there to maintain his ethical and spiritual equilibrium. He was able to retain his popularity with the young men of his own age in spite of his refusal to join them in their drinking bouts and carousals. That he didn't succumb was due to wise friends such as Mentor Graham.

Among these influences were people such as Jack Kelso, an educated ne'er-do-well who had an aversion to gainful employment. It was he who first introduced Lincoln to Shakespeare, Burns, and Byron. Kelso lived to fish. Though Lincoln considered it a waste of time, he was willing to fish just to hear Kelso ramble through the hitherto unknown world of great literature. No small thanks to Kelso, for the rest of Lincoln's life the writings of Shakespeare would be ever at his side.

A Life-Changing Day in Boonville

The leading rule for the lawyer, as for every other calling, is diligence.
Leave nothing for to-morrow which can be done today.

—Abraham Lincoln

By now, Lincoln was the most popular man in the region. Though he was strong enough to take on most any man he met, he never sought out a quarrel. He was everyone's friend yet used neither liquor nor tobacco. He was extremely poor and had less than a year's education in him, yet he was the best-informed young man in the village. He'd grown up in the rough wilderness world of Kentucky and Indiana, yet his speech was gentle, clean, and free of cursing.

Not least of his charm, to parents at least, was his love of children. He'd even stop his beloved reading to play marbles with little boys, one of whom later declared that Lincoln kept the boys running in all directions picking up marbles he'd scattered. Once, when he found a barefoot urchin chopping wood to get money to buy shoes, Lincoln did the chopping himself and quickly raised the needed money. Indeed, all the children of New Salem clustered around him whenever he appeared, clearly idolizing him.

Always, it seemed, Lincoln had been fascinated by lawyers and the dramas that took place in frontier courtrooms. Since Boonville, the Warrick County seat, was not far from Pigeon Creek and Gentryville, every time the boy heard that an interesting case was being tried, he did his best to take it in—*especially* when John A. Brackenridge, the star regional prosecutor, was on deck.

In 1828, the chief topic of discussion in the county was a big murder case. Abe determined to be there. It proved to be everything he'd hoped it would be—and more. After Brackenridge had brilliantly won his case, among the admirers who pressed forward to congratulate him was a tall, gangly boy in shabby clothes who told the prosecutor, "Your speech was the best I have ever heard!" Brackenridge was anything but impressed, and showed it. Imagine how stunned Brackenridge was, thirty-four years later, when their paths met again in Washington, and the president of the United States told him it was during that long-ago court trial that he had "formed a fixed determination to study law and make it his profession.[12]

But it was not until the New Salem years that Lincoln was finally able to find someone who would mentor him in law: Justice of the Peace Bowling Greene. Although he mastered most books with ease, Lincoln found law books much more difficult to internalize. Even before immersing himself in Blackstone's Commentaries and other law books, Lincoln began arguing a case now and then before Squire Greene.

At first, Greene allowed Lincoln to speak in his court mainly because he was so funny. Greene, an enormously fat man weighing well over 300 pounds, would shake with laughter at the young man's droll humor. Over time, however, Greene became ever more impressed with Lincoln's reasoning powers.

So it was that when Lincoln declared his candidacy for the legislature in August 1834, he was elected one of four Sangamon County members of the Illinois Legislature. He was in fact the top vote-getter.

The Ann Rutledge Love Story

In this sad world of ours, sorrow comes to all; and, to the young,
it comes with bitterest agony, because it takes them unawares.
The older have learned to ever expect it.

—Abraham Lincoln

Ann Rutledge was generally acknowledged to be the prettiest girl in New Salem. Her hair was so light that it appeared golden, and she had large blue eyes, a delicate, rather rosy complexion, and cherry-red lips. Contemporaries considered her to have been both sweet and friendly to everyone she met and very intelligent. She dressed simply but in perfect taste, loved to sew and quilt, and was a superb housekeeper.

Naturally she had lots of suitors. Of them all, the enigmatic young storekeeper John McNiel won out. During Lincoln's time, being engaged had a permanency to it that it no longer has in the twenty-first century. Once one had given his or her word, it was binding—like an oath. Ann told John McNiel (an assumed name; it was really McNamar) she wouldn't marry him until she'd completed additional schooling. Just as she was getting into her studies, her fiancé received word that his father in New York was gravely ill and his finances in disarray. He needed to go home at once but would return to marry her as soon as possible.

According to William Herndon, as months passed, each succeeding letter to Ann was less ardent and correspondingly more formal. The gaps between letters grew wider—then ceased altogether. Ann began asking herself, *Has his love for me died like a morning wind?* Compounding the problem was the town: word spread that her fiancé had lived among them with an assumed name and had jilted her.

When McNamar arrived in New York, he found his father's financial affairs in shambles and his father dying. But Ann, having no way of knowing the truth, became frustrated, embarrassed, and despondent. Lincoln, being both lonely and often in her company (including joint study sessions with Mentor Graham) began, after an entire year had gone by without a single letter from her fiancé, to squire her around town. Anyone with an eye to see could tell he was in love with her.

So it was that the two of them walked back and forth between home and the schoolhouse, and he'd accompany her to quilting bees, corn-huskings, and on horseback rides, and sit with her each evening by the Rutledge fireplace. There they'd sing from the *Watt's Psalm Book* and *The Missouri Harmony* hymn books. He would also accompany her to the Rogers home, four miles away, where Mrs. Rogers tutored Ann.

Herndon noted that at one quilting bee—during which affairs men usually waited outside—Lincoln came in and watched her stitch. At one point, he leaned over and whispered "the old, old story," which so affected her that her fingers momentarily lost their skill—so much so that older quilters noticed the resulting irregular stitches. In 1866, that quilt was still being viewed and talked about in the Springfield area.

When Lincoln was elected as one of the four Sangamon County members of the Illinois Legislature, he now had someone to share the joy of victory with. Nevertheless, it was not until the spring of 1835, two years after

McNamar left and a year after she'd last received a letter from him, that Ann conditionally accepted Lincoln's proposal. In keeping with the code of the times, however, there could be no announcement of their engagement until McNamar agreed to release her from his promise. Complicating the situation was Ann's realization that though she now loved Lincoln, she had never fallen out of love with McNamar.

Ann found herself engaged to two men, both of whom she dearly loved. Perhaps it is not surprising that this strain, which continued for over a year, seriously weakened her health. She finally found herself unable to eat or sleep, for McNamar neither wrote nor showed up so that the matter could be brought to resolution one way or another.

The spring and summer of 1835 were both wet and sizzling hot. In its wake came an epidemic of typhoid. Few New Salem households were spared. Several of the Rutledges came down with it, including Ann. Lincoln ministered to the family night and day, contracting the disease himself, but kept going in spite of it.

On August 25, 1835, Ann Rutledge succumbed to the disease and died. Lincoln collapsed. Many years later, after talking with people who had personally known Lincoln, biographer Ida Tarbell wrote these words:

> The girl's death came to him as a supreme tragedy—the failure of the most beautiful hope he had ever entertained. It is little wonder that, ill as he was in body, stricken as he was in mind and heart, he should have gone through a period of terrible despair.[13]

One thing is absolutely certain: whether Lincoln was actually engaged to Ann when she died, so precious was she to him that he was changed forever after her passing. For a time, his grief was almost uncontrollable, and he went again and again to Ann's grave and wept. He cried out that he could not bear the thought that rain and snow would beat upon her grave.

Lincoln was still reeling from the death of Sarah, his only blood sibling, and Ann's death broke him. Was he always to lose those he loved most? It caused him to reevaluate all that he believed in, giving his face a melancholy cast from that day forward.

Not long afterward, Dr. Jason Duncan placed in Lincoln's hands the poem that came to mean more to the grieving young man than any other poem; all his life it remained constantly by his side—not that it needed to be, for he often recited all fourteen stanzas from memory. It is virtually impossible to understand fully all that Lincoln would become without coupling these melancholy lines to his story—the ever-present awareness of the transitory nature of this thing called life. Here is the poem:

Oh! Why should the spirit of mortal be proud?
Like a swift fleeting meteor, a fast-flying cloud,
A flash of the lightning, a break of the wave,
Man passeth from life to his rest in the grave.

The leaves of the oak and the willow shall fade,
Be scattered around, and together be laid;
And the young and the old, and the low and the high
Shall molder to dust and together shall lie.

The infant a mother attended and loved;
The mother that infant's affection who proved;
The husband that mother and infant who blessed—
Each, all, are away to their dwellings of rest.

The maid on whose cheek, on whose brow, in whose eye,
Shone beauty and pleasure—her triumphs are by;
And the memory of those who loved her and praised,
Are alike from the minds of the living erased.

The hand of the king that the scepter hath borne;
The brow of the priest that the mitre hath worn;
The eye of the sage, and the heart of the brave,
Are hidden and lost in the depth of the grave.

The peasant whose lot was to sow and to reap;
The herdsman, who climbed with his goats up the steep;

The beggar, who wandered in search of his bread,
Have faded away like the grass that we tread.

The saint who enjoyed the communion of heaven,
The sinner who dared to remain unforgiven,
The wise and the foolish, the guilty and just,
Have quietly mingled their bones in the dust.

So the multitude goes, like the flowers or the weed
That withers away to let others succeed;
So the multitude comes, even those we behold,
To repeat every tale that has often been told.

For we are the same our fathers have been;
We see the same sights our fathers have seen,—
We drink the same stream, and view the same sun,
And run the same course our fathers have run.

The thoughts we are thinking our fathers would think;
From the death we are shrinking our fathers would shrink;
To the life we are clinging they also would cling;
But it speeds for us all, like a bird on the wing.

They loved, but the story we cannot unfold;
They scorned, but the heart of the haughty is cold;
They grieved, but no wail from their slumbers will come;
They joyed, but the tongue of their gladness is dumb.

They died, aye! they died: and we things that are now,
Who walk on the turf that lies over their brow,
Who make in their dwellings a transient abode,
Meet the things that they met on their pilgrimage road.

Yea! hope and despondency, pleasure and pain,
We mingle together in sunshine and rain;

And the smiles and the tears, the song and the dirge,
Still follow each other, like surge upon surge.

'Tis the wink of an eye, 'tis the draught of a breath,
From the blossom of health to the paleness of death,
From the gilded saloon to the bier and the shroud—
Oh! why should the spirit of mortal be proud?

—"Oh! Why Should the Spirit of Mortal Be Proud?" by WILLIAM KNOX[14]

As one studies Lincoln's life and notes his insistence on treating everyone the same, his empathy with all human suffering, his unvarying and absolute kindness, and his rather fatalistic attitude to death itself, it is hard not to factor in the impact of these words.

Soon after Ann Rutledge's death, into New Salem drove the long-absent John McNamar, with his mother, brothers, sisters, and family possessions stacked high in the wagon. He'd come at last to claim his fiancée. For well over a year of unfeeling silence he now paid the ultimate price. Lincoln commiserated with him, but apparently said nothing about what the loss of lovely Ann meant to *him*. McNamar decided to stay anyway, and later married another.

Mary Todd Lincoln

LIFE
Goes On

*It is said an Eastern monarch once charged his wise men to invent him
a sentence to be ever in view, and which should be true and appropriate
in all times and situations. They presented him the words:
"And this, too, shall pass away." How much it expresses! How chastening
in the hour of pride! How consoling in the depths of affliction!*

—ABRAHAM LINCOLN

VANDALIA INTERLUDE

Ann Rutledge was gone, but life for Abraham Lincoln had to go on. It was
time he concentrated on what was happening in Vandalia.

In 1834 Vandalia was the capital of Illinois. It was on the famed National Road, America's first interstate highway. There were about a hundred
buildings in the town, and normally around eight hundred inhabitants. But
when the legislature was in session and the Supreme Court convened, the
otherwise sleepy little town came to life, becoming the social center of the
state. Wealthy members brought their wives along, and dancing and social
gaiety enlivened the evenings. Indeed, when the legislature was in session,
the state's wealth, fashion, beauty, and its entrepreneurs would all be found
in Vandalia.

Here were issues Lincoln had never dealt with: state banks, public education, tariffs, public lands, court creation, railroad and canal construction,
slavery, abolitionism, and much more. If New Salem's six years had provided
him with his basic college education, Vandalia's years represented a graduate
degree in politics, government, and statesmanship.

Lincoln, the freshman Sangamon representative, listened and watched much and spoke little that first session. There was *so much* to learn. It didn't take him long before he discovered just how complex the machinery of government could be. Lobbying groups, each with pet agendas, were there to influence. Prime movers from inside the state and apparently every other quarter of the nation were there to get their slices of the pie. Needless to say, all those pushers and shovers congregating in one small city at the same time created the need for legislative prioritizing—known more familiarly as "You scratch my back and I'll scratch yours."

Lincoln knew that if he was ever to achieve his dreams of success, it would begin here. He would need to learn how to rub shoulders with the great of Illinois—and to weigh his words carefully.

There were other freshmen just like him hoping to be noticed. One of those lobbying for power was the shortest man of all, Stephen A. Douglas, soon to be known far and wide as "The Little Giant." Neither he nor Lincoln could have known when they first met that they'd be in each other's hair as long as they lived, the fortunes of each dramatically affected by the words and acts of the other.

In order to secure a place for himself among the state's high and mighty, Lincoln resorted to a skill that had helped him throughout his life: storytelling. Imagine him telling this one as he and his audience stood around the fireplace in the inn late in the evening:

[I'm reminded] of a fellow who lived just out of town, on the bank of a large marsh. Well, one day, he conceived a big idea in the money-making line. He took it to a prominent merchant, and began to develop his plans and specifications. "There are at least ten million frogs in that marsh near me, an' I'll just arrest a couple of carloads of them and hand them over to you. You can send them to the big cities and make lots of money for both of us. Frogs' legs are great delicacies in the big towns, an' not very plentiful. It won't take me more'n two or three days to pick 'em. They make so much noise my family can't sleep, and by this deal I'll get rid of a nuisance and gather in some cash."

The merchant agreed to the proposition, promised the fellow he would pay him well for the two carloads. Two days passed, then three, and finally two weeks were gone before the fellow showed up again, carrying a small basket. He looked weary and "done up," and he wasn't talkative a bit. He threw the basket on the counter with the remark, "There's your frogs."

"You haven't two carloads in that basket, have you?" inquired the merchant.

"No," was the reply, "and there ain't no two carloads in all this blasted world."

"I thought you said there were at least ten million of 'em in that marsh near you, according to the noise they made," observed the merchant. "Your people couldn't sleep because of 'em."

"Well," said the fellow, "accordin' to the noise they made, there was, I thought, a hundred million of 'em, but when I had waded and swum that there marsh day and night fer two blessed weeks, I couldn't harvest but six. There's two or three left yet, an' the marsh is as noisy as it uster be. We haven't catched up on any of our lost sleep yet. Now, you can have these here six, an' I won't charge you a cent fer 'em."[1]

By the time the following legislative session rolled around, Lincoln was ready to begin making a difference. Before it adjourned in January, it had passed an apportionment act. By this act Sangamon County became entitled to seven representatives, rather than four, and two state senators.

During 1836, Lincoln permitted himself to be maneuvered into a relationship with Mary Owens, a cousin of Mentor Graham. As time passed, and it became clear he didn't love her, he felt more and more boxed in. Eventually, he proposed to her several times merely because he felt he owed it to her as a gentleman. Not being either dense or dumb, she saw through his charade and turned him down—to his vast relief.

Less than twenty months after Ann's death, Lincoln would leave New Salem for Springfield. Nevertheless, during that intervening period, he continued to study with Mentor Graham.

After noting Lincoln's tendency sometimes to take liberties with accepted grammar, Graham told him a thorough knowledge of correct grammar was essential to anyone who wished to advance politically and appear well in society. Lincoln immediately responded, "Where can I find such a treasure?" By that evening, after a six-mile walk, Lincoln was knocking on the door of the farming house of John Vance. After borrowing Kirkham's *Grammar* from him, Lincoln all but memorized the book.

Thirty years later, Graham wrote to William Herndon, declaring that, in his entire forty-five-year teaching career, during which he had taught or mentored over five thousand students, he'd never encountered another student as diligent or studious as Lincoln. In his reading and studying, Lincoln was a miser of time, never wasting a moment. Between customers, clients, or constituents, he was invariably reading. Whenever he was walking anywhere, almost always he'd be reading. He'd read until late at night and be reading again at dawn.[2]

SPRINGFIELD

*The way for a young man to rise is to improve himself every way he can,
never suspecting that anybody wishes to hinder him.*
—ABRAHAM LINCOLN

It was during the Tenth General Assembly that Lincoln came into his own as a legislative manipulator. As the leader of the famous Sangamon "Long Nine" (all six feet tall or taller), Lincoln led out in a brilliant series of pitched battles in order to achieve one coveted surprise at the end.

The bill that was the linchpin for the entire monstrosity was the Illinois boondoggle to end all boondoggles, the innocuous-sounding Internal Improvement Bill. The enthusiastic legislators, convinced Illinois would become the New York State of the heartland, decided to gamble on that hope by enacting this public works bill in order to construct a vast grid of roads, canals, and railroads. Unfortunately, no prophet arose to tell them that a financial panic would smash the nation's economy in 1837. The $9 million note would all but bankrupt the state.

Lincoln and the rest of the Long Nine, taking advantage of their increase in representation from four to seven, shrewdly structured a master plan Byzantine enough to have made Machiavelli chuckle. Realizing that the $9 million pork barrel would arouse greed in every municipality in the state, they concluded that it would be stupid to give away their votes. When approached about supporting a specific pork-barrel request with their votes, they'd agree to do so, *providing*, should the subject come up of moving the capital, they'd promise to cast all their votes for the motion to move the state capital to Springfield.

So when the boondoggle passed, the Long Nine breathed a collective sigh of relief. At the end, they eked out the desired victory: the capital would be moved from Vandalia to Springfield in 1839. Needless to say, the Vandalia supporters were livid, as were those from other cities coveting the honor.

When the stagecoach brought them back to Springfield from Vandalia, the Long Nine were greeted with dinners, speeches, songs, and congratulations. And everyone knew that behind the scenes, Lincoln had been the one guiding the ship. He was urged to leave New Salem and come to live in the new capital.

So when Lincoln again rode into Springfield about a month after the close of that historic session, he knew he already had many friends in the city. And the very next day after the capital city victory, he received the glad news: after several years of study—he'd passed the bar!

But on that bright April 15, 1837, morning, his big question must have been: *Where can I live? I am all but broke—every spare penny being applied on that store debt.*

He rode up to Joshua Speed's general store. Speed, who had known Lincoln for some time, watched his friend riding up on a horse that turned out to be borrowed; his total personal effects consisted of a pair of battered-looking saddlebags containing a couple of read-to-death law books and a few pieces of worn clothing.

Having already discovered that a single bedstead would cost $17, after walking into the store, Lincoln told Speed about his dilemma.

"I can loan you the money," Speed said.[3]

"Oh, the price is probably cheap enough, but I don't have enough money to pay it back," Lincoln said. "And if I fail here as a lawyer, I won't be able to pay you at all."

Then Speed surprised even himself by offering to share his large double bed.

"Where is your room?" Lincoln asked.

"Upstairs," said Speed, pointing to a stairway. Without saying a word, Lincoln picked up his saddlebags, carried them upstairs, set them down on the floor, came down again, and with a face beaming with pleasure, exclaimed, "Well, Speed, I'm moved."

The world was so different in the 1830s. Space was at such a premium that many one-room cabins housed twelve to fifteen people. Travelers as well as those who needed a place to live and sleep fully expected to share beds with others. In fact, it was customary for *more* than two to sleep in the same bed.

Though Joshua Speed came from a wealthy Louisville, Kentucky, family, his father owning a plantation and seventy slaves, and Lincoln came from the poorest of the poor, they soon became fast friends. During the next four years, Speed would become the one and only such friend and confidant Lincoln would ever have.

By Eastern standards, 1830s Springfield was little more than a frontier town. Like Vandalia, the wide, unpaved roads were quagmires in the winter and strangling dust storms in the summer; there were no sidewalks, and street crossing could be perilous. Typical of most towns and cities across the country, livestock—most notoriously, hogs—rooted around in the streets and alleys. Yet Springfield, with almost twice the population of Vandalia, was the most cosmopolitan city Lincoln had ever lived in.

It was now that John T. Stuart, himself battling Stephen A. Douglas for a seat in Congress, invited Lincoln to join him as a partner in his law firm. Thus Lincoln didn't have to wait for clients to find him. In the end, Stuart defeated Douglas by the razor-thin margin of thirty-six votes (one of Douglas's few political defeats).

On December 16, 1839, Lincoln was one of the organizers of the cotillion party held at the prestigious American House. The guests included the very attractive twenty-one-year-old Mary Todd of Lexington, Kentucky, who had come to reside with her sister, Mrs. Ninian W. Edwards.

Lincoln had a hard time taking his eyes off her.

MARY TODD

I have now come to the conclusion never again to think of marrying, and for this reason: I can never be satisfied with anyone who would be blockhead enough to have me.

—ABRAHAM LINCOLN

Lincoln had never met a woman quite like her. In the past, the only women he'd felt comfortable with were older, married, or otherwise taken. But now that Ann was gone forever and the Mary Owens trauma had passed, Lincoln once again hoped that he would find *the* woman.

Once Lincoln had set eyes on Mary Todd, he determined to see her again. The opportunity came sooner than expected. The occasion: a dance at the Ninian Edwards mansion. Even more so than before, at the dance Lincoln was captivated by her quick wit, repartee, sparkling blue eyes, creamy complexion, thick brunette hair, and dimpled smile. After finally getting up his nerve, he shyly said to her, "I want to dance with you in the worst way." When she returned to her seat, one of her companions asked mischievously, "Well, Mary, did he dance with you in the worst way?"

"Yes," she answered, "the very worst."[4]

Since Mary quickly became one of the belles of the city, Lincoln was not alone in wishing to know her better. What he learned about her did little to shore up his courage: Mary had been educated at a private academy and the exclusive school of Madame Mentelle, where she'd been immersed in French, music, dancing, and drama, her specialties being language and literature. Her great-uncle, John Todd, generally considered to be the founder of Illinois, had been acting governor and was killed at the Battle of Blue Licks on August 18, 1782. Her wealthy father moved in the highest social circles of the South.

But a cloud had come over her life: her mother had died, her father had remarried, and her new stepmother was cold to her. So she'd come to Springfield to be with her sister Elizabeth, who was married to Ninian Edwards, the son of an Illinois governor and a leader of society.

So *who am I*, wondered Lincoln, *to attract such a woman?* Listening to her, watching her, he was fascinated by everything about her. Never having met anyone remotely like her, he struggled to keep a conversation going. He'd have been amazed at how much her quick mind learned from his halting answers. He was both surprised and pleased to discover they both liked some of the same poets, had memorized some of the same poems, were both Kentuckians, both supported the Whig political party, and were both ambitious. (The Whig Party [1824–1854] rose as a counterforce to the Democratic Party. It would founder on the issue of slavery.)

And so a courtship began. Some of Mary's friends were amazed she'd be interested in someone so completely out of her social class as Abraham Lincoln. Those who knew her better, however, were not surprised, knowing her keen mind ran deep. When people asked her about the prospects of Lincoln and Douglas and which she'd choose if they both proposed to her, she answered without pausing a second, "He who has the best prospects of being president."

Sometime in 1840, Lincoln asked Mary to marry him, and she said yes. But strangely enough, the engagement failed to bring the expected joy to Lincoln. He was tormented by fears, doubts, and reservations. How could he support a woman who'd always had everything? The partnership with Stuart was coming to an end. No small thanks to the public works boondoggle, the state's fiscal credit rating was collapsing—so he'd most likely not run for the legislature again. Speed was selling out and returning to Kentucky, thus Lincoln would lose both a place to stay and his companionship. And he couldn't help but be troubled by Mary's pride: if they married, he doubted whether she'd even condescend to meet his parents and relatives.

Overwhelmed by panic, he asked to be released from the engagement. Kindly, but sadly, she granted it. Then Lincoln felt even worse! He, who could not bear to see the least of God's creatures suffer, could not stand the thought that he'd brought pain to her. Speed told him to be a man and go to Mary and explain. He did, but when she cried, he took her in his arms—and they were engaged again. But seeing how tormented he was, again she released him.

Now Lincoln tumbled into one of the deepest depressions of his life. To his law partner he wrote:

> I am now the most miserable man living. If what I feel were equally distributed to the whole human race, there would not be one cheerful face on the earth. Whether I shall ever be better I cannot tell; I am fully forebode I shall not. To remain as I am is impossible; I must die or get better, it appears to me.[5]

As time passed, a matchmaker got them to meet together. Mary, it appears, loved him enough to swallow her pride. To herself, she must have said, *I can only hope he'll come back to me—I know no one who could possibly take his place.*

Enter the unlikeliest of all possible romance salvagers.

The Duel with James Shields

Quarrel not at all. No man resolved to make the most of himself can spare time for personal contention. Still less can he afford to take on the consequences, including the vitiating of his temper and the loss of self-control.

Yield larger things to which you can show no more than equal right;
and yield lesser ones, though clearly your own. Better give your
path to a dog than be bitten by him in contesting for the right.

—ABRAHAM LINCOLN

It all started out as a joke. A group of Springfieldians with more time on their hands than sense cast about for ways of spicing up the pages of the *Sagamon Journal*. One of them (Lincoln, most likely) came up with the idea of cranking out a series of anonymous columns to poke fun at people who deserved such treatment. As fate would have it, the initial target was a handsome, dashing, thin-skinned, and vain Irishman named James Shields. Shields was state auditor at the time.

The editor of the *Sagamon Journal*, eager to increase circulation, agreed to the plan. The conspirators (including Mary Todd, Julia Jayne, Dr. Elias Merryman, and Lincoln) took turns writing columns ostensibly written by a mythical countrywoman by the name of Rebecca. Merryman, feeling that the first few letters were too easy on Shields, added a telling phrase here and there to give the letters a little more *bite*.

And bite they certainly had! Imagine yourself as James Shields waking up one morning, picking up the newspaper, and reading the likes of "Dear Girls, *it is distressing*, but I cannot marry you all. Too well I know how you suffer; but do, *do* remember, it is not my fault that I am *so* handsome and *so* interesting."

The columns became a hit, for they were not only funny, they were also bitingly sarcastic and skewered the state auditor while the entire state read and chuckled. But Shields wasn't chuckling. After one particularly offensive column, he sent a friend to demand of the editor the name of the perpetrator. When the editor came to Lincoln asking how he should respond, Lincoln's heart sank. *It was just a joke!* And thinking of the humiliation for Mary and Julia should the truth of the authorship get out, he decided to shoulder all the blame himself.

Next thing he knew, he'd been challenged to a duel.

As the challenged party, Lincoln knew he could choose the weapons. He is said to have quipped, "How about cow dung at five paces?" He quickly ruled out pistols, for with them he'd be quickly dead, just as was Alexander Hamilton at the hands of Aaron Burr. He finally settled on large broadswords, since he'd had a little experience with them in the Black Hawk War. Being six feet four to Shields's five feet nine, he felt he'd have a "slight" advantage in reach.

Lincoln knew full well that the Illinois penalty for dueling was up to five years in prison and a permanent ban from political office. Therefore the duel was set to take place across the border in Missouri. Lincoln and his seconds headed for the Missouri border in order to fight the duel there, about three days of hard riding away. Only moments before it would have been too late, the duelists heard the sounds of galloping horses: three friends had ridden all that way just to try to restore some sanity to the minds of the duelists. Sheepishly both men laid down their swords.

There were several crucial turning points in Lincoln's life. The Shields duel was one of them. Never in his life had Lincoln been this embarrassed, and he had no one to blame for his stupidity but himself. He'd always prided himself on being the ultimate peacemaker—the one who settled quarrels, not started them! Had it not been for three faithful friends willing to ride night and day for several days in order to restore him to some semblance of sanity, either he or Shields would quite possibly be dead or maimed for life—and certainly destroyed politically. Or it could have ended as a farce, with both men laughed out of a political future.

Furthermore, he realized that the problem went far deeper than just a few anonymous letters. He recalled a day two years earlier in which he exacted revenge on a certain Jesse B. Thomas, who had disparaged him in a campaign speech.

Lincoln had always been such a wicked mimic that he could convulse audiences with his impersonations. On that day—July 20, 1840—he'd more than got his revenge on Thomas. The only problem was that right in the middle of his merciless public mimicry of Thomas's idiosyncrasies, with his audience almost rolling in the aisles, Lincoln chanced to look up and spot Thomas's face in the crowd. The absolute misery on that face kept him awake most of the night. Next day, he sought out Thomas and abjectly apologized. The damage, however, was already done, and Lincoln's revenge on that day came to be called "the skinning of Thomas."[6]

So this was a recurring problem with him. What was he going to do about it?

During the several days spent riding back to Springfield, Lincoln had a lot of time in which to reorder his life's priorities. It took a while, for Lincoln always had to think a matter through slowly before he arrived at a conclusion, but in the end this almost-duel with Shields proved to be a Rubicon for Lincoln. That moment separated the thirty-three floundering years of his youth from the twenty-three thoughtful, focused years that remained to him.

First, he was through with anonymous letters forever! Had he been in Shields's shoes, and not been born with a sense of humor, how would *he* have felt? For the first time in his life, he took a long look at this lesser self that would knowingly wound—perhaps even kill—someone, and for no valid reason. Beveridge observed:

> Thus ended the most lurid personal incident in Lincoln's entire life, the significance of which in his development is vital. He had received a badly needed lesson in humility. At last his habit, formed in boyhood, of ridiculing other people through offensive, anonymous writing, had been sternly checked. He had needlessly and heedlessly assailed a brave and honest man, and the insulted Shields had resented it, in the terms and manner of the times. Never again did Lincoln forget that experience. Never again did he write an anonymous letter, never again say an insulting word about any human being. From the time of the Shields duel Lincoln was infinitely circumspect and considerate in his dealings with others.[7]

Not least of his resolutions had to do with his foolishly permitting two of his seconds to persuade him to go through with such an uncharacteristic act. Lincoln determined henceforth to steer his own course, realizing, with a sigh, that the soul-mate relationship he'd enjoyed with Speed would most likely never be replicated with anyone else. In years to come, he would listen to input but would ask no advice and became a man everyone thought they knew but whom no one person ever would.

His growing-up years were over.

Mary Todd had been so touched by Lincoln's chivalrous behavior in shielding her from the effects of her own poison pen that when Lincoln rode back into Springfield, she rushed to him. The long period of alienation and misunderstanding was over. The engagement was on again.

But that didn't mean Lincoln no longer had reservations about the marriage. He did.

First, there was still Mary's pride. She'd already made it clear that marrying him did not mean accepting his family. No, should he marry her, most—if not all—of his interactions with his family would take place when Mary was not with him. Never had he hidden his roots from society, never had he passed up an opportunity to visit the folks in Coles County. That would never change. It would merely mean he'd never have the joy of introducing Mary to his family. And when children came . . . that would be worst of all, for he knew Mary would do her utmost to keep the children from interacting with their Lincoln and Hanks cousins.

Second, there was the not-so-small matter of Mary's quick temper, the tantrums she'd throw when she didn't get her way in all things.

Third, could she handle becoming the wife of a poor man? Years would pass before his mercantile debts were paid off and they'd have money for extras.

He just didn't know. True, he loved her unreservedly, but did he love her enough to compensate for the loneliness and verbal abuse he was certain to get?

Perhaps Speed could help him decide. For Speed had almost backed out of his engagement to the beautiful Fanny several years ago. And—irony or ironies!—it had been Lincoln who'd shored up his friend's courage and urged him to go through with it. So he wrote Speed and asked him these questions: "Are you happy?" and "If you were to do it over again, would you marry Fanny?" Day after day passed, and still Lincoln did not know if he should go through with it. Finally, the long-awaited letter! Yes, he and Fanny were very happy . . . and, were he to face the question again, most certainly he'd marry her. And, yes, Lincoln should swallow his doubts and marry Mary Todd. It was high time he settled down and got serious about life.

And so, on November 4, 1842, Abraham Lincoln and Mary Todd were married. Charles Dresser, an Episcopal minister, performed the ceremony in the Ninian Edwards home. The groom placed on the bride's finger a ring on which were engraved the words, "Love is eternal."

Time to Straighten Up

I want you to open the case, and when you are doing it talk to the jury as though your client's fate depends on every word you utter. Forget that you have anyone to fall back on, and you will do justice to yourself and your client.

—Abraham Lincoln

A year and a half earlier, on April 14 of 1841, Lincoln's law partnership with Stuart was dissolved. Lincoln accepted a junior partnership with Stephen T. Logan. Lincoln had been blessed by two strong mentors in his life: Andrew Crawford and Mentor Graham. Now, in the person of Logan, his third and last mentor came on the scene.

Judge David Davis, later a justice of the U.S. Supreme Court, maintained that Logan was "the greatest natural lawyer of his day." Albert Woldman, in his landmark book about Lincoln the lawyer, points out that:

> Logan was perhaps the most constructive influence in Lincoln's life. Stuart had been indifferent to Lincoln's carelessness, lack of method, and slipshodiness. Placing politics before law, Stuart had been inclined to rely on his own native wit and ability, rather than on study and preparation, to win cases. He trusted the spur of the moment; and the junior partner had adopted the same haphazard methods.[8]

But now Lincoln was confronted with a stern senior partner who had a history of not tolerating anything less than what he expected of himself. By being:

> methodical, industrious, particular, painstaking, and precise himself, Logan spread out before Lincoln a new pattern. Furthermore, instead of stumbling into law cases, as Lincoln had before, Logan expected—and demanded—that Lincoln dig deep into the principles underlying a given lawsuit; to study the authorities, precedents, and carefully prepare each case in advance.

If Logan had a mantra he expected of Lincoln, it was that he would become known for his attention to detail, thoroughness, and exactitude, all three of which had been foreign to Lincoln before (and not just to Lincoln, for he was merely reflective of the legal norms in 1841).

Woldman maintains it was Logan who unknowingly prepared Lincoln to take on Stephen Douglas in the greatest series of debates in American history. As Lincoln studied Logan's courtroom performances and questioned him afterward, Lincoln was amazed at how Logan could see through the forest to the trees, how he could single out the strongest points in his case and the weakest in his opponent's. Indeed, before Logan ever stepped foot in the courtroom, he not only knew how he would prove his case, but far more important, he knew his opponent's case inside out, its strengths as well as weaknesses. Rarely, if ever, was Logan surprised in a courtroom.

By the time Lincoln had studied under Logan for four years, he wasn't the same careless, sloppy, somewhat insecure young man he'd been in 1841. Needless to say, Logan was both pleased and surprised by the transformation. Early on, he'd wondered if perhaps he'd made a mistake in making Lincoln partner. Instead, the partnership now became known as one of the top law firms in the state, leading to retainers from other law firms, not only in Illinois but across the nation. During the 1841 term alone, Lincoln argued fourteen appeals before the Illinois Supreme Court, losing only four. All told, during his four pivotal years with Logan, Lincoln participated in thirty-nine Supreme Court cases.

The Globe Tavern Newlyweds

My wife is as handsome as when she was a girl and I a poor nobody,
then fell in love with her, and what is more, I have never fallen out.

—ABRAHAM LINCOLN *(said to a war correspondent in a White House receiving line)*

Lincoln's marriage to Mary came during his partnership years with Logan. After the wedding Abraham and Mary Lincoln settled down in a room in the Globe Tavern. By the time he'd slipped the ring onto her finger, Lincoln had a pretty good idea what he was walking into. The wedding had been arranged in haste: even her sister Elizabeth hadn't known when or if it would take place until the actual morning of the wedding! And it was remarked at the wedding that Lincoln looked miserable.

Lincoln knew Mary would be exceedingly difficult to live with. From an early age, she'd played a very dangerous game with her mind: when she failed to get her way for any reason, the rational part of her brain would knowingly release the irrational tiger within her. When she was young, these episodes could be excused as childish tantrums, but when she got older, they became a far more serious matter.

Of course there were excuses and provocations, such as the excruciating migraine headaches that would recur during their married life. Far more serious, however, would be the gradual drift into mental illness. In the early years of the marriage, fortunately the good periods would far outweigh the bad. And there would *always* remain one constant: Lincoln dearly loved his wife, and she not only loved him unreservedly, she also revered him.

There was never even a shadow over his lifetime commitment to her. He would not have been human, however, had he not sometimes wondered: *What if?* According to Lincoln biographer David Donald, shortly after Lincoln was elected president, he and an old friend, Isaac Cogdal, were chatting about the good ol' days in New Salem and questioning each other as to the whereabouts of people they'd known back then. When the name of Rutledge came up, Cogdal ventured to ask if it was true that Lincoln had fallen in love with Ann. "It is true—true indeed I did," Lincoln replied. "I loved the woman dearly and soundly: she was a handsome gal—would have made a good, loving wife. . . . I did honestly and truly love the girl and think often—often of her now."[9]

It is intriguing to speculate what might have happened to Lincoln had he married Ann Rutledge or someone else besides Mary Todd. More and more, Lincoln scholars appear to be moving toward a consensus that since she represents a sizable portion of the seething crucible in which the Lincoln of 1861 was forged, without the Mary Todd relationship it is distinctly possible he might have been less able to survive the maelstrom of the Civil War.

Sadly, no person in the Lincoln story has been treated more harshly than has Mary—both during her lifetime and afterward. So many writers and biographers have portrayed her as a virago, a she-devil, almost satanic. The truth of the matter is that she was extremely loving, devoted to her husband, and supportive of all his career plans. And she was equally devoted to the children. As we shall see, she did a lot of things right, especially early on.

One of Lincoln's early fears proved groundless. Though the Globe

Tavern room was a real comedown from the home she'd grown up in Lexington and the Edwards's luxurious mansion, and though for the first time in her life she had neither servants nor slaves and barely space enough to turn around in, Mary did not complain—not even when her sisters, who'd warned her what she would expect if she married out of her class, were quick with their "told you so's." So much did Mary love and admire her husband, rarely did she ever complain about what she'd given up for him.

And she had to come to terms with the undeniable truth that her husband was not forthcoming with displays of affection. As she put it many years later, he "was *not* a demonstrative man; when he felt most deeply, he expressed the least." This being the Victorian Age, when she referred to him, it was as "Mr. Lincoln." He, on the other hand, tended to choose among "Molly," "Mary," and, in private, "Puss," "Little Woman," "Child Wife," or, after the first child, Robert, was born on August 1, 1843, "Mother."

The Lincolns took stock of their options. With little Robert now in the picture, they needed larger living quarters. And what with Lincoln's financial obligations to his parents and his determination to continue chipping away at the New Salem debts, there wasn't much extra to draw from. By May 2, 1844, however, the Lincolns felt they could afford to buy the Rev. Charles Dresser's home on the corner of Eighth and Jackson. It would remain their home as long as they lived.[10] They certainly needed the extra room when their second child, Edward Baker Lincoln, was born on March 10, 1846.

Lincoln and Herndon

The better part of one's life consists of his friendships.

—Abraham Lincoln

In December 1844, Lincoln left Logan and set up his own law firm. He took young William Herndon as his partner. Herndon proved to be a nearly perfect fit, and the partnership lasted the rest of Lincoln's life. Lincoln referred to his new partner as "Billy," but Herndon, who almost idolized Lincoln, always referred to the senior partner as "Mr. Lincoln."

Neither man was a good housekeeper, and consequently the office was invariably a mess. Since neither partner excelled at bookkeeping or financial details, they just split whatever money came in. If Herndon had a pet peeve, it would be what he called "the Brats," the Lincoln boys, who would reduce the office to even more shambles than normal whenever they came in. Lincoln, the most permissive of parents, would say nothing while war raged around him.

As for Mary, Herndon got off on the wrong foot the first time he met her. So fascinated had he been by her sinuous grace as she moved across the dance floor that he complimented her, likening her smooth movements to those of a serpent. Taking the comment as an insult, she never forgave him. That was all right with Herndon, as he eventually grew to loathe her. Because of this mutual hatred, getting the two families together proved a near impossibility.

Congressman Lincoln

If there is anything that links the human with the divine, it is the
courage to stand by a principle when everybody else rejects it.

—Abraham Lincoln

Lincoln believed wholeheartedly in the Whig Party. It was founded on the principles of growth, development, progress, and freedom—principles he ascribed to. He looked forward to representing that party in Washington one day, perhaps in Congress. Though he failed in his congressional bid in 1844, he was successful in 1846. In that campaign he capitalized on the beauty of rotation in office: after one term, give someone *else* a chance. Once he was in office, however, that concept lost some of its beauty to him.

In December 1847, the Lincolns journeyed to Washington, which then had a population of 40,000. Houses were generally far apart, with privies, pigsties, cowsheds, and geese pens in backyards. Pigs, cows, and geese wandered and rooted at will in the garbage tossed out into the streets and alleys. The cobblestones paving broad Pennsylvania Avenue were at such odd angles that no one in his right mind drove a carriage over it unless it was covered with snow. Neither wing of the Capitol building had been constructed yet, and the temporary dome was wooden. In the streets, coffles of shackled slaves were a common sight.

Since Washington was not considered much of a family town, few government officials brought their wives and families with them. Women who lived in the city much preferred to do their shopping in Baltimore. Yet with all this squalor and ugliness, Washington was the one planned city in America and thus had the potential for great beauty.[11]

The Lincolns settled in at Mrs. Sprigg's boarding house, the usual place for Whig congressmen. But it quickly became apparent that shutting up lively Robert into a box of a room all day would be a disaster. So in March of 1848, Mary and the boys left for Louisville, Kentucky, remaining there until the end of Lincoln's term in Congress.

It is almost always risky politically to criticize a popular war. Lincoln took that risk because he felt the recent war with Mexico was based on greed for Mexican land rather than on principle. He would pay a heavy price for this stand back home in Illinois.

Due to his campaign emphasis on office rotation and the undeniable erosion of his support back home, Lincoln concluded that it would be unwise to run for reelection. But being out of step with the forces of Manifest Destiny left him few viable options. Though he missed his family, he really wasn't anxious to return to Illinois right then. So he looked to see what other office he might obtain.

He tried to secure the job of commissioner of the General Land Office but failed. He was offered an appointment as secretary—then governor—of the Oregon Territory. Lincoln was inclined to accept, but Mary was not. It would, of course, require that they relocate to the Pacific Northwest. As Mary perceived it, not only would they lose contact with friends and family with such a move, they'd also lose contact with the burning issues of the day. By the time newspapers got to Oregon, the news would be old indeed. In those days, Europe was less remote than Oregon!

If Lincoln had stayed in Congress, he would almost certainly have succumbed to the way of thinking we now refer to as the "Beltway mind-set." He would likely have become so fascinated by the machinations of Washington that he would have lost touch with heartland issues. Accepting the Land Office job almost certainly would have turned him into just another bureaucratic hack. And the Oregon Territory job would have taken him far away from the explosive issues of the day.

But none of these made any sense to Lincoln at that time. As he perceived it, he was just adding three more failures to his growing list of dead ends.

But once again we see Providence, always working behind the scenes, stepping in to alter the course of Abraham Lincoln's life.

Presbyterian Church in Springfield, Illinois, attended by the Lincolns

THE ROAD
Back to God

*I can see how it might be possible for someone to look down upon
the earth and be an atheist, but I cannot conceive how
he could look up into the heavens and say there is no God.*

—Abraham Lincoln

Picking Up the Pieces of Life

*Now I don't know what the soul is, but whatever it is,
I know that it can humble itself.*

—Abraham Lincoln

And so Lincoln left the seats of power in Washington and returned to the
plains of Illinois, ready to pick up where he left off. He returned to his family
and the house on Eighth Street, returned to the people who gave him his
strength. Or, as Woldman put it:

> His political fortune at low ebb, his finances attenuated by its pur-
> suit, disillusioned and deeply humiliated, a politician repudiated by
> his own party, a lawyer without a practice. It was indeed a new and
> chastened man who now retreated from the world at large to seek
> solace by burying himself in the law.[1]

We are indebted to King James Bible translators for two related terms
that have become familiar to millions: "the wilderness" and "the fullness
of time." When God was about to hammer someone into shape for a great
responsibility, chances were good that the chosen crucible would be a wilder-

105

ness. Moses was sent there, as were Elijah and Paul. Even Christ Himself went there. It was a place of suffering, a pentathlon of the soul. Only when the chosen one made it through, purged of hubris, was the other term, "the fullness of time" brought into play.

It is extremely unlikely that any man or woman in human history has ever faced a more daunting task than that which would face Lincoln in 1861, still more than ten years in the future. Neither the Lincoln of "The Skinning of Thomas" nor the Lincoln of the Rebecca letters lampooning James Shields would have been ready for such an ordeal. Nor would the cowed politician now returning from Washington and looking for a place to hide.

A friend of Lincoln's, Grant Goodrich, was a prominent member of the Chicago bar with a lucrative law practice. Goodrich urged Lincoln to join him. But Lincoln told his friend that he couldn't stand confinement in a big city law office—and that he'd been longing for the open road of the Eighth Judicial Circuit.

With a growing family to support, as well as house, office, and past debts, Lincoln took a long, hard look at his life and career. Since his political life had apparently come to a dead end, what should he do now?

He'd mistakenly assumed that with nine years of Eighth Judicial Circuit experience and a private law practice, which had led to the U.S. Congress, he had a bright future. But now he was in worse shape than when he'd originally set off for Washington. Not only did he feel discredited, but he'd also lost his clients. Furthermore, the legal profession had dramatically changed since he was admitted to the bar. As Woldman put it, "Lawyers were learning that a broad and profound knowledge of legal principles were more important than the pyrotechnics of the courtroom and ear-splitting stump oratory."[2]

Furthermore, his sojourn in Washington had significantly raised the bar in his own mind. What a long way he had to go before he matched the standards of the legal giants he'd met in the East.

Always suspicious of rhetoric exploiting emotion-based audience manipulation, Lincoln turned to a serious study of mathematics, poetry, and astronomy. In his determination to master logic he reached back almost twenty-two centuries to the great Greek mathematician Euclid. Incredibly, Euclid's scientific textbooks are the only ones still in classroom use two millennia later.

Speaking of Lincoln's methodical and thorough mastering of the first six books of Euclid, Lord Charnwood pointed out that there followed from this intensive study significant results:

> The faculty which he had before shown of reducing his thought on any subject to the simplest and plainest terms possible, now grew so strong that few men can be compared with him in this.[3]

Thanks to this mastery of Euclid and continued study of the principles undergirding the profession of law, during the ten years following his return from Washington a dramatic development occurred in him that wouldn't have occurred had he remained in the political arena. According to Woldman:

> his constitutional interpretations, his understanding of the broad principles of law and justice, and his fine legal conscience and reasoning power are causing jurists like Lord Shaw of Dunfermline, a leading English legal authority, to rank Lincoln, with Pampinianus, Grotius, and Lord Mansfield, among the greatest lawyers in history.[4]

INTO THAT GREAT SILENCE

In regard to the great book [the Bible], I have only to say it is the best gift which God has ever given man. All the good from the Savior of the world is communicated to us through this book. But for this book we could not know right from wrong. All those things desirable to man are contained in it.

—ABRAHAM LINCOLN

Like his father, little Edward Lincoln loved kittens. During their long sojourn with his grandfather in Lexington, Eddie, discovering a kitten, had become ecstatic. Unfortunately, Mary's stepmother, despising the entire feline race, ordered a servant to "throw it out!" Two-year-old Eddie sobbed uncontrollably.

In mid-November of 1849, back in their Springfield home, Eddie came down with pulmonary tuberculosis, for which there was then no known cure. All the parents could do was hope. Days and weeks passed, and still the little boy suffered on, coughing and coughing.

Finally, after fifty-two days of acute illness, Eddie died. It was February 1, 1850, and he was not quite four years of age.

Mary, who'd been nursing Eddie night and day, and who had recently lost her beloved father and grandmother as well, collapsed. For weeks afterward, she remained in her bedroom weeping. And when she finally *did* come out, she was more overanxious, more insecure, more given to sudden explosions of temper than ever.[5] As for Lincoln, once again death had taken someone dear to him. It was all the more wrenching for both husband and wife in that God seemed so far away. In all his adult life Lincoln never officially joined a church.

Not that they were the exception. Even in 1860, ten years later, only 23 percent of Americans belonged to a particular church. Which didn't mean they didn't believe in God, for the Bible was the most read and referred-to book in the land, but rather that they didn't have a church family and pastor to gather around them and provide spiritual comfort at a time like this.[6]

In Lincoln's day, 77 percent of the population did not belong to any particular church. To his generation, what was far more important was reading and knowing the Bible, the number one source of allusions during that century. Ironically, today we see the reverse: high church membership coupled with an abysmal ignorance of what is in the Bible.

Lincoln had never forgotten his birth mother's dying words to him and had done his best to follow her parting admonitions. Yet he had to admit that frontier preaching did not attract his rational mind. William Barton pointed out that the Baptist churches of that period featured:

> a very unprogressive type of preaching. The preachers bellowed and spat and whined and cultivated an artificial "holy tone" and denounced the Methodists and blasphemed the Presbyterians and painted a hell which even in the backwoods was an atrocity. Against it the boy Abe Lincoln rebelled.[7]

In New Salem, Baptists, Methodists, and Presbyterians had been continually attacking one another over doctrinal hairsplitting.[8]

While in New Salem, Lincoln had read Thomas Paine's *Age of Reason* and Constantin de Volney's *Ruins of Civilization*, books that postulated that religion's value to society was merely moralistic. During the New Salem and Vandalia years, Lincoln had been rather desultorily searching for a viable philosophy of life. He had not found it. Neither had he felt much of a need to do so. Because of this increasingly secular outlook, Eddie's untimely death now came as almost a knockout blow.

The Reverend Dr. James Smith, pastor of Springfield's First Presbyterian Church, conducted the funeral for little Eddie. The brokenhearted parents listened intently to every word, searching for a life raft of hope. And while Mary might have responded to emotion, her husband would not.[9]

After the funeral, Lincoln sought out the pastor and questioned him as to his own personal journey. He was intrigued to discover how open and honest the pastor was. Smith admitted to once having strong doubts about God and, unwilling to accept pat answers, he had determined to put God to the test. Over time, with the help of prodigious study, one by one he had been able to put his doubts aside. Not content with this, he had even written a ponderous defense of Christianity, titled *The Christian's Defence* [sic]. Lincoln asked if he could borrow it.

Back home, Lincoln pondered over every word in the book, challenging each assumption, reading the text painstakingly as he would were he preparing a brief for an important legal trial. When he'd finished, he leaned back in his chair and breathed a giant sigh of relief. At long last the simple faith in the Bible he'd had as a child was validated by his logical mind: he could now rest in the faith that the Bible was truly the inspired word of God.

Not long after, Mary became a member of the congregation. Lincoln rented a pew for the family. From this time on, whenever he was not on the road, almost every Sunday would find him sitting with Mary and Robert in church.

On the Road Again

Justice is not a fiction; and though it is often held to be a sentiment only, or a remote idea, it is real, and it is founded and guarded on all sides by the strongest powers of Divine and human law.

—Abraham Lincoln

Once again, the life of the Lincolns settled down to the rhythm of law. Before his term in Congress, Lincoln had accompanied Judge Samuel Treat on the Eighth Judicial Circuit. Now the reign of Judge David Davis had begun, and Lincoln would be in his retinue for about eleven years. The circuit, made up of fourteen county seats, entailed a journey of about 500 miles and covered one fifth of the state. The group of lawyers and the judge would be gone three months in the spring and three months in the fall.

It was a vagabondish traveling circus. For rural settlers in those days, there was precious little entertainment to offset the drudgery of farming—except when the court came to town. Everything else in the county then stopped. From all over the countryside they would stream in: men, women, children, on foot, on horseback, in wagons and buggies. Before the advent of railroads, telegraphs, telephones, and daily newspapers, lawyers were the rock stars; consequently the crowds assembled mainly just to hear and watch the court proceedings. Because of his unfailing good humor and large stock of stories, Lincoln was almost always the center of attention wherever the court went.

In September 1857 word came to Lincoln that Hannah Armstrong (widow of Jack Armstrong, of the Clary's Grove Boys of New Salem) badly needed his services. Her son, Duff, had gotten in with the wrong crowd and had been accused of a murder she did not believe he had committed. Could Lincoln help? She didn't feel the other attorney would save her son. "But," she warned him, "we have no money to pay you with."

On May 7, 1858, the big day arrived in Beardstown, Illinois. As Lincoln listened to the testimony, it was clear that the circumstantial evidence had all but hanged Duff, short of a miracle. According to Albert Woldman:

> The State's star witness was Charles Allen. He had already testified at the trial of James H. Norris, also accused of participating in the murder. Norris was found guilty of manslaughter largely through Allen's testimony that under the bright moonlight he had seen Norris hit James Metzker on the back of the head with a club-like object and Armstrong strike him in the right eye with a sling-shot. Now Allen repeated the same story, and the prosecution's case was seemingly clinched.
>
> "Lincoln sat with his head thrown back, his steady gaze apparently fixed upon one spot of the blank ceiling, entirely oblivious to what was happening about him, and without a single variation of feature or noticeable movement of any muscle of his face," is the recollection of Judge Abram Bergan, then a young lawyer present in the courtroom.

Lincoln took over the witness for cross-examination. With apparent unconcern he questioned Allen regarding unimportant details. Then as to the fatal blows themselves; tell about them again.

"Did you actually see the fight?"

"Yes."

"Well, where were you standing at the time?"

"About one hundred fifty feet away from the combatants."

"Describe this weapon again." The sling-shot was pictured in detail.

"And what time did you say all this occurred?"

"Eleven o'clock at night."

"How could you see from a distance of one hundred and fifty feet, at eleven o'clock at night?"

"The moon was shining real bright."

"A full moon?"

"Yes, a full moon, and as high in the heavens as the sun would be at ten o'clock in the morning." He was positive about that.

Then with dramatic suddenness Lincoln requested the sheriff to bring him an almanac for the year 1857. Turning to the date of August 29, the night of the murder, he pointed a long forefinger to the page and bade Allen to read. Did not the almanac specifically say that the moon on that night was barely past the first quarter instead of being full? And wasn't it a fact that the almanac also revealed that instead of the moon being high in the heavens in the position of the morning sun, it had actually disappeared by eleven o'clock? And wasn't it a further fact that it was actually so dark at the time that it was impossible to see distinctly from a distance of fifty feet, let alone one hundred and fifty feet?[10]

Needless to say, those revelations caused a tremendous sensation in the courtroom. After having discredited the star witness' testimony, Lincoln gave one of the most impassioned and moving pleas to the jury of his career.

Duff Armstrong was acquitted. And Lincoln refused to accept a cent from the widow, who was weeping tears of joy.

Today, 150 years later, Lincoln pilgrims still come to Beardstown to see the courtroom where the Armstrong murder case was tried and the cage Duff Armstrong was locked into. Even the famous almanac can still be seen.

Woldman noted that the lawyers who followed the presiding circuit judge from town to town inescapably became close friends. When not in court, the judge and lawyers usually assembled in the vicinity of the fireplace if the town had an inn, otherwise in the barroom of a tavern. There they'd talk, play cards, sing, or tell stories. Some carried guitars, violins, or banjos.[11]

Often, in order to provide entertainment for the lawyers and towns-people, Judge Davis would call into night session what he called an "Or-gamathorical Court," a mock tribunal. Here various members of the bar, to the great delight of the spectators, would be tried for sundry "high crimes and misdemeanors," amid much pretended severity and seriousness. Lin-coln would sometimes be tried for the high crime of setting his fees so low his competitors couldn't match them without forcing their families into starvation.

Since many of these county seats had only a few hundred inhabitants, the lawyers were frequently forced to sleep in crude farmhouses or wretched country taverns. Often they'd have to sleep on the floor. If they were lucky enough to stay at an inn, the lawyers usually slept two to a double bed—ex-cept, of course, Judge Davis. Since he tipped the scales at over 300 pounds, no lawyer lean enough to sleep with him could be found.

When moving to the next county seat, in most cases the court would leave town long before dawn, and it was usually late into the night before their caravan arrived at their destination. If the weather was good, the best rate their plodding horses could make would be four to five miles an hour—if the roads were bad, perhaps one to two miles an hour. By early 1850, Lincoln would often hitch "Old Buck," or later, "Old Tom," to his own ramshackle buggy. In rainy weather, horses would have an extremely difficult time mak-ing it through at all, and buggy wheels would sink down to their axles.

In sparsely settled areas, bridges were scarce, consequently the lawyers had to be ready to wade or swim, depending on conditions. Lincoln, because of his extremely long legs, was often selected as the scout to test the creek or river depths. Taking off his boots and socks and rolling up his trousers, he'd lead the party across. After one severe rainstorm, a party of lawyers, including the portly judge, was led by Lincoln into waters so deep that all of them had to strip buck naked and carry their clothes over their shoulders.

It would be mainly on this circuit during these busy years that Lincoln would accumulate the stories he'd be telling for the rest of his life. It was a seasonal cycle that earned him enough money finally to pay off the New Salem debts and his business and home expenses in Springfield. But he was away from his wife and family half of every year. Truly, life had passed him by. The mere thought that this dusty—often muddy—circuit rider had ever aspired to be president of the United States would once in a while strike him with grim humor.

PART THREE

ABRAHAM LINCOLN IN THE

White House

AND THE

Civil War

Abraham Lincoln during the darkest days of the Civil War

Abraham Lincoln, June 1860, candidate for president

COUNTDOWN TO THE
Civil War

We are now on the threshold of Lincoln's years in the White House. Therefore it is important that we take a moment to understand some of the causes and underpinnings of the Civil War. Without a little historical and political background, the rest of our story would be confusing at best. In short, here is what had been happening as our story has been unfolding.

Ever since the dawn of the republic, a most uneasy truce had existed between the power brokers of the slave states and the uncoordinated leadership of the free states. The nation's wake-up call came in 1820, when Lincoln was only eleven. Indeed, the nation's thirtieth birthday was almost its last.

When, in 1819, Missouri applied for admission into the Union as a slave state, the twenty-two states were evenly divided at eleven free and eleven slave. The debate over the issue grew increasingly rancorous and raged on into 1820. This early in the century the South was already threatening to secede from the North. Finally, Henry Clay of Kentucky brokered what hereafter became known as the Missouri Compromise: Maine would be admitted as a free state and Missouri would be admitted with no restrictions on slavery. Of the rest of the vast tract of land known as the Louisiana Purchase, anything north of the parallel 36° 30' was mandated to be free. Thanks to this landmark compromise, the South backed off from its threat to secede.

As time passed, each time a territory became populated enough to ask for admission into the Union, the same bitterly fought process would begin all over again. In 1850 California asked to be admitted as a free state. Though it's south of the Missouri Compromise line, the forty-niners steadfastly refused to compete with slaves for mining claims. So once again there was an impasse. And once again Clay, the Great Compromiser, stepped in to save the nation from breaking apart.

The so-called Compromise of 1850 was truly a cut-and-paste job worthy of Henry Clay. California would be admitted as a free state *providing* that the territories of New Mexico and Utah could both choose slavery if they so desired and the North would be willing to accept the toughest-yet fugitive slave law, this one mandating high fines and imprisonment for any citizen who helped a runaway slave get away from his owner. (This law would soon cause many moderates to turn into abolitionists.)

Hardly had the furor over that issue died down when a veritable earthquake rocked the nation and then the world. Harriet Beecher Stowe, wife of a Presbyterian minister and sister of famed preacher Henry Ward Beecher, had for some time felt convicted that she should write a novel depicting the horrors of slavery. From the account that has come down to us, there was no gimmick involved. She just felt that a Higher Power was impressing her to speak out on behalf of the millions of Negroes enslaved in America.

By pure instinct, Stowe gave birth to a new genre: a series of incidents or scenes in which characters, white and black, are portrayed as being typical in the South. Beveridge writes:

> The distinct and emphatic idea was conveyed to the reader that, as a class, the slaves were frightfully abused and yearning for freedom; that Southern men, with tepid exceptions, were tyrannical and vile; that, in general, Southern women were incompetent, sluggish, and cruel.[1]

Initially, the gripping story was published serially in the pages of *The National Era*, an antislavery magazine. But in 1852 *Uncle Tom's Cabin* was published in book form, and three hunded thousand copies were sold in only twelve months (unprecedented in a nation of only 24 million). After sweeping the nation, it kept going around the world, being translated into twenty-three languages and setting sales records wherever it went.

The result was that millions of readers now perceived slavery not as the abstraction that previously had left them cold and unresponsive but as personal as Uncle Tom, Simon Legree, Eliza, Topsy, and Eva St. Clare, who now achieved the ultimate pinnacle of literary fame: becoming character types.

Years later, when Mrs. Stowe came to the White House to see President Lincoln, he is reputed to have strode to her with outstretched hands, saying, "So you're the little woman who wrote the book that made this great war."[2]

Not surprisingly, however, the average Southerner perceived slavery

very differently. When an institution has been part of a culture for almost a quarter of a millennium, those who live with it on a day-to-day basis are extremely unlikely to view it objectively.

The stage was now set for the Kansas-Nebraska Act of 1854, the political event that brought an end to the "wilderness" years of Abraham Lincoln and the arrival of the biblical "fullness of time" that would propel him to center stage of the greatest drama of the age.

The Freedom/Slavery Teeter Totter

Many people today are unaware that many states entered the Union (the United States) as slave states. Indeed, six of the thirteen original colonies were slave states. To help the modern reader better understand the events leading up to the Civil War, here is a table laying out the sequence of free and slave state admissions into the Union.

The Original Thirteen Colonies	
Free States	**Slave States**
New York	Virginia
Massachusetts	Maryland
Connecticut	Delaware
Rhode Island	North Carolina
Pennsylvania	South Carolina
New Jersey	Georgia
New Hampshire	
States Entering the Union after 1776 but before the Civil War	
Vermont (1791)	Kentucky (1792)
Ohio (1803)	Tennessee (1796)
Indiana (1816)	Louisiana (1812)
Illinois (1818)	Mississippi (1817)
Maine (1820)	Alabama (1819)
Michigan (1837)	Missouri (1821)
Iowa (1846)	Arkansas (1836)
Wisconsin (1848)	Florida (1845)
California (1850)	Texas (1845)
Minnesota (1858)	
Oregon (1859)	

This was the situation when the Civil War began. There were eighteen free states and fifteen slave states. The territory of Kansas wanted to join the Union as a free state, but the South resisted; it would have given the North an even greater advantage. If Kansas came in free, the South felt, the game would be over. Southern states planned to counter either by dividing Texas into four to six slave states—or by seceding.

During the Civil War three more states joined the Union, all as free states siding with the North: Kansas (1861), West Virginia (which broke away from Virginia, a slave state, in 1863), and Nevada (1864).

This brief survey of the sentiments about slavery and the distribution of free and slave states helps provide a glimpse of the situation the nation faced at the dawn of the Civil War.

Abraham Lincoln Wakes Up

I know there is a God and that He hates injustice and slavery.
I see the storm coming and I know that His hand is in it. If He
has a place for me, and I think He has, I believe I am ready.

—Abraham Lincoln

Five long years after slinking back from Washington and escaping into the time warps of the circuit and total immersion into law, one morning in mid-May of 1854, Abraham Lincoln was jolted into the present.

The catalyst: Illinois senator Stephen Douglas, "the Little Giant," a man who had been his rival for Mary Todd's hand in marriage, a man who had been Lincoln's debate opponent for many years, was ramming the Kansas-Nebraska Act down the throats of Congress and in the process destroying the Missouri Compromise. The Missouri Compromise had alone kept the North and the South together for thirty-four years. By that seemingly inexplicable act, Douglas wrenched open a long-closed door to slavery, making it possible to introduce it not only into the last open spaces in America—the Kansas, Nebraska, and Dakota territories—but also into the other free states as well. The very existence of America, land of the free, was now placed in jeopardy.

All his life Lincoln had detested the dehumanizing institution of slavery but had felt powerless to do anything about it—after all, it had been entrenched in America for 235 years, long before the birth of the nation itself. He'd also gritted his teeth that constitutionally, though slaves were considered nonpersons, they gave their owners immense political power. Since each slave was considered the equivalent of three-fifths of a free person, one man owning five thousand slaves could outvote three thousand voters in the North.

But thanks to his mastery of Euclid and the law, Lincoln was a different person from when he left Congress. Reasoning from cause to effect, he was now able to take an abstraction like the Kansas-Nebraska Act and chart its effect far into the future.

The great man and the great opportunity were about to merge.

As one studies this time period, it is almost impossible to disagree with Lincoln's later perception that God, not man, was orchestrating events with a script and timetable that were uniquely His own. For without that concept, nothing made sense.

Here was Lincoln, a failure at almost everything he'd tried, facing Stephen Douglas, considered the greatest orator of his day, who rarely failed at all. Why should this time be different from the others? Furthermore, without a sequence of events that was mind-bogglingly improbable, Lincoln would never have made it to the White House.

These improbable events, lined up like an array of dominoes, now began toppling—and didn't stop until the election of 1860.

The first miracle was that Lincoln was there at all. Had he drowned in Knob Creek, or died from the horse's kick at his head, or been murdered by the Mississippi River pirates, or been killed in a duel, he would not have been there. Had he pursued any other career except law, had he remained in Congress, had he been given the bureaucratic land office job in Washington, had he accepted the Oregon Territory governorship, had he been elected senator . . . the list could go on and on. Without all these failures, Lincoln would not have been in the right spot at the right time when destiny came calling.

Without question, the lead domino had to be the Kansas-Nebraska Act. Without it, Lincoln would have remained on the Eighth Judicial Circuit. And here was Stephen Douglas, the most popular political figure in America, acknowledged as the most feared debater in the nation, with bags of tricks up his sleeves—the man whom no politician in his right mind dared to debate, a man all but assumed to be a future president of the United States.

Lincoln returned to Springfield and challenged Douglas to a debate on the issue of the Kansas-Nebraska Act, and Douglas accepted. In those days, if the people wanted you to debate someone, a politician didn't dare say no. And the people wanted Lincoln and Douglas to debate. The two of them had been and would continue to be rivals for the same political posts in Illinois, and their debates were always good entertainment.

If Douglas thought about Lincoln at all, it would have been to chalk him up as just one of many little people left behind in his glorious climb to the top. *So what is he doing here at the Springfield State Fair this October fourth? I thought he'd been left in the dust five years ago! Oh well, if he dares to debate me—we've been doing that sort of thing for twenty years now—he'll tell more of his funny stories, but they won't hurt me.*

That early autumn day, Douglas took the offensive in building a case for why the Kansas-Nebraska Act was good for the country. It all sounded so plausible, such a good thing, the way Douglas described it. But when it was Lincoln's turn, he took a different view. He described the act as the most needless, incendiary bill in American history, with the potential to transform the land of the free into the land of the degenerates.

According to Joseph Fort Newton, the last thing Douglas expected was a Lincoln he'd never encountered before:

> For four hours the circuit-riding lawyer unfolded and described the great issue with a mastery of facts, a logical strategy, and a penetration of insight that astonished even his friends. Evidence of careful study was apparent in the compactness of his thought and the lucidity of his style, and there was a total absence of the story-teller, of the grotesque humor, which had marred his earlier efforts. . . . For the pet dogma of Douglas he had a profound scorn, and his epigrams pierced it like flashes of lightning. He turned it over and over, inside and out, tearing off its mask and exhibiting it in such a light that no one could fail to see the deception embodied in it. No political dogma ever received a more merciless exposure, while the Senator himself sat on a front bench, not 12 feet away, intently listening.[3]

When he'd finished, men of all parties realized a new force had arisen from the plains of Illinois. At last, here was a man who could hold his own with the greatest debater of the age. (For a fascinating story about Lincoln's enduring humility, even amidst the acclaim this series of debates had brought him, see Appendix A.)

Despite Lincoln's heroics, the Kansas-Nebraska Act of 1854 was passed and the Missouri Compromise of 1820 was repealed. This act was a major factor leading to the Civil War. Even now Lincoln was opposing the actions that would split the nation.

The second domino to fall in the sequence of events that led Lincoln to the White House was Kansas. This territory was set to enter the Union in the free column—and this had the South in an uproar. Another state on the free side would make the North that much stronger if it came to war. To prevent this, the South invaded the Kansas Territory with thugs from adjoining slave states.

The Kansas Territory was plunged into chaos for six long, bloody years as unprincipled villains such as William Quantrill led his brutal guerilla bands back and forth across the land, killing at will. In one attack—the sacking of Lawrence, Kansas—they killed over 150 of the citizens. After defeating a federal cavalry unit, Quantrill slaughtered all the troops who surrendered. The Southern power brokers even forced through a bogus "government" and constitution (the Lecompton Constitution) in a desperate attempt to steal the state by outright fraud. Unquestionably, the chaos in Kansas hastened the Civil War.

The third domino fell on May 22, 1856, eighteen days after John Brown's attack in Kansas. This day saw the most brutal attack ever to take place on the Senate floor.

Senator Charles Sumner of Massachusetts was not known as being shy or retiring. In fact, three days before, in a fiery speech, Sumner had likened South Carolina's Senator Andrew Butler to a chivalrous knight who'd chosen as a mistress the "harlot Slavery," and had accused Butler of plotting to lead South Carolina out of the Union.

South Carolina representative Preston Brooks, feeling his uncle Andrew (Butler) had been greatly maligned, strode up to Sumner's Senate desk, called him by name, declared that his speech libeled South Carolina and his uncle, and then beat Sumner to such a bloody mess with his walking stick that many thought he was dead. He was not, but it took three years before he could recover enough to resume his senatorial duties. He was in a wheelchair for four years.

With this act—still considered the most significant attack on a legislator in our history—the nation realized that not only was the issue of slavery not going away, but the strife was getting worse. This attack on Sumner illustrated how bad things had become. The conflict had reached the point of violence on the Senate floor and was rapidly approaching a point of combustion on the national stage.

In the middle of this turmoil, Lincoln cast his lot with the new Illinois Republican Party, organized in Bloomington on May 29, 1854. But who knew if this new party would even last? So many others had come and gone; why should *this* one have staying power? After arriving as a delegate, Lincoln became concerned because preliminary reports indicated that the radicals might end up dominating the young party. If that happened, there would be no future in such a party for him. So he helped draft a moderate platform that went on record against the repeal of the Missouri Compromise.

Before adjournment, from all over the hall came two thousand calls of "Lincoln! Lincoln! Lincoln!" Though Lincoln knew he'd be asked to speak to the delegates, he uncharacteristically decided to do what he did worst: speak extemporaneously, so he'd leave no record of what he said behind. He knew if the delegates left the city without drawing together in common cause, the fragmented party would fall apart. According to Beveridge, Lincoln:

> had to use the passions of the crowd and yet hold them in check; he had to satisfy and even arouse the reluctant Whigs, and yet not repel the excited radicals. He had to enlist the Germans and secure the Know-Nothings—without either group the new party could not win. He had to make all factions forget past differences and present dissensions and remember only the one outstanding practical issue on which all agreed: opposition to the extension of slavery.[4]

As Lincoln began to speak, Herndon tried to take notes for his newspaper but got so excited he gave up trying. Because no transcription was made of it, this oration became known as Lincoln's "Lost Speech." As Lincoln got into the heart of his speech, he gained in power and passion, especially when he thundered: "Slavery must be kept out of Kansas!" Lincoln cautioned delegates to avoid extreme measures lest they alienate those who might otherwise join forces with them. As for Southern Disunionists (another term for secessionists), in ringing tones, Lincoln threw down the gauntlet, "We will say to the Southern Disunionists, we won't go out of the Union, and you shan't!!!"

Cheering madly, the crowd rose as one, waving handkerchiefs and throwing hats in the air. The floor shook with stamping feet. At the end, the convention went wild. The throng rushed to Lincoln. All struggled to shake his hand. As long as Herndon lived, he contended that Lincoln's speech was "the grand effort of his life. . . . At Bloomington that day he was seven feet high." As he walked out, delegate Jesse Dubois said to fellow delegate Henry Whitney: "That is the greatest speech ever made and it puts Lincoln on the track for the Presidency."

Without question, the fourth domino was toppled by one of the most significant rulings ever made by the U.S. Supreme Court: the Dred Scott decision.

The case dealt with the status of Dred Scott, a slave, who'd been taken by his master from Missouri (a slave state) to Illinois and later to the Minnesota Territory (both free), and then back to Missouri. In 1846, with the help of antislavery lawyers, Scott sued for freedom, not only for himself but also his wife and family, on the basis that his residence in a free state and a free territory made him a free man. Scott's request had been denied by the Missouri Supreme Court and the Federal District Court. Then, due to prodding from Southern politicians, who were hoping for an all-encompassing ruling they could use to take slavery *everywhere*, it was appealed to the U.S. Supreme Court.

On March 6, 1857, Chief Justice Roger Taney, in an almost inaudible voice, read his majority decision. The decision declared that: (1) Negroes were not citizens, and thus could not sue in federal courts; (2) a slave's residence in a free state did not make him a free man; and (3) the Missouri Compromise of 1820, which had forbidden slavery in that portion of the Louisiana Purchase (except Missouri) lying north of latitude 36° 30', was an unconstitutional exercise of congressional power.

To abolitionists, everything about the decision smelled. President-elect Buchanan obviously knew about it before it had been announced; in fact, it was suspected that he'd urged Chief Justice Taney to delay announcing the decision until after the election so it wouldn't impact the election results, for the eyes of the entire nation had been riveted upon the case for some time.

Naturally, the South was jubilant at the ruling, for they could now take slavery *everywhere*. In the North, the Court's ruling seriously eroded belief in the Supreme Court's objectivity—especially since the Court's invalidation of the Missouri Compromise wasn't justified by the case. With this ruling, coupled with the parallel rage at the Kansas-Nebraska Act, the stage was now set for the Civil War.

Abraham Lincoln in early 1861 (earliest photo of him growing out his beard)

To the
White House

Only events can make a president.
—ABRAHAM LINCOLN

While the nation was beginning to tear itself in two, Abraham Lincoln's road turned ever more directly to the presidency.

AT HOME WITH THE LINCOLNS

Marriage is neither heaven nor hell; it is simply purgatory.
—ABRAHAM LINCOLN

Soon after the death of little Eddie, Mary told her husband she was expecting. On December 21, 1850, William Wallace Lincoln was born. Less than three years later, on April 4, 1853, Thomas (Tad) Lincoln was born, completing the family.

At the Lincoln home on Eighth and Jackson, husband and wife had carved out their personal comfort zones. Both loved politics and enjoyed discussing it. Mary read widely and often reviewed with her husband books she thought he'd be interested in. She was an excellent judge of human nature, better able to read men's motives than her husband and quick to detect those who sought to use him.

Of course they both idolized their children. Mary, a devoted homemaker, soon learned to make the most of what income came in. Her life was strenuous, with five pregnancies, nursing each child a year and a half, keeping up the house, cooking, sewing, and struggling with servants when they could afford them.

Lincoln understood that his wife was volatile, and he had adjusted to it. He was invariably kind to her and catered to her fears. If a thunderstorm blew in, and if he was in town, he'd hurry home in order to be a refuge. The long periods of time when he was riding the circuit were very difficult for her—for they meant she had to fill both parental roles. At night, when everything was dark (the streets were then unlighted), she'd become afraid if her husband wasn't with her. Especially did she panic when a child got sick and Lincoln wasn't there to help her.

Mary was an excellent hostess, and her table was famed for splendid cooking, ambiance, and witty conversation. But she had a difficult time retaining servants because she quarreled incessantly with them. And Lincoln got more of her negativity than was his fair share. Benjamin Thomas postulates that:

> It was unquestionably a factor in shaping Lincoln's character. For over the slow fires of misery that he learned to keep banked and under heavy pressure deep within him, his innate qualities of patience, tolerance, forbearance, and forgiveness, were tempered and refined.[1]

The Great Debates and Speeches

Ambition has been ascribed to me. God knows how sincerely I prayed from the first that this field might not be opened. I claim no insensibility to political honors, but today could the Missouri restriction be restored, and the whole slavery question be placed on the old ground of "toleration by necessity," where it exists with unyielding hostility to the spread of it, on principle, I would, in consideration, gladly agree that Judge Douglas should never be out, and I never in, as long as we both, or either, live.

—Abraham Lincoln

On June 16, 1858, the Republican Party of Illinois nominated Lincoln as their choice for U.S. senator. There was wisdom in this, as Lincoln was one of the only men in America foolhardy enough to take on the wiliest politician in America, Stephen A. Douglas, in debate.

Stephen A. Douglas, a Vermont transplant who had moved to Illinois in 1833, had experienced one of the most meteoric rises in American political history. As chairman of the powerful Committee on Territories, he'd been virtual czar of the nation's territories and statehood process. The ablest Democrat of the age, he was aggressive, brilliant, daring, and perhaps the slipperiest debater America has ever known. For good measure, he was married to Adele Cutts, generally considered to be one of America's most beautiful women.

The last thing Douglas wanted right then was to debate the only man who'd been able to hold his own with him. To friends, Douglas confided:

The whole country knows me and has me measured. Lincoln . . . is comparatively unknown, and if he gets the best of this debate— and . . . he is the ablest man the Republicans have got—I shall lose everything. Should I win, I shall gain but little. I do not want to go into a debate with Lincoln.[2]

But eight debates were set up in cities across Illinois. More than debates, they were spectacles, as the following shows:

On August 21, 1858, the sun rose on a scene of commotion in the thriving town of Ottawa and the rich farm lands, thickly settled, that surrounded it. Daybreak revealed wagons filled with farmers and their families moving on every road that led to the little city. Here and there were buggies, and men and women came on horseback, too. Many were on foot. As time wore on, more vehicles, horsemen, and pedestrians filled the roads. Soon delegations and cavalcades appeared. Banners, mottoes, flags, floats, and other campaign devices advertised the purpose of the outpouring. The day was hot, the dirt roads very dry, dust rose in thick clouds. By 10 o'clock Ottawa was in a haze. But the town was full of noise. Cannon roared, bands played, rural fife and drum corps rattled and shrilled, men shouted and hurrahed. "Hurrah for Lincoln!" "Hurrah for Douglas!" "Hurrah for Old Abe!" "Hurrah for Little Doug!" Peddlers hawked their wares—Douglas badges, Lincoln badges, "Hurrah!"

Mounted marshals and their aids, elaborate sashes about their waists, dashed to and fro, arranging rival processions to greet and escort their respective chiefs. Nor were the two leaders neglectful of the dramatic. Lincoln came on a special train of 14 cars crowded with shouting Republicans. It arrived about noon and when the

Republican champion alighted a dense crowd sent up such loud and repeated cheers that "the woods and bluffs rang again." Into a carriage which the "fair young ladies of Ottawa" had decorated with evergreens and mottos climbed Lincoln, and, preceded and followed by military companies, bands, and other units of the political parades of the time, was taken through crowded streets to the house of Mayor Glover, where once more, three "mighty" cheers were given.

Douglas came from Peru in a grand carriage drawn by four "splendid" horses. Four miles from Ottawa a reception committee of several hundred horsemen bearing flags and banners met him and escorted him to town. Once more artillery thundered, martial music blared, excited partisans cheered. With utmost difficulty the Douglas carriage and escort made their way through the shouting throng to the Geiger House.

At two o'clock the debate began. The crowd filled the square, swarmed over the platform, climbed upon the covering above it. Douglas, the light of battle in his eye, looked "imperiously" over the assemblage, tossing back his heavy mane; Lincoln appeared to be placid and humble. It was a big assemblage; at least 12,000 people were there.[3]

In each of the seven debates, a somewhat similar scenario played out, each candidate trying his best to put the other on the defensive.

Lincoln had recently, at the state Republican Convention, given one of the pivotal speeches of his career. It later became known as the "House Divided speech," because in it he quoted seven words by Christ that were familiar to all: *A house divided against itself cannot stand.* Lincoln followed up with:

> I believe this government cannot endure, permanently half *slave* and half *free*. I do not expect the Union to be *dissolved*—I do not expect the house to *fall*—but I do expect it will cease to be divided. It will become *all* one thing, or *all* the other.[4]

In the present debates, Lincoln felt it would be a grave mistake to let Douglas escape without going on record as to whether he felt a territorial people (as opposed to the people in a state that had entered the Union) had the right to exclude slavery.

Lincoln was warned that forcing Douglas to answer such a question could cost him the senatorial election. According to Nicolay and Hay, Lincoln answered: "Gentlemen, I am killing larger game; if Douglas answers, he can never be president, and the battle of 1860 is worth a hundred of this."[5] When warned that the speech might kill his senatorial chances, Lincoln replied:

> Friends, this thing has been retarded long enough. The time has come when these sentiments should be uttered; and if is decreed that I should go down because of this speech, then let me go down linked to the truth—let me die in the advocacy of what is just and right.

Sure enough, Douglas answered as he had to in order to win the senatorial election. He said that a territorial people *did* have the right to exclude slavery. This got him the votes he needed in Illinois but cost him his power base in the South, which he had to keep if he wanted to win the presidency in 1860. Lincoln's question and Douglas's answer thus changed the course of American history.

But the Lincoln who lost the race for senator was not the Lincoln people of his time assumed they knew. In fact, unbeknownst to almost everyone, Lincoln had been reborn into someone who considered the cause to be everything and the position merely an opportunity to serve. Somewhere along the way in the wilderness, he'd been purged of self.

Because of this new sense of purpose and his new God-given strength and wisdom, he was ready for the unexpected invitation to speak in New York.

The Cooper Union speech had more to it than met the eye. Lincoln was fully aware that he had no perceptible following in the East, without which his chances for the presidency were dismal. Thus, when he was invited to give a lecture at Henry Ward Beecher's Plymouth Church in Brooklyn in February of 1860, he quickly accepted. Knowing that he'd be appearing before a sophisticated Eastern audience, he devoted more effort to the research for the speech than he had for any other in his career.

By the time Lincoln arrived in New York City, sponsorship of the address had been taken over by the Young Men's Central Republican Union, an organization that included the likes of William Cullen Bryant and Horace Greeley. Some in the organization hoped that one of the chosen speakers in their series might exhibit sufficient stature to challenge the front-runner for the Republican Party's presidential nomination, William Seward. Lincoln was not informed until he arrived in New York that the event had been moved away from the church to an even more prestigious location, the Cooper Union Institute. That meant Lincoln had to change the tone of his speech to one more secular.

It is said that Lincoln gave the greatest speech of his life that night. Many came out of mere curiosity, wondering if they would see some sort of frontier freak. Even the Republicans in the audience expected to be embarrassed. Instead they, as well as critics, newspaper editors, scholars, and thought leaders, were dumbfounded. For, through exhaustive research, Lincoln did what no scholar in history had ever done before: he dismantled the South's position on slavery.

Like a lawyer in court well fortified with briefs and precedents, he took up in proper order each and every argument the Southern leaders were making against the North at that time. He:

> proceeded to prove that a majority of the "thirty-nine" who signed the Constitution were opposed to Douglas's local control of slavery. On the contrary, he argued, the "fathers" favored federal control. They had marked slavery, he said, as "an evil not to be extended." One after another, with impregnable arguments, he answered the southern complaints against the North.[6]

Then Lincoln moved to the present and postulated that the South would be satisfied with nothing less than the North's unconditional acceptance of slavery and that the next step likely to be taken by the South would be to push for the right to bring slavery into all the free states and territories, thus achieving the goal of a slave nation.

Lincoln awoke next morning famous, the speech having being published across the country. The exhaustive research paid off, for now the East was beginning to accept the idea of Abraham Lincoln as a presidential candidate.

THE NIGHT OF A THOUSAND KNIVES

When not a very great man begins to be mentioned for a very great position, his head is very likely to be turned. . . . As you request, I will be entirely frank. The taste is in my mouth a little.

—ABRAHAM LINCOLN

But the odds of Lincoln getting the Republican nomination for president were prohibitive. Everyone knew that William Seward of New York had the nomination all but locked up. In fact, it was such a foregone conclusion that Seward's backers had become more than a little complacent—and cocky.

Lincoln and his campaign team, led by the wise and wily Judge David Davis, discussed at length the odds against them. They concluded that in order for Lincoln to have a ghost of a chance, they'd have to make certain things happen. First, they'd need to bring the convention to Chicago. Lincoln was popular in Illinois but would have no chance anywhere else. Second, they should not let anyone else know that Lincoln was a strong contender. Third, they must not alienate anyone, so that Lincoln would be everyone's second choice.

Incredibly, they pulled it off. Chicago edged out St. Louis by one vote. As train-loads of delegates disembarked in Chicago, straw polls revealed that of the leading candidates (William Seward, Salmon Chase of Ohio, Simon Cameron of Pennsylvania, Edward Bates of Missouri, and Lincoln), Lincoln's delegate strength was second only to Seward's.

Chicago had constructed a rectangular building worthy of housing the new party's chiefs, hence its nickname: "The Wigwam." Chicago, a city of one hundred thousand, was the fastest-growing city in America. Even so, forty thousand visitors represented far more people than there were rooms for.

Only twenty-seven of the thirty-three states had sent delegates. Ever present in each delegate's thinking was what had happened to the Democratic Convention in Charleston, South Carolina, in April. Because Douglas, the front-runner, had been unable to undo the damage of his answers to Lincoln's question, the party had split at the seams: the cotton states of the South—Alabama, Mississippi, Louisiana, South Carolina, Florida, Texas, and Arkansas—walked out. The eventual results were that the Southern

Democrats nominated John C. Breckinridge, and the Northern Democrats Stephen Douglas.

Lincoln himself did not attend the Republican Convention. But he and his backers stayed in contact with one another by telegrams. One of his read, "I authorize no bargains and will be bound by none." After much negotiating, Indiana agreed to add its votes to those of Illinois on the first ballot. Because the Seward camp had arrogantly taken for granted Pennsylvania's earlier pledge to transfer Cameron's votes to Seward on the second ballot, Cameron's camp now told Lincoln's men that if he (Cameron) were to be offered a top Cabinet position, the votes might go to Lincoln instead.

Given Lincoln's telegram, that was a deal-breaker—unless they fudged a bit. So they did. When Lincoln later found out, he'd complain, "They have gambled me all around, bought and sold me a hundred times. I cannot begin to fulfill the pledges made in my name."[7]

In spite of this, it remained a foregone conclusion that Seward would receive the nomination. And he would have, had the nominations been made Thursday, as expected. But they were unexpectedly delayed until Friday, thus making possible the "Night of a Thousand Knives," during which something unforeseen took place.

The legendary New York newspaper tycoon Horace Greeley—always and forever a firm supporter of Seward in all his campaigns—had for a number of years been secretly brooding about Seward's and Thurlow "Boss" Weed's unwillingness to offer him a party position (or even the opportunity to run). As fate would have it, it would be on this particular night that Greeley's cup of bitterness would run over and his admiration of Seward would curdle, then coagulate into hatred. Greeley stunned delegation after delegation by knocking on their doors—nobody was sleeping much that night anyway—and sharing with them his conviction that Seward could not carry the border states, without which they could not win.

So the morning of Friday, May 18, dawned, and the bleary-eyed Lincoln men were ready. Weed and Seward had filled an entire thirteen-car train with vociferous supporters. Lincoln's men, not to be outdone, capitalized on Illinois Central's new Chicago-to-Cairo (700 miles long—the longest in nation) train route and arranged a special reduced rate on all Illinois trains connecting with Chicago.

Second, Lincoln's organizers Jesse Fell and Ward Hill Lamon took it upon their consciences to sneakily oversee the printing of a large number of duplicate tickets for Friday's session. They then distributed them to supporters who promised to claim them early and be prepared to shout like they'd never shouted before. The Seward men were so overconfident that they marched over a thousand supporters through the streets of the city behind their blaring band. Imagine their rage when they later discovered the Wigwam all but full, with only their delegates guaranteed admission.

Furthermore, the Lincoln men, not taking any chances, craftily sandwiched the entire Pennsylvania delegation between the Illinois and Indiana delegations, in order to make sure Pennsylvania didn't change allegiance.

The great moment finally arrived. During the first two days, the Lincoln men had permitted the Seward men to have free reign on the Wigwam floor—but not the third. On the third day, Lincoln shouters were shoved through the doors until they filled all the nondelegate seats as well as the standing-room seats.

When Seward was nominated, the shouting and shrieking from his supporters defied description. It seemed to people vainly covering their ears that it was not humanly possible to assault eardrums any worse. But the Lincoln men had known that the presidency might indeed come down to this, and they were ready to answer. According to Isaac Arnold:

> There was then living in Chicago, a man whose voice could drown the roar of Lake Michigan in its wildest fury; nay, it was said that his shout could be heard on a calm day, across the lake.[8]

They also found another, a Dr. Ames, who was unequaled in shouting power. These two men were told to organize a body of men, many of them champion hog-callers, to be prepared to cheer and shout. They were positioned on opposite sides of the Wigwam and told to watch for their signal. When Chairman Burton C. Cook (who would be conspicuous on the platform) took out his white handkerchief, they were to shout and cheer and shriek and stomp their feet, and not dare stop until Cook returned the handkerchief to his pocket.

At the first wave of Cook's handkerchief, there went up such a shout as had possibly never been heard on this planet before. One person described it thus:

> The shouting was absolutely frantic, shrill and wild. No Comanches or panthers ever struck a higher note or gave screams with more infernal intensity. Imagine all the hogs ever slaughtered in Cincinnati giving their death squeals together, and a score of big steam whistles going. [9]

When the New Yorkers tried to do the same for Seward, their voices were instantly drowned out by the white handkerchief.

With bated breaths, thousands listened intently to the delegation spokesmen. At the end of the first ballot, Seward had a commanding lead. He had 173½ votes of the 233 needed for nomination. Lincoln was second with 102 votes. He was followed by Cameron with 50½; Chase with 49; and Bates with 48 votes. Back in Springfield, Lincoln received these numbers by telegram immediately after the results were confirmed.

Now began the fateful second ballot: Who would gain? Who would lose? Would this one put Seward over the top? Pencils scribbled furiously as delegates attempted to keep up with the changing votes. Sure enough, Seward's total rose 11 votes to 184½. But Lincoln, gaining 79 votes (largely because of the transfusion of Pennsylvania votes), now stood at 181, only 3½ behind Seward.

When the third ballot began, the tension in the Wigwam was so thick it was almost palpable, for everyone knew the race had been reduced to two candidates. In this poll Seward lost 4½ votes—and Lincoln gained 50½. Now Seward stood at 180 votes and Lincoln had 231½—way out in first place and only 1½ votes short of nomination!

A deathly silence followed. Finally it was broken by delegate Cartter from Ohio, who, in a voice trembling with excitement, announced the transferal of four votes to Lincoln. The nomination was Lincoln's.

The boom of a cannon on the roof of the Wigwam announced the nomination to the tens of thousands in the streets. Inside the convention, the Lincoln river now swelled into a torrent as delegation after delegation, amidst continuing shouting, changed its vote to the victor. Hannibal Hamlin of Maine was then chosen as nominee for vice president.

In Springfield, Lincoln was waiting with some friends in the office of the *Sangamon Journal*. Suddenly a messenger from the telegraph office rushed in and handed him a slip of paper. Lincoln first read it silently, then out loud to his friends. Then, without stopping to receive their congratulations, said quietly, "There is a little woman at our house who will like to hear this. I'll go down and tell her."[10]

The Election

Every man is said to have his peculiar ambition. Whether it be true or not,
I can say for one that I have no other as great as that of being truly
esteemed of my fellow men, by rendering myself worthy of their esteem.

—Abraham Lincoln

Of the campaign that followed, Isaac Arnold writes, "This presidential campaign has had no parallel. The enthusiasm of the people was like a great conflagration, like a prairie fire before a wild tornado."[11] Lincoln's backers took full advantage of their candidate's homespun roots during their campaigning. To be able to field a candidate who actually *had* been born in a log cabin and actually *had* split hundreds—perhaps thousands—of rails was almost too good to be true.

How very much had happened since Owen Lovejoy had stood over the newly dug grave of his brother Elijah (an abolitionist editor slain for daring to criticize slavery). Whittier, Bryant, Lowell, Longfellow, and other poets had all championed the cause of liberty. Stowe's *Uncle Tom's Cabin* continued to speak to hearts and minds everywhere. Charles Sumner's fiery eloquence had nearly cost him his life. Henry Ward Beecher, Wendell Phillipps, and William Ellery Channing had added their voices to the cause, as had Salmon Chase with his logic, and Lincoln with the clearest voice of all. All of these voices now blended and found expression at the ballot box. The nation declared that slavery should go no further.

In the national election Lincoln received 180 electoral votes, with a popular vote of 1,866,452. Stephen Douglas, Lincoln's old debate partner, received 12 electoral votes and 1,375,157 popular votes. Breckinridge received 72 electoral votes and 847,953 popular votes, and John Bell (of the newly formed Constitutional Union Party) got 39 electoral votes and 590,631 popular votes.

Abraham Lincoln was elected the sixteenth president of the United States.

The South had dominated the American Republic for most of its existence. But now the nation's executive power passed out of the hands of those who believed the Negro to be a nonperson and into the hands of those who believed that the Declaration of Independence and Constitution applied to *all* people.

TREASON IN WASHINGTON

I only wish I could have gotten there [Washington, D.C.]
to lock the door before the horse was stolen.

—ABRAHAM LINCOLN

There is a general perception that the Civil War did not begin until Fort Sumter—after Lincoln became president. That is not true. The rebellion was anything but sudden: it had been planned and replanned for thirty years.

When John Nicolay and John Hay researched this period, they discovered that the war actually began during the Buchanan presidency. A cabal consisting of John Floyd of Virginia, Howard Cobb of Georgia, Jacob Thompson of Mississippi, and W. H. Trescott of South Carolina operated from within the Buchanan Cabinet. It was as though there were four giant black widow spiders draining the lifeblood of the nation, leaving but empty shells behind—all to position things in the nation so that the South would have the advantage in the eventual, unavoidable war. [12]

The once robust Treasury was looted and left in shambles. The army and warships were sent too far away to be quickly recalled. The best military equipment and supplies from arsenals across the nation were "requisitioned" and sent south. The federal fortifications and armories in the South were plundered. The nation's reputation abroad was trashed by operatives of the South so that the Confederacy would be quickly recognized by the great powers.

The plan was to invade Washington before Lincoln's votes could be officially counted. With the capital in their hands, the victory would belong to the South without a fight.

Once again, South Carolina threatened to secede. The last time that had happened, Andrew Jackson had been president, and South Carolina had meekly backed down. But there hadn't been a really strong president since. Buchanan merely whimpered, wrung his hands helplessly, and bleated that though the Constitution gave him the power to stop secession, he really didn't see how he could. So South Carolina and the South took him at his word.

When loyalists in the Cabinet belatedly took a stand in late December 1860, Buchanan in essence abdicated. The cabal resigned and the cotton states of Mississippi, Florida, Alabama, Georgia, Louisiana, and Texas seceded. Buchanan labeled himself "The last American president."

Lincoln, watching the collapse of the nation from Springfield, told Joseph Gillespie, "Buchanan . . . is giving away the case, and I have nothing to say, and can't stop him."[13] So Lincoln had to watch from the sidelines when, on February 9, 1861, Jefferson Davis and Alexander Stephens were elected president and vice president of the Confederate States of America.

Abraham Lincoln during the Civil War

IN THE MIDST OF
Enemies

I will suffer death before I will consent . . . to any concession or compromise which looks like buying the privilege to take possession of this government to which we have a constitutional right.

—ABRAHAM LINCOLN

MR. LINCOLN GOES TO WASHINGTON

For months after the election, well-wishers, gawkers, and office seekers flooded to Springfield to see the face of the president-elect. On the surface he was the same affable Lincoln but beneath he was deeply troubled. Already the weight of his awesome responsibilities was beginning to leave its imprint on him.

If the president-elect was to survive the next four years, he would need a Cabinet like no other. He was determined to get his two principal rivals for the nomination on board: William Seward of New York and Salmon Chase of Ohio, two gentlemen who heartily disliked each other. For starters, Seward and Boss Weed were determined to force Lincoln to choose a Seward-Weed cabinet, and Chase was equally determined to push for a Chase cabinet. In the stormy days ahead, Lincoln needed a stellar Cabinet to be his eyes and ears into the nation. He needed leadership, integrity, and stature. There had to be balance.

In the end, he balanced his Cabinet with East and West, former Democrats and Whigs, hard-liners and conciliators. In short, the Cabinet had a perfect balance representative of all the divisions in the nation. When someone asked him if a Cabinet full of rivals wouldn't eat him up, Lincoln smiled and said that rather they'd eat one another up. He never doubted his ability to hold his own. In weaker hands, this would have been a den of snarling tigers; in Lincoln's hands, it became a tower of strength.

William Seward of New York became secretary of state; Salmon Chase of Ohio, secretary of the treasury; Edward Bates of Missouri, attorney general; Simon Cameron of Pennsylvania, secretary of war; Gideon Wells of Connecticut, secretary of the Navy; Caleb Smith of Indiana, secretary of the interior; and Montgomery Blair, postmaster general.

Lincoln had one last pilgrimage to make: to see his mother once more. He would make this trip alone, as Mary never deigned to visit his family.

Sarah Lincoln had heard so much about her famous son that she'd even made a special trip to one of his Douglas debates. Among the thousands thronging the streets, she thought she'd be unnoticed by anyone. But no—his eagle eye spied her, and he stopped his carriage and pressed through the crowd to kiss her.

Now, on January 31, 1860, after traveling via passenger train, freight train, and buggy, he finally got to the house where she was living with her daughter. They had a wonderful visit. As he got up to go, she clung to him and wept, overcome by a feeling that she'd never see him again, that *something would happen to him in Washington.*[1] This kind of foreboding was occurring more and more frequently in Lincoln and those around him. Sarah Lincoln never did see him alive again.

Another poignant parting was with his faithful law partner, William Herndon. As they parted, Lincoln suggested that Herndon not remove the partnership sign that hung at the foot of the stairs:

> "Let it hang there undisturbed," he said, "Give our clients to understand that the election of a president makes no change in the firm of Lincoln and Herndon. If I live I'm coming back some time, and then we'll go right on practicing law as if nothing happened." Then Lincoln's mood changed, and a shadow came over his face. "He said the sorrow of parting from his old associations was deeper than most people would imagine, but it was more marked in his case because of the feeling which had become irrepressible that he would never return alive."[2]

ONE MAN'S RESOLUTION

Must is the word. . . . *You* can *not fail if you resolutely determine that*
you will *not*. . . . *Always bear in mind that your resolution to succeed*
is more important than any other thing.

—ABRAHAM LINCOLN

Scholars continue to marvel at Lincoln's first six months as president. Here he was, a man without administrative experience, suddenly becoming president of the United States at the most terrifying moment of its history. And yet somehow he thrived.

The cotton states had already seceded from the Union and elected their own president and vice president. The slightest misstep or ill-advised word on Lincoln's part could cost him the border states, too. These states—Missouri, Kentucky, Maryland, and Delaware—were buffers between the Confederate and Union states. Kansas was still a political wild card. Without these states aligning with the North it would be all but impossible for the Republic to survive.

As we have noted, Buchanan considered himself to be the last president of the United States, the Confederacy had set up shop as a separate state on the North American continent, and the South intended to seize Washington before Lincoln could get there, and furthermore planned to make sure he'd never get there at all—alive, that is.

So it was that when Lincoln looked out at the crowd thronging the Springfield train station on that bleak February 11, America was only one man's heartbeat away from chaos, anarchy, and disintegration. One man's will, one man's resolution, was all that held a people together.

As for the people of the North, Lincoln was still an unknown quantity. The odds were he'd turn out to be just another in a long line of spineless, lackluster presidents. Even the Confederate leaders laughed at his chances for success. *Everyone* underestimated him and would continue to do so for years to come.

This actually turned out to be the salvation of the Union. Had Southern leaders realized early on that Lincoln's courageous resolution and firm hand on the tiller were all that kept the republic together and that assassinating him would bring them almost immediate victory, the temptation to take such action would have been almost irresistible.

Which brings to the reason that didn't happen. Lincoln would have summed up that reason in one word: "Providence."

And so Lincoln arrived at the station in Springfield to board the train that would take him to Washington, D.C. Many supporters gathered to see him off:

It was a cloudy, stormy morning, which served to add gloom and depression to their spirits. The leave-taking became a scene of subdued anxiety, almost of solemnity. Mr. Lincoln took a position in the waiting-room, where his friends filed past him, often merely pressing his hand in silent emotion.

The half-finished ceremony was broken in upon by the ringing bells and the rushing train. The crowd closed about the railroad car into which the president-elect and his party made their way. Then came the central incident of the morning. Once more the bell gave notice of starting; but as the conductor paused with his hand lifted to the bell-rope, Mr. Lincoln appeared on the platform of the car, and raised his hand to command attention. The bystanders bared their heads to the falling snow-flakes, and standing thus, his neighbors heard his voice for the last time in the city of his home, in a farewell address so chaste and pathetic that it reads as if he already felt the tragic shadow of forecasting fate:

"My friends, no one, not in my situation, can appreciate my feeling of sadness at this parting. To this place, and the kindness of these people, I owe everything. Here I have lived a quarter of a century, and have passed from a young to an old man. Here my children have been born, and one is buried. I now leave, not knowing when or whether ever I may return, with a task before me greater than that which rested upon Washington. Without the assistance of that Divine Being who ever attended him, I cannot succeed. With that assistance, I cannot fail. Trusting in Him, who can go with me, and remain with you, and be everywhere for good, let us confidently hope that all will yet be well. To His care commending you, as I hope in your prayers you will commend me, I beg you an affectionate farewell."[3]

He would never see them again. The train that would bring him back would move ever so much slower than the one taking him away.

Indianapolis, Columbus, Cincinnati, Cleveland, Pittsburgh, Buffalo, Albany, New York, Trenton, Philadelphia, Harrisburg—each with a vast crowd of people with but one goal, to see the man representing their only hope in the dark days all knew lay ahead. In his great humility he knew he was but a symbol to them—a symbol of hope.

And there were, of course, many short stops. At Westfield, New York, the president-elect addressed the crowd, saying, "I have a correspondent in this place, and if she is present, I would like to see her. Her name is Grace Bedell." [4]

As the blushing eleven-year-old girl was led through the crowd to the train platform, Lincoln continued, "She wrote me that she thought I would be better looking if I wore whiskers."

By then she had reached him. He looked down at her from his great height and said, "You see, I let these whiskers grow for you, Grace."

Then he kissed her.

The story was carried by newspapers all across the country.

SCOTT AND BRECKINRIDGE SAVE THE NATION

Necessity knows no law.

—ABRAHAM LINCOLN

Two men, both Southern-born, now step into our story.

John Cabell Breckinridge of Kentucky had been a Democratic presidential candidate running against Lincoln. He had had received seventy-two electoral votes. He was also the outgoing vice president. As such, he had the opportunity to deny the presidency to Lincoln and throw the nation into chaos.

Everyone knew he was a secessionist. In fact, he would soon become brigadier general, then major-general, then secretary of war in the Confederate cause. Yet he was a man of impeccable integrity and so honored his oath of office that he worked out a plan with General Scott.

Seventy-five-year-old Winfield Scott of Virginia, one of the most colorful figures of his time, ought to have long since retired. Yet here he was, like a 300-pound bird of paradise, bedecked in a gorgeous uniform topped off with a multiplumed hat. Affectionately known as "Old Fuss and Feathers," this hero of the War of 1812 had been in every war since then. He had been the commander in chief of the war with Mexico, had run for president in 1852, and for twenty years had been the nation's only lieutenant general. Though frail and frequently ill, he still served the nation he loved.

Because the cabal in Buchanan's Cabinet had made certain that Scott wouldn't have enough men to protect Washington against an insurgent attack, Scott had known he might be forced to explore other alternatives.

February 13, 1861 ("seizure day"), was the day Washington was to have fallen. Armed bodies of men had been enlisted and drilled. Many had entered the city and reported for orders. For several days, trains had been disgorging passengers from all over the South. By 8 o'clock that cloudless Wednesday morning, crowds were climbing the gallery steps where the two Houses of Congress were to meet in joint assembly. The plan was to incite a riot, keep Lincoln's votes from being counted, and in the confusion take the city. The secessionist organizers anticipated little trouble in accomplishing this.

But General Scott, knowing that the District of Columbia forces often could not be trusted, had brought in plainclothes policemen from as far away as Philadelphia and New York. These men were now scattered through the galleries and corridors, armed and ready for action.

Thus the plan to incite a riot never got off the ground. The mob that was to enter the Senate building and create bedlam never made it inside. At every entrance Scott's men met them. A guard force of civil but inflexible soldiers barred admission to all except senators, representatives, and those with written tickets of admission signed by the speaker of the house or the vice president. Not even friends or family of senators were allowed in. Needless to say, the seething crowd outside, acres in extent, had much to say about this, almost all profane, but to no avail. They could not get inside.

When all had been seated, it was quickly obvious that Southerners were in the vast majority. L. E. Chittenden (soon to be Register of the Treasury) was one of the favored few to be let in.

Then entered Vice President Breckinridge and the Senate. The members of the House stood until the senators took their seats in a semicircle. Chittenden was proud of the vice president that day. Though a Kentucky secessionist, Breckinridge was not false to his duty:

He knew that the day was one of peril to the Republic—that he was presiding over what appeared to be a joint meeting of two deliberative bodies, but which, beneath the surface, was a caldron of inflammable materials, heated almost to the point of explosion. But he had determined that the results of the count should be declared, and his purpose was manifested in every word and gesture. Jupiter never ruled a council on Olympus with a firmer hand. . . .

One member rose—"Except questions of order, no motion can be entertained," said the presiding officer. The member exclaimed that he wished to raise a point of order. "Was the count of the electoral vote to proceed under menace? Should members be required to perform a constitutional duty before the janizaries of Scott were withdrawn from the hall?" "The point of order is not sustained," was the decision which suppressed the member, more by its emphasis than by its words.

After all the votes had been tabulated, the vice president arose and, standing erect and dignified, declared "That Abraham Lincoln, of Illinois, having received a majority of the whole number of electoral votes, is duly elected President of the United States for the four years beginning on the fourth day of March, 1861."

The Senate retired to its own chamber—and the room exploded in shouts, curses, vituperation. All the venom of the secessionists in the room was directed at General Scott. One of their own had prevented them from doing the very thing he said he supported. They screeched for Scott to remove his "minions," "janizaries," "hirelings," "blue-coated slaves" from the Capitol. Eventually, through sheer exhaustion, the howling subsided and the danger inside the building passed.

Outside, the entire avenue in the direction of the Treasury was choked with an angry, howling mob. They had heard what had happened—or, rather, what had not happened—and they were furious. The mob maintained possession of the avenue far into the night. There was much street fighting and many arrests.

Scott and Breckinridge saved the nation from revolution that day. Chittenden wrote:

> A perfect understanding existed between them. General Scott knew he could rely on the promised assistance of the vice president, who had repeatedly declared that until the end of his term he should perform the duties of his office, under the sanction of his oath. ... These two men, both southern-born, on the 13th of February conducted the republic safely through one of the most imminent perils that ever threatened its existence.[5]

If Confederate leaders had managed to take possession of Washington that day, the Civil War would have been over before it was officially declared. With Virginia already leaning toward secession, with Maryland a powder keg of a state with thousands of secessionists eager for an excuse to precipitate action in the capital city, a takeover of Washington that "seizure day" would have been like spontaneous combustion. Lincoln would have had no capital to go to and the republic would have had no credibility with its own people or the world at large.

Nine days later, Scott affected the outcome again. While Lincoln was still in Philadelphia, Allan Pinkerton, head of the Pinkerton Detective Agency, warned Lincoln that when he and his party reached Baltimore, a city seething with secessionists, he was to be assassinated. At first Lincoln felt Pinkerton was overreacting, but then in rushed Frederick W. Seward with a message from his father and General Scott, confirming the plot to kill Lincoln, and he felt it would be foolish to reject the urgent messages from the head of his Cabinet, the nation's chief detective, and the chief of America's armed forces. He agreed to follow their advice.[6]

Later it was discovered that a mob of twenty thousand roughs and plug-uglies was to have made sure he'd never leave Baltimore alive. What sends chills up one's spine has to do with one of the six paid assassins lying in wait: "One of them is an actor who recites passages from *Julius Caesar* in their conclaves."[7] Even back in 1861, John Wilkes Booth was already on Lincoln's trail.

Foiling them all, the president-elect arrived on February 23 (on a different train from that scheduled) in Washington, a hostile Southern city riddled with secessionists who fully expected to see the Confederate flag flying over the capital by May 1.

Yet Lincoln had already accomplished more than he knew. In the thousands of conversations and interviews he'd had since his nomination, how had he known what to say or what not to say? In his psyche was a marvelous gyroscope that enabled him to keep near-perfect balance. For this ability, Stephen Douglas was due a great vote of thanks. In the twenty-some years of Lincoln's life spent debating the "Little Giant" ("the most subtle juggler of words ever known to American politics"[8]) Lincoln had learned to avoid vague phrases that lent themselves to twisting or misinterpretation.

Of all the known candidates for Northern leadership, only Lincoln could have kept the Union from self-destructing. Chase's rigid self-righteousness would have been just as fatal as Seward's conciliation. Had Lincoln freed the slaves too early, there would have been disastrous results; had he not done so when he did, the great European powers would in all likelihood have recognized the Confederacy.

How had he known?

Unfinished U.S. Capitol, inauguration of Abraham Lincoln, 1861

SUNLIGHT AND
Shadow

Of all the trials I have had since I came here, none begin to compare with those I had between the inauguration and the fall of Fort Sumter. They were so great that could I have anticipated them, I would not have believed it possible to survive them.

—ABRAHAM LINCOLN

THE GUNS OF APRIL

The city of Washington had changed little in the twelve years since Lincoln had lived there. Cobblestoned Pennsylvania Avenue was still the only paved road in the city. Like ancient Rome, it was not a fragrant city: open drains emptied into the streets; an open canal bred mosquitoes, malaria, and tadpoles; and Goose Creek was stagnant. The only completed public edifices in the city were the weather-beaten Little State Department, the War and Navy building on Seventeenth Street, the Post Office Department, the Interior building, and the White House. Neither the wings nor the dome of the Capitol had been completed.

The extensive open spaces of the capital city were covered with building stones, lumber, and huge iron plates for the Capitol dome. House member Albert Riddle pointed out that "Nothing more conclusively showed the predetermined destruction of the Republic than this deliberate suspension of the completion of the Capitol and Treasury building."[1] The Capitol was also unfinished inside. Even the Potomac bridges were in terrible condition. Money that might have been used for all this had been sent south into secessionist coffers. The population of Washington was now 61,000, including 3,000 slaves.

Another grave danger awaited the president-elect on March 4, Inauguration Day. Even at an early hour a dense multitude had already assembled in the corridor between the executive mansion and Capitol Hill. According to L. E. Chittenden, barricade cables had been stretched on either side of the carriageway, and watchful police were positioned. General Scott fielded an even larger force than before. Armed men in plainclothes were positioned all over the city, many traveling great distances to be there. Sharpshooters were placed strategically where they could command the best views.

The procession started at the executive mansion, where President Buchanan entered a carriage drawn by four horses. Led by the Marshall of the District with his aides on horseback, they were followed by a select company of the sappers and miners of the regular army, all formed as a hollow square, with the carriage in its center. More companies joined in, until five hundred mounted soldiers surrounded, preceded, and followed the presidential carriage.

At Willard's Hotel, the procession stopped. Mr. Lincoln walked through the parting crowd to the carriage, and sat down next to Buchanan.

> The venerable form, pallid face, and perfectly white hair of Mr. Buchanan contrasted powerfully with the tall figure, coal-black hair, and rugged features of Mr. Lincoln, and suggested that the exhausted energies of the old were to be followed by the vigorous strength of the new administration.

According to Chittenden, now followed the most dangerous moment of the day:

> I learned afterwards that the tall form of Mr. Lincoln was exposed the whole distance, so that a shot from a concealed assassin from any one of the thousand windows would have ended his career.

Stretching out almost half a mile, the crowd had been waiting expectantly for the president-elect. Because of a rumor that the secessionists were planning to blow up the platform, Scott had stationed a guard under it throughout the previous night. In the distance two batteries of horse artillery stood ready for action.

Behind the marshal came the tall, bent form of Chief Justice Taney, arm in arm with Lincoln. Senators, congressmen, officers of the army and navy followed—but the crowd had eyes only for the president-elect. Suddenly, the silvery voice of Lincoln's cherished friend, Senator Edward Baker, rang out over the multitude: "Fellow citizens, I introduce to you Abraham Lincoln, the president-elect of the United States of America!"

A slight ripple of applause followed. Who could have known that Baker would be one of the first to fall in days to come?

Lincoln now stood and looked around for a place to lay his hat—and then occurred one of the most moving acts of America's heroic age. Senator Stephen Douglas, Lincoln's career-long nemesis and debating partner, who had just been defeated by Lincoln in Douglas's lifelong quest for the presidency, made a magnificent gesture. That proud "Little Giant" never stood taller than when he stretched out his hand for Lincoln's hat. That hat he would humbly hold in his lap during the next half hour.

Chittenden notes that, accustomed as they were to perfunctory speeches from politicians, few had even an inkling that they were about to hear one of the world's greatest speeches:

> It needed the light of subsequent events for its comprehension. I count it as one of the valued opportunities of my life, that seated only a few yards from the speaker, I heard distinctly every word he uttered, watched the play of his strong features, and noted the effect of his emphatic sentences upon the persons around me. A flash of light swept over the field as the faces of the multitude were turned toward Mr. Lincoln, when the words, "Fellow citizens of the United States" fell from his lips. Few of those faces were turned away until his last words were spoken.

The speaker's voice was heard with clarity into the farthest margins of the crowd. There was absolute silence as everyone strained to hear every word he spoke.

Chittenden wondered how Lincoln's words would play out, for few here had ever heard him speak. The silence stretched until it actually became painful, beginning to break only with lines such as, "I hold that in contemplation of universal laws, and of the Constitution, the Union of these states is perpetual!" and "I shall take care, as the Constitution itself expressly enjoins upon me, that the 'laws of the Union shall be faithfully executed in all the states!'" When he continued on with "The power confided in me will be used to hold, occupy, and possess the property and places belonging to the government," a great wave of enthusiasm rolled through the audience, "as the united voices of the immense multitude ascended heavenward in a roar of assenting applause."

From that moment on, the president-elect had his audience. Lincoln had consulted with Seward and others ahead of time, testing every word the address contained, knowing full well it would be scrutinized in the South and around the world. He had all but panicked when Lincoln's son Robert forgot to safeguard it and it got lost on the train. (Happily, it was found in time.) Especially had they labored over the last lines, lines that have since become one of the treasures of the American people. With them he specifically addressed all those living in the South:

> I am loath to close. We are not enemies, but friends. We must not be enemies. Though passion may have strained, it must not break our bonds of affection.
>
> The mystic chords of memory, stretching from every battle-field and patriot grave to every living heart and hearthstone, all over this broad land, will yet swell the chorus of the Union, when again touched, as surely they will be, by the better angels of our nature!

According to Chittenden, there was no hesitancy in the judgment that the audience was prepared to pronounce upon this inaugural address. From the farthest limits of East Capitol Square, from the distant street where General Scott and his batteries were posted as a corps of observation, and from every foot of the enclosed space, a burst of applause arose that made loyal hearts beat more rapidly, and the blood in loyal arteries leap joyously to their extremities. Over and over again the cheer was repeated. Grave senators and judges "joined in the rapturous cry, and even the ranks of *slavery* could scarce forbear to cheer!"

The aged chief justice of the United States came forward to administer the presidential oath of office for the ninth and last time in his career:

> He extended an open Bible, upon which Mr. Lincoln laid his left hand, and uplifting his right arm, he slowly repeated the words of

the Constitution. "I do solemnly swear that I will faithfully execute the office of President of the United States, and will, to the best of my ability, preserve, protect, and defend the Constitution of the United States. So help me God!"

As Citizen Buchanan was driven down the road to Washington's only railroad station and the crowds peacefully melted away, it was the united opinion of close observers that for the third time in only three weeks, the life of the nation and its leader had been preserved by Lieutenant General Winfield Scott.

No small thanks to him, Abraham Lincoln was now the sixteenth president of the United States.[2]

The Road to War

War is a crime against humanity. Criminals who transgress laws made by men sometimes escape the penalty; those who break the laws ordained by God, never. Whether nation or individual, their punishment is inevitable.

—Abraham Lincoln

Before Lincoln had even taken office, most of the federal forts in the South had already been commandeered by the South. One that had not was Fort Sumter in Charleston Bay. It would have been, had outgoing Secretary of War John Floyd had his way. Floyd had even commanded Major Robert Anderson to take no steps to protect, reinforce, or reprovision his men. Anderson, disdaining such treasonable counsel, in the dead of night moved his men behind the impregnable walls of Fort Sumter.

The first thing that was handed to Lincoln after he returned from the inauguration was a letter from Major Anderson, relayed by outgoing Secretary Floyd. The news from Fort Sumter was dire and unexpected: there was food enough for only another twenty-eight days!—a direct result of Floyd's determination to starve out the garrison so they'd have to surrender the fort. Lincoln must have often muttered, *Buchanan, Buchanan, what an unbelievable mess you left behind!*

What a baptism of fire for the new president and Cabinet. The more they discussed Sumter options, the more they realized all the good ones had been wasted by Buchanan. Only consequences remained. Seward pointed out that any attempt at this late date to send in enough forces to protect the fort would automatically trigger a civil war—and the Union would be considered the aggressor, a position Lincoln had promised not to take.

Neither were the leaders of the Confederacy eager to start a war. Jefferson Davis and his cabinet, sitting in their offices in Montgomery, much preferred to negotiate until they got their way. They always had, after all. In fact, Southerners in general considered Northerners to be incapable of standing up to them. They had seceded thinking the North would "just let them go." Should it come to civil war they were confident that the great European powers, desperately needing cotton for their mills, would intervene on the side of the Confederacy. The one possibility the South never considered was the one that actually happened: that the North would fight an all-out civil war rather than let the Union be shattered and that England and France would not come to the aid of the South.

Lincoln's adroit handling of the matter left Montgomery with few choices. If they attacked Fort Sumter, they'd lose both their moral high ground and their Northern allies. If they backed down, their people would be back in the Union in only days. They decided to make the first move, before the reprovisioning ships reached Charleston.

On April 11, 1861, General P. G. T. Beauregard sent an officer out to the fort, demanding its surrender. Anderson refused, telling him that if they just waited, they'd be starved out if relief ships didn't arrive very soon. After Anderson heard back from Montgomery twice, a little after 3:00 A.M., on April 12 the ultimatum came: surrender, or the firing would begin within an hour's time.

The rebels (secessionist troops) had set up as many as nineteen artillery batteries around the bay, mounting a total of thirty guns and seventeen ten-inch mortars, each capable of dropping large shells into the fort. Though Anderson had forty-eight guns, twenty-seven were on the parapet, a death trap for any soldiers who dared to man them; and he had no mortars at all. Of his 128 men, eight were musicians and forty-three were noncombatant laborers, compared to Montgomery's six thousand soldiers on the shore.

Bombardment from the shore was continuous all day. Anderson's return fire from the fort was only intermittent, thanks to Floyd. During the afternoon the relief ships arrived, but a storm that night kept them from reaching the fort.

At about 9:00 a.m. on April 13, thanks to a red-hot shot, the fort's roof caught fire, and the men were unable to put it out. To avoid being killed by exploding gunpowder, all fifty remaining barrels of gunpowder were heaved into the bay. With no gunpowder for their guns, Anderson had no choice but to surrender. The gallant garrison was permitted to board the *Baltic* and be taken north.[3]

The rebels were jubilant and again predicted their flag would be flying over the U.S. Capitol in Washington by May 1. What they didn't realize was that Lincoln had pulled off a miracle. According to Nicolay and Hay:

> When he finally gave the order that the fleet should sail he was master of the situation; master of his Cabinet; master of the moral attitude and issues of the struggle; master of the public opinion which must arise out of the impending conflict; master if the rebels hesitated or repented, because they would thereby forfeit their prestige with the South; master if they persisted, for he would then command a United North.[4]

Lincoln's inaugural had been a clarion call to the nation. One man had courageously stood up, in a city where secessionists vastly outnumbered those faithful to the Union, and had declared in ringing tones, "So far—and no farther. We have retreated for seventy-two years, but we are now drawing a line in the sand. One step over that line and the South will have to answer for the consequences."

The North had listened. The South had, too, but with laughs of derision. They neither believed Lincoln meant what he said nor that the rest of the country would back him if he did. Seventy-two years of Northern subservience to the South was proof that this backwoodsy hayseed was braying in the wind.

But they were wrong. The guns of the Fort Sumter bombardment woke the country from its seventy-two-year sleep. The length of time its people had swallowed insults and ridicule in order to placate the imperialistic South now resulted in proportional bellows of outrage, fury, and vengeance. The South couldn't believe the docile, lamblike North could morph into a great lion whose roars now shook the earth.

It is to Lincoln's credit that he knew instinctively that sooner or later a day of reckoning had to come. If the Confederacy—which commanded a landmass twice as big as any European nation other than Russia—became a separate nation, it could be counted on to be a perpetual enemy of the United States that remained. So Lincoln concluded that the showdown might as well take place "now."

Lincoln was convicted that liberty and democracy were also at stake. If democracy could not survive in America, it was doomed around the world. This was also how the monarchs of England, Spain, and France viewed the struggle. The collapse of the American experiment would free them from the Monroe Doctrine, and they'd be able to replicate throughout the Americas the kind of empires that Maximilian and Carlotta had created in Mexico.

And so Lincoln led the nation into the Civil War.

WASHINGTON CUT OFF FROM THE WORLD

When the people rise in masses on behalf of the Union and the liberties of their country, truly may it be said, "the gates of hell shall not prevail against them."
—ABRAHAM LINCOLN

North Carolina, Tennessee, Arkansas, and Virginia now joined the Confederacy, bringing its total to eleven states. Lincoln's patient refusal to panic eventually paid off, enabling the Union to hold on to Missouri, Kentucky, and what became known as West Virginia. But Lincoln didn't have the luxury of waiting for Maryland to decide which side it wanted to align with. For if it seceded, Washington would be lost.

Now came the darkest week of the Lincoln presidency, that week in April 1861 when it appeared certain the capital would be taken by rebel troops before it could be reinforced by recruits coming from the North.

All communication between Washington and the rest of the world was cut off by the South. But the last train to make it through the blockade contained a regiment of New York volunteers. Changing trains in Baltimore, one hundred recruits were cut off from the rest of the regiment by a mob of "plug-uglies" (idle, vicious, muscular brutes who survived on whiskey and crime) said to number over ten thousand. Forming a square, the recruits, with fixed bayonets and moving in double-quick time, somehow made it through the mob, with most of them surviving to tell the story. All mail into Washington now stopped, and the telegraph lines were cut.

What news got through from then on was all bad. Because of the incendiary situation, Maryland forces refused to let Union reinforcements across its borders. The railroad line from Annapolis to Washington was torn up, the rails sunk in deep water. And rumor had it that rebel troops were massing for an attack on Washington.

General Robert E. Lee, who had been serving in the Union army, rejected the offer to lead that army against the South. Instead, he joined the Confederates and became commander of their armies.

The disasters kept piling up. Virginia seceded from the Union on April 17. Harper's Ferry burned on the eighteenth. Baltimore endured a riot and destruction of railroad bridges on the nineteenth. The great navy yard and all its ships were abandoned and destroyed on the twentieth. Day after day passed and the telegraph lines remained down. Mail did not get through, trains could not get through, ships did not arrive, and even messengers failed to get through.

The city became a ghost town as people fled, many on foot. Secessionists, vowing to return as soon as the rebels captured the capital, left first. It appeared that perhaps the rebels had taken over the entire state, even closing the Chesapeake Bay to incoming ships.

Remembering back to that week of despair, John Nicolay and John Hay (Lincoln's secretaries) noted that Lincoln's inner anxiety must have approached torture:

> In the eyes of his countrymen and of the world he was holding the scales of human destiny; he alone knew that for the moment the forces which made the beam vibrate with such uncertainty were beyond his control. In others' society he gave no sign of these inner emotions. But once, on the afternoon of the 23rd, the business of the day being over, the Executive Office deserted, walking the floor alone in silent thought for nearly half an hour, he stopped and gazed long and wistfully down the Potomac in the direction of the expected ships; and unconscious of any presence in the room, at length broke out with irrepressible anguish in the repeated exclamation, "*Why don't they come! Why don't they come!*"

Nicolay and Hay continue:

> Those who were in the Federal capital on that Thursday, April 25, would never, during their lives, forget the event. An indescribable

gloom and doubt had hung over Washington for nearly a week, paralyzing its traffic and crushing out its very life. As soon as their coming was known, an immense crowd gathered at the depot to obtain ocular evidence that relief had at length reached the city. Promptly debarking and forming, the [New York] 7th marched from the Capitol up Pennsylvania Avenue to the White House. As they passed up the magnificent street, with their well-formed ranks, their exact military step, their soldierly bearing, their gaily floating flags, and the inspiring music, they seemed to sweep all thought of danger and all taint of treason not only out of that great national thoroughfare, but out of every human heart in the Federal city. The presence of this single regiment seemed to turn the scales of fate. Cheer after cheer greeted them, windows were thrown up, houses opened, the population came forth upon the streets as for a holiday. It was an epoch in American history. For the first time, the combined spirit and power of liberty entered the nation's capital.[5]

Bull Run

If Hell is not any more than this, it has no terror for me.

—Abraham Lincoln *(said to John Defrees after the Battle of Bull Run)*

As we have noted, the South went into the war with huge advantages over the North, especially in its leadership. For generations, the young men of the South had tended to train for two vocations: politics and the military. Consequently, the top officers in America's armed forces were from the South. Rather than remaining loyal, most of them resigned and took up arms against the very armies they'd been leading. Because of this, the Confederacy began the war with legendary leaders such as Robert E. Lee, Thomas J. "Stonewall" Jackson, James Longstreet, J. E. B. Stuart, P. G. T. Beauregard, Albert Sidney Johnston, Joseph E. Johnston, and Nathan Bedford Forrest.

Against this galaxy, the North had . . . well, the aged Winfield Scott and a host of leaders who as yet had not earned their spurs. Lincoln, being a rookie at war, had a steep learning curve ahead of him. It didn't take his team long to learn that in war there can be no substitute for trained, seasoned leadership. Later, strong military leaders such as Ulysses S. Grant, William Tecumseh Sherman, Philip Henry Sheridan, David Glasgow Farragut, David D. Porter, and George H. Thomas proved their worth. But the Union was not led by their ilk early on.

During the first half of the war, Lincoln would replace general after general in a desperate search for winners with staying power, generals who would actually fight. Some of them promised the moon but were unable to deliver an asteroid.

Three months after the fall of Fort Sumter, the Battle of Bull Run took place. This was the first serious confrontation between North and South. It turned out to be a real wake-up call for Lincoln and the North, for the general assumption had been that the conflict would be a cakewalk for the North. With their spirits lifted in Washington, people assumed that tens of thousands of the boys in blue would chase the foolish boys in gray clear back to the Gulf. Except that it didn't work out that way: the chase went the other way.

So self-confident were they that the North would win the Battle of Bull Run that many Washingtonians trotted along behind their soldiers, picnic baskets in tow, eager to see the ignominious retreat of the rebels.

General Irvin McDowell's orders had been clear: attack General P. G. T. Beauregard's 35,000 troops at Manassas, Virginia, on July 9, 1861. Again and again it would happen in the early years of the Civil War: fatal slowness on the part of the federal generals. It happened now. Not until a week after his due date was McDowell finally ready to move. By that time, Confederate general Joseph E. Johnston had joined forces with those of Beauregard. Stonewall Jackson's men came just in time as well.

The result was that instead of the victory that would have been theirs a week before, McDowell's troops were the ones that retreated—and among them the panic-stricken picnickers, who now fled for their lives. All night long on July 21, the president listened to firsthand reports from terrified eyewitnesses.

There was plenty of blame to go around, but Lincoln coolly took responsibility for the debacle. The day after the battle he asked General George B.

McClellan from western Virginia to take command of the Union armies. Lincoln charged him with taking the thousands of recruits and forging an army capable of winning battles. But what hurt Lincoln most was the knowledge that had the Union forces delivered a crushing defeat to the Confederate army at Bull Run, they could have ended the war right there.

McClellan would go on to do just what the president wanted him to do: forge a capable, well-disciplined army. No one, in fact, could have done a better job at it than he. The problem would come when Lincoln asked him to be equally effective at fighting battles—or, more to the point, actually *winning* them.

Lincoln receiving visitors at a White House reception

LIFE IN THE
White House

*This struggle and scramble for office, for a way to live without work,
will finally test the strength of our institutions.*

—ABRAHAM LINCOLN

Though the war was ever first on Lincoln's mind, still he had other business to attend to. He had a nation to run, a Cabinet to establish, political groups to assure, and, not least, a young family to move into the White House.

It took a strong constitution, incredible patience, kindness beyond belief, and a strong sense of humor to handle the never-ending lines of people asking for "just five minutes" of the president's time. Lincoln found them impossible to get away from—they'd even accost him on the street for jobs! They'd be standing outside the White House at dawn and still clogging the halls at midnight. Sometimes there were so many inside that it was almost impossible to climb the stairs to the second floor.

The patronage system, less euphemistically called "the spoils system," is almost as old as society itself. In the United States, the practice had taken this form: the political party that won a given election was expected to reward its active supporters by appointment to public office. When a given party remained in power through a number of administrations, office-changing was kept to a minimum. But when a party lost power and a new one replaced it, free-for-alls could and did result.

Increasingly, the element of "competency" for a given job was not even considered. Eventually, long after Lincoln's day, civil service reform bills were passed, and life became much easier for new administrations. But those far-off days were of little comfort to Lincoln and his pathetically small staff, who now had to make replacements for thousands of positions (postmasters, port collectors, marshals, superintendents, paymasters, doorkeepers, etc., each having deputies and assistants).

THE FIRST FAMILY

It is my pleasure that my children are free and happy, and unrestrained by parental tyranny. Love is the chain whereby to bind a child to its parents.

—ABRAHAM LINCOLN

To Mary Lincoln, 1861 was a happy year. She had achieved her heart's desire: being mistress of the White House. Congress had entrusted her with $20,000 to refurbish the White House, and thus the executive mansion was now beautiful inside. Having always loved entertaining, she now had enough money to put on dinners that were the talk of the city. The Lincolns would also have weekly levees for the public. Last and foremost, her two boys were happy.

When the Lincolns had moved into the executive mansion, they'd been almost overwhelmed. Thirty-one rooms—not counting stables, outbuildings, and a conservatory! Their entire Springfield house could have fit in the East Room alone. Once they settled in, though, they realized that all that space was anything but theirs. It belonged to the people. In the entire first floor, only the family dining room was off-limits to the public. Even on the second floor, half the rooms were public. Though the aged doorkeeper, Edward McManus, was supposed to screen the public, in reality anyone who wanted to come in could come in—and did.[1]

America had never before had children in the White House, and the nation took to the boys warmly. Though the Lincoln lads were already thoroughly spoiled by their indulgent parents, now they became more so, as they were showered with toys, pets, and other presents.

Of the three Lincoln children still living, Robert (now eighteen years old) had been shortchanged the most in fatherly interaction. His father had been away half the time on the court circuit when he was young, and when Robert had gotten older, he was away at college. Robert would always feel he'd never gotten to know his father the way his brothers had. Now a student at Harvard, Robert would be dubbed by his classmates "the Prince of Rails." And for good reason, for Robert was the mirror image of his aristocratic Todd forebearers and "to the manor born." Robert's preference for the trappings of wealth may have been another reason he and his father were always a little distant from each other.

Willie (who turned eleven that December) was everyone's favorite. He was good-looking, always cheerful, and mature for his age. He had light-brown hair, fair skin, and blue eyes. Perhaps because he mirrored his father in so many ways, his mother adored him and called him "my comfort." In fact, both parents instinctively felt that with Eddie dead, Robert a bit distant, and Tad afflicted by slowness of mental growth, Willie would be their mainstay when they got old.

Willie Lincoln was obsessed with the wonder of the age: railroads. By the age of ten, being fascinated by mathematical figures and machines, he'd constructed a virtual railroad from Chicago to New York, keeping his time-tables to the minute. Willie would always beg his father to take him along on all railroad trips. He also loved hotels and theaters.

Willie was also the most deeply spiritual of the Lincoln boys. He loved to play church with Tad and declared that he would be a preacher when he grew up. And, like his father, he loved poetry.

Willie and Tad were inseparable and together turned the White House upside down. Not until Teddy Roosevelt's rambunctious family came along would the executive mansion be subjected to this many indignities.

Thomas, known as Tad (eight when they moved into the White House), was happy, lovable, and exasperating. Ruth Painter Randall noted that Taddie would burst into the room where his father was sitting, looking for something, and having found it, throw himself on his father "like a small thunderbolt," give him a wild, fierce hug, and then rush from the room before his father could put out a hand to detain him.

Tad had always been slow at his lessons. His parents, recognizing his limitations, had wisely permitted him to grow at his own pace. His speech impediment made the boy extremely frustrated because most people couldn't understand him. But his father *always* did. As had been true with little Eddie, Tad had a tender heart and was intuitively sympathetic to those who suffered. Each of the four Lincoln sons had absolute integrity as the bedrock of his character.

Upon arriving at the White House, Willie and Tad investigated every room, alcove, and closet. Once settled in, they moved from one prank to another. Shortly after moving in, the boys were strongly attracted to three visitors: Bud, Julia, and Holly Taft. Mary, knowing how lonely her boys were for child companionship, invited the Taft children back the next day. They soon became inseparable.

Julia came with instructions: "Don't let those young rascals tear down the White House." The four boys paired off: Bud and Willie being thoughtful and usually showing restraint, Tad and Holly being completely irresponsible. One day Tad and Holly thought it would be a great idea to take Tad's toy cannon and bombard the room where the president was meeting with his Cabinet—and did so.

Holly and Tad threw the White House into an uproar one morning when they mysteriously disappeared. They were brought back in a carriage after dark, having spent the day investigating the Capitol building. Deciding to find out just how deep a certain stairwell was, they "went down steps pretty near to China." There were rats, and it was "awful dark."

On one of their expeditions, Willie and Tad discovered the White House bell system. Tad, like his father, loved to investigate the inner workings of things. He found out how the bells worked, and bedlam resulted, as Lincoln's secretaries, John Nicolay and John Hay "were rushing to the president's office with visions of a sudden national emergency or presidential ire; old Edward, the doorkeeper, was hurrying up the stairs; everyone was running somewhere to answer the violent ringing." The boys, of course, had a wonderful time.

Once, when Tad ate up all the strawberries the cook had been preparing for a state dinner, he was dubbed "the madam's wildcat."

The Lincoln boys also graciously gave measles to Colonel Elmer Ellsworth, a guest and dear friend. This magnetic and intense young leader of the Zouaves (named for French infantry drawn from the Berbers in Algeria), with his North African–looking uniform, would be one of the first casualties of the war. His funeral would be held in the East Room.

On June 3, 1861, came the shocking news that Stephen A. Douglas, "the Little Giant," had died. The president and his wife had remembered Douglas and his wife, Adele, being among the first to welcome them to Washington after the inauguration. In spite of their political differences, Lincoln and Douglas had always remained friends.

At Lincoln's request, Douglas had agreed to undertake a mission to the border states and the Northwest to rouse the spirit of Unionism. He'd already spoken in West Virginia, Ohio, and Illinois, when he died on June 3 in Chicago at the age of forty-eight. Douglas had always been a roman candle, living at an explosive intensity. Apparently this, plus the stress of the times, losing the presidency, the collapse of the Democratic Party, and the war, was more than his overburdened heart could handle.

Both of the Lincoln boys living at the White House loved attending Sunday school and church: Willie because of his plans to be a preacher, and Tad because he refused to be separated from his brother.

Once, while their mother was in New York buying furnishings for the White House, the four boys and some friends put on a circus. When Julia Taft came over to see if they were behaving, she found the servants and White House staff grinning broadly. Admission charge was five cents. She discovered that Bud and Willie were to be lovely Victorian ladies in the show. She saw each one struggling into Mrs. Lincoln's dresses. Julia pinned up the train of Willie's dress, the surplus folds of Bud's, and also straightened up his bonnet. In Julia's words:

> The show opened patriotically with a rousing rendition of "Hail Columbia" by the entire "troupe." Billy Sanders and Tad Lincoln then sang "The Star-Spangled Banner." Loyal Unionism having thus been demonstrated, there followed a duet of "Dixie Land" by Joe Corkhead and Bud Taft, Bud doubtless an irresistible Southern belle in Mrs. Lincoln's white morning gown and a stylish bonnet. Willie, in a voluminous lilac silk of his mother's, cut very décolleté, probably stirred deep emotions in the audience when he joined in a duet of "Home Sweet Home."

In later years, Julia also remembered once coming in and finding the president sitting in a big chair telling the boys exciting stories of hunters, settlers, and Indians. Willie sat on one of his knees, Bud on the other, Holly on the arm of the chair, and Tad perched on the back. A long arm then reached out and drew Julia into the circle.

Another time, hearing a terrific racket in a nearby room, Julia raced in to find the president flat on the floor with the four boys doing their best to hold him down. Seeing her come in, Tad shouted, "Julia, come quick and sit on his stomach." Mr. Lincoln's twinkle and wide grin showed he was enjoying every minute of it. (For a delightful story of Abraham Lincoln's kindness toward another Julia, see Appendix B.)

When Washington had been cut off from the world and tensions had been so high, the boys had had to lay low. But when that terrible scare was over, they built a protective fort on the White House roof and searched the Potomac for "enemy cruisers" with an old spyglass.

Lincoln enjoyed taking his sons with him when he visited military camps, though some frowned on it. One time he did leave the boys behind because it was a cold day and both boys had colds. But the boys tapped into that Lincoln resourcefulness and found a way to get there after all. They called the Taft children together and pulled out the money they'd made on their circus. Then off they went into the city:

> [A]s the president and dignitaries passed solemnly and ceremoni-
> ously down the line of soldiers, just after them came a rickety, mule-
> driven cart driven by a small, grinning coachman, and containing
> Willie, Bud, Holly, and Tad, each stiffly holding a battered sword
> at salute.

On one occasion, the Sanitary Commission in New York sent Tad a sol-dier doll, which he named "Jack." The doll was dressed in Zouave uniform. Sadly, Jack had unfortunate character traits, causing the boys to have to frequently court-martial him—for sleeping at his post, or desertion, or some other crime—always sentencing him to be shot at sunrise. Tad, with his toy cannon, would act as firing squad. Afterward the dishonored Jack would be buried, undeservedly with full military honors, in the White House rose garden.

One day, Julia was in Mrs. Lincoln's room when "a strange and dreadful sound came through the window."

"What is that noise, Julia?" Mrs. Lincoln asked her.

"It's probably the 'dead march,'" Julia answered. "I suppose the boys are burying Jack again."

Mrs. Lincoln told Julia to hurry out and tell the boys to cease, as it would kill the roses. She obeyed, even though she knew that previous warn-ings hadn't worked. Outside, Julia found a band of "a broken-down fiddle, a dented horn, a paper over a comb, and Tad's drum." The irate gardener,

Major Watt, arrived on the scene. Desperate for the survival of his precious roses, inspiration came to him: "Why don't you boys get Jack pardoned?"

The boys felt this was a capital idea, and ran upstairs, Julia vainly trying to keep them from interrupting the president. John Hay had no better luck stopping them. Hearing all the commotion outside his office, Lincoln came out to see what the trouble was. After hearing Tad's request, the president told Tad that pardons weren't granted without a hearing, and it was up to them to tell him why Jack deserved a pardon.

Tad characteristically delivered his argument in a rush of words. Almost every day, he said, they tried Jack for being a spy or deserter or something and then they shot him and buried him and Julia said it spoiled his clothes and Major Watt said it dug up his roses so they thought they should get Pa to fix up a pardon.

The president considered these facts with due gravity and then told Tad he thought he'd made a case. It was a good law, he said, that no man shall twice be put in jeopardy of his life for the same offense. Since Jack had been shot and buried a dozen times, he was entitled to a pardon. He turned to his desk, on which so many pardons were to be signed, and wrote on his official paper: "The Doll Jack is pardoned by order of the President. A. Lincoln."

And so poor Jack was saved from execution. However, it is sad to relate that even the presidential pardon failed to reform the incorrigible Jack. In less than a week, he was again convicted of being a spy. This time, however, they decided he should be hanged from a tree in the Taft garden.[2]

Lincoln looking out from the south portico of the White House

THE EARLY
War Years

If we shall suppose that American slavery is one of those offences which, in the providence of God, must needs come, but which having continued through His appointed time, He now wills to remove, and that He gives to both North and South, this terrible woe due to those by whom the offence came, shall we discern there in any departure from those divine attributes which the believers in a living God always ascribe to Him?

—ABRAHAM LINCOLN

STANTON TAKES CHARGE

Stanton is the rock upon which are beating the waves of this conflict. . . . I do not see how he survives—why he is not crushed and torn to pieces. Without him, I should be destroyed.

—ABRAHAM LINCOLN

Nobody had ever insulted Lincoln like Edwin M. Stanton. At $400,000, it was the biggest case Lincoln had ever prepared: Cyrus H. McCormick versus John M. Manning. McCormick was represented by the lawyers E. N. Dickerson and Reverdy Johnson. Manning had retained George Hardin, Stanton, and Lincoln.

When Stanton first set eyes on Lincoln, he spat out, "Where did that long-armed baboon come from?"[1] He followed that up by saying that he most certainly wouldn't associate with "such a damned, gawky, long-armed ape as that." At the trial, after all Lincoln's preparation, Stanton wouldn't even look at his brief, but just plain froze him out. Lincoln, however, listened to every word Stanton said in the courtroom and left convicted it was one of the greatest courtroom performances he'd ever seen.

Years later, Lincoln, now president, decided he needed that same Stanton at his side.

As 1861 ticked away, Lincoln became convinced that his instincts were right about his secretary of war, Simon Cameron. The job was a brutal one, with pressures enough to break anything less than a titan, and Cameron just wasn't up to it. He was breaking and had already proven himself unable to control corrupt suppliers from bleeding the Treasury Department dry. To save Cameron's pride, Lincoln persuaded him to accept the position of minister to Russia. When the press blamed Cameron for the corruption, Lincoln gained his undying gratitude by shouldering the blame himself.

But having removed Cameron, to whom could Lincoln turn? Certainly no one would have recommended Edwin Stanton, who was even then bad-mouthing and ridiculing the new president every chance he got. Nevertheless Lincoln was convinced that Stanton was the only man who could handle the job of secretary of war. He offered it to him, doubtless surprising Stanton and the whole city. Just as surprising was that Stanton accepted.

A very serious man was Edwin M. Stanton. At his father's knee he had sworn an oath he would fight slavery until the day he died. He'd worked night and day so he could complete a degree at Kenyon College. When defending a client accused of murder, he swallowed poison so he could describe its effects, saving his client from hanging.

Life had been difficult for him. First, a cherished little daughter had died from something and the doctors knew not what. He kept her ashes in an urn by his bedside; her passing almost paralyzed him with grief. Two and a half years later, his wife died. Then his brother Darwin, sick with a fever, cut his throat and died. The consecutive deaths left him a hardened man. Eventually he married again. Ellen Stanton was sixteen years younger than her husband. Hay described her as "a frail, aristocratic woman, 'white and cold as marble' whose rare smiles seemed to pain her."[2] Yet Lincoln liked her. In fact, she was one of only three people to whom he ever gave a copy of his treasured poem "Mortality."

Stanton proved to be what Lincoln so desperately needed: an incorruptible, indefatigable workhorse of a man who soon put the War Department in order. He could not be bought for any amount of money. In fact, he was suspicious of anyone who even complimented him. Very quickly he stemmed the hemorrhage in the Treasury, forcing suppliers to accept fair remuneration. He operated strictly on principle: even when a weeping mother would beg him not to shoot her son for sleeping on sentry duty, he refused to bend.

He paid a terrible price for this rigidity. A clerk remembered years later seeing late one night a little group consisting of a:

> mother, wife, and children of a man condemned to be shot as a deserter, on their knees before Stanton, pleading for the life of their loved one. He listened standing, in cold and austere silence, and at the end of their heart-breaking sobs and prayers answered briefly that the man must die. The crushed and despairing little family left and Mr. Stanton turned, apparently unmoved, and walked into his private room. The clerk thought Stanton an unfeeling tyrant until he discovered him moments later, leaning on a desk, his face buried in his hands, and his heavy frame shaking with sobs. "God help me to do my duty; God help me to do my duty!" he was repeating in a low wail of anguish.[3]

Undoubtedly, in such cases, Stanton was grateful that it was the president who had life and death authority over 2 million men—not he. (For a story of when Lincoln pardoned some deserters, see Appendix C.)

TEAM OF RIVALS

We need the strongest men of the party in the Cabinet. We needed to hold our own people together. I had looked the party over and concluded that these were the very strongest men. Then I had no right to deprive the country of their services.

—ABRAHAM LINCOLN

As time passed, Lincoln's wisdom in choosing what Doris Kearns Goodwin called "a team of rivals" became more and more apparent. As the Cabinet members represented the entire spectrum of American life, each with his own support group, Lincoln remained fully informed as to the mood of the country. But only an extremely strong president would have dared do such an audacious—some said "foolhardy"—thing.

He'd been right about Cameron, however. And now Stanton proved to be the perfect choice for secretary of war. Salmon Chase, secretary of the treasury and the number two man in the Cabinet, did a superb job as well. Yet as time passed Chase began to actively campaign for the presidency while still professing allegiance to Lincoln. Of course, trouble resulted.

The power struggle over who would dominate the Cabinet didn't last very long. To Seward's and Chase's surprise, it was neither of them—but rather the president. Lincoln alone kept them from each other's throats. His secretaries never ceased to be amazed by the chief executive. In private they referred to him as "the Tycoon." More than once Lincoln articulated one of his management mantras: "Some single mind must be master, else there will be no agreement in anything."

Strangely enough, a strong bond developed between the president and Stanton, the irascible secretary of war with such poor people skills. In fact, as Chase began spending more and more of his time plotting how he could make himself president, Lincoln, Seward, and Stanton, working so well together, understanding one another and respecting one another, became the central dynamo propelling the Cabinet and nation. However, Stanton would often say no to Lincoln:

> Mr. Lovejoy, heading a committee of Western men, discussed an important scheme with the president, and the gentlemen were then directed to explain it to Secretary of War Stanton.
>
> Presenting themselves to the Secretary, and showing the president's order, the Secretary said: "Did Lincoln give you an order of that kind?"
>
> "He did, sir."
>
> "Then he is a d——d fool," said the angry Secretary.
>
> "Do you mean to say that the president is a d——d fool?" asked Lovejoy, in amazement.
>
> "Yes, sir, if he gave you such an order as that."
>
> The bewildered Illinoisan went at once to the president, relating the conversation.
>
> "Did Stanton say I was a d——d fool?" asked Lincoln at the close of the recital.

"He did, sir, and repeated it."

After a moment's pause, Lincoln said: "If Stanton said I was a d——d fool, then I must be one, for he is nearly always right, and generally says what he means. I will slip over and see him."[4]

But when the president felt strongly on a given matter, Stanton always deferred to his wishes.

With Seward, Lincoln had an even tighter bond. Here was a man who appreciated literature and the arts, the kind of Renaissance man Lincoln longed to be. On documents and sensitive negotiations with foreign powers, each helped the other. Were it not for the combined wisdom of Seward and Lincoln, the Trent Affair (in which a Union captain had stopped a ship carrying two Confederate negotiators to England) would have unquestionably resulted in British recognition of the Confederacy, Union war with England, and the collapse of the United States.

Seward, like Lincoln, was an incurable punster. Once when the two men were walking down Pennsylvania Avenue, Seward called Lincoln's attention to a sign bearing the name of T. R. Strong. "Ha," said Lincoln, his face lighting up with a peculiar smile, "T. R. Strong but coffee are stronger."

HEARTBREAK IN THE GREEN ROOM

I have been driven many times to my knees by the overwhelming conviction that I had nowhere else to go. My own wisdom and that of all about me seemed insufficient for the day.

—ABRAHAM LINCOLN

Early in the summer of 1860, little Willie Lincoln had come down with scarlet fever. As was often the case with that debilitating disease, even when he'd recovered, his health was never again as strong.

January of 1862 was cold, rainy, and muddy, so Mary tried to keep her boys inside, but that was especially hard now that Willie had a new pony—and both boys loved horses. Willie became ill with typhoid. Since tens of thousands of soldiers camping along the Potomac generated a lot of waste, and the White House used water from that river, uncontaminated water was in increasingly short supply.

As the weeks passed, Willie's fever ebbed and returned. Each time it returned, it would get worse (and with it came diarrhea, painful cramps, internal hemorrhaging, vomiting, exhaustion, and delirium). His companion, Bud Taft, was constantly at his side, refusing to be parted from him. In early February, Tad came down with typhoid, too. Lincoln would come into the room, stand there drinking in the feverish face of his son, lean over to smooth the light brown hair, and go out without saying a word. Mary was up night and day with her two boys, generating dark circles under her eyes.

Newspapers were covering the story of Willie Lincoln, the little boy who had captured the city and nation's heart. Over and over people would ask, "Is there any hope?" "Not any. So the doctors say."

Willie seemed better on Thursday morning, February 20, 1862. But that afternoon the fever worsened again, and by 5 o'clock it was all over. John Nicolay, exhausted from the pressures of the day, was dozing on his office couch when the president walked in: "'Well, Nicolay,' said he, choking with emotion, 'my boy is gone—he is actually gone!' and bursting into tears, turned and went into his own office."

Elizabeth Keckley, Mrs. Lincoln's seamstress, would never forget the sight of Lincoln coming into that room:

> I never saw a man so bowed down with grief. He came to the bed, lifted the cover from the face of his child, gazed at it long and earnestly, murmuring, "My poor boy, he was too good for this earth. God has called him home. I know that he is much better off in heaven, but then we loved him so. It is hard, hard to have him die!" Great sobs choked his utterance. He buried his face in his hands, and his tall frame was choked with emotion. . . . I did not dream that his rugged nature could be so moved. I shall never forget those solemn moments—genius and greatness weeping over love's idol lost.

Three years later—just days before his own death, actually—while Lincoln was on board a ship en route to Fort Monroe, he was still thinking of little Willie:

[A]fter reading passages from *Macbeth* and *King Lear* to an aide, the president then, from *King John*, recited Constance's lament for her son:

"And father cardinal, I have heard you say / That we shall see and know our friends in heaven: / If that be true, I shall see my boy again."

His voice trembled, and he wept.

Willie's body was embalmed, placed in a metal coffin (finished in rosewood and silver), and carried into the Green Room, adjacent to the East Room where the services would be held. Beautiful even in death, he was dressed in evening clothes, eyes closed, hands crossed on his chest, one hand holding a small bouquet of exquisite flowers.

One look at that small beloved face sent Mrs. Lincoln into convulsions. According to Elizabeth Keckley:

Mrs. Lincoln's grief was inconsolable. . . . Around him, love's tendrils had been twined and now that he was dressed for the tomb, it was like tearing the tendrils out of the heart by their roots.

Mrs. Keckley also witnessed one sadly prophetic scene:

In one of her paroxysms of grief, the president kindly bent over his wife, took her by the arm, and gently led her to the window. With a stately solemn gesture, he pointed to the lunatic asylum: "Mother, do you see that large white building on the hill yonder? Try and control your grief, or it will drive you mad, and we may have to send you there."

Even Congress shut down on the day of Willie's funeral. The service was conducted by the Reverend Dr. Phineas D. Gurley, pastor of the New York Avenue Presbyterian Church, which President and Mrs. Lincoln attended. Officers in uniform and all of official Washington was represented there, including Seward, with quivering lips, and McClellan, with misty eyes. More would have attended but nor'easter winds came up that morning, blowing off roofs and toppling chimneys and steeples.

After the funeral service, the casket was removed to the hearse. Behind the pallbearers followed a little group of children, the members of Willie's Sunday school class, which he'd always so faithfully attended.[5]

LINCOLN'S DARK AND LONESOME VALLEY

I have felt His hand upon me in great trials and submitted to His guidance, and I trust that as He shall further open the way, I shall be ready to walk therein, relying on His help and trusting in His goodness and wisdom.

—ABRAHAM LINCOLN

Life would never be the same, neither in the White House nor in the Lincoln marriage. Thomas notes that without question, of all the multitudinous sorrows life dealt Lincoln, none could compare to the death of Willie. As for Mary:

> The defiant courage with which she had faced the gibes of society and the cruel spotlight of a hostile press wilted at the loss of a second child. She never again entered the guest room where Willie died or the Green Room, where his body had been embalmed. All except the necessary functions of the White House stopped.[6]

For the next three years, Lincoln "would live in virtual seclusion and it became the fate of the overburdened president to walk alone, haunted by the fear that his distraught wife might go insane." Mary spent more and more time in the sanctuary of her bedroom, often weeping uncontrollably. Fewer people came to see her now, and she refused to see most of those who did.

The impact of all this on little Tad was devastating. Though he had finally recovered after a lingering illness, he never returned to his previous strength. Now he was parted from Willie—the light of his life—and his mother, who couldn't look at him without thinking of Willie. Nor did he have the consolation of Holly, Bud, and Julia Taft, for since they, too, reminded Mary of Willie, she never invited them to the White House again.

That left him only one refuge—his father. After Willie's death, deprived of the companionship of playmates his own age, Tad could rarely stand any kind of absence from his father. Now, instead of sleeping in a bed with his brother, he insisted on sleeping with his father. Government officials, staff, and visitors found themselves saddled with the presence of Tad whether they wanted him around or not.

THE DEEPEST SPIRITUAL AWAKENING

Clergyman: *I hope the Lord is on our side.*

Lincoln: *I am not at all concerned about that, for I know the Lord is always on the side of the right. But it is my constant anxiety and prayer that I and this nation should be on the Lord's side.*

—ABRAHAM LINCOLN

The death of his beloved Willie in 1862 brought about the deepest spiritual awakening of Abraham Lincoln's life. Never had Lincoln felt his own inadequacies more than now: the war was not going well, and criticism of him and his administration mounted every day. The desperate search for a competent general continued. Each new candidate led to another unmitigated disaster.

Lincoln had felt his need for God in Springfield. He'd felt it ten times more on the train en route to Washington. But now he felt it a hundred times more—now, when he and his Cabinet tried to steer the Union through mapless waters.

It was because of this fierce inner need that back in 1860 on Lincoln's very first Sunday in Washington, he'd taken his family to the New York Avenue Presbyterian Church. He and the pastor, Dr. Phineas D. Gurley, had quickly bonded. The church became home to the Lincolns, and Willie and Tad became regular members of the Sunday school. They selected as their pew B-14, seventh row from the front, vacant since Buchanan had left Washington.[7]

Lincoln liked Gurley's old-school Presbyterian preaching. Being suspicious of emotionalism, Lincoln much preferred the rational religion articulated in the Westminster Confession of Faith. After Willie's death, Lincoln's relationship with his pastor deepened, and Gurley was a frequent visitor to the White House. The untimely death of Lincoln's son enabled him better to empathize with the thousands of other bereaved parents and prompted questions such as "What is the meaning of life?" and "What is the meaning of death?"

No Agenda

It was a time when a man with a policy would have been
fatal to this country. I have never had a policy; I simply
tried to do what seemed best each day as each day came.

—Abraham Lincoln

The war news in 1862 was mixed. Union forces had won in faraway places such as Fort Henry, Fort Donelson, and New Orleans, but those victories were more than offset by the awful defeat at Shiloh. There, General Ulysses S. Grant had been caught napping, and 24,000 troops were killed in two days. That's more than the American losses in the entire Revolutionary War.

During four months of bloody fighting in the Peninsula battles in Virginia, 47,000 had died, but McClellan had no victories to show for it. Even the naval battle between the ironclads *Merrimac* and *Monitor* had ended in a draw. That battle had accomplished one thing, however: now all the wooden navies in the world were obsolete.

So, as the second year of the war wore down, who was winning? Psychologically, the South. Not by territory conquered, for the North had made some gains, but by the undeniable fact that the South had consistently better generals than the North. Even when the rebels were outnumbered three to one, they still managed to avoid defeat or even win. This is what depressed the people of the North most: seeing the flower of their youth cut down with so little to show for it.

The South had more than its fair share of strong generals. And two can be classified as "great": Robert E. Lee and Stonewall Jackson. Lee, of course, was the great mastermind, *the* premier Confederate strategist. But Jackson was the general who struck the most fear in the hearts of Union troops for he could be counted on to do the unexpected—even the supposedly impossible.

When Jackson arrived at the last moment at Bull Run and rallied the fleeing Confederates, he saved the day for the South. In the Peninsula Campaign, when it appeared that McClellan would take Richmond, it was Jackson who, in a series of lightning strikes from all directions, would so demoralize McClellan that Jackson's 17,500 men neutralized the action of

175,000 Union men. At Manassas Junction, another of Jackson's lightning strikes would help to utterly defeat General John Pope. It was Jackson who would save the Confederates from disaster at Antietam. At Chancellorsville, Lee and Jackson would orchestrate one of the boldest strokes of the war. Today military strategists consider Lee and Jackson to be two of the world's greatest military tacticians.

In the midst of all this turbulence, Lincoln visited his old friend General Winfield Scott, who was summering in West Point, New York. Disappointed in almost every Union general, Lincoln sought Scott's objective opinion about the quagmire the Union was mired in. Undoubtedly, too, the president unburdened his soul in terms of the loss of his son.

Whatever Scott said or didn't say, one thing is absolutely certain: the Lincoln who returned from that visit to West Point was a changed man. From now on we see the Lincoln who took command, who became proactive, who became ever more spiritual. We see the Lincoln who was at last determined to free the 4 million slaves. From now on we see the Lincoln who articulated to the American people just what they were fighting for and why they must not settle for anything less than total victory.

Lincoln in military camp, greeting Union soldiers

ANXIOUS TO MEET
Their President

The battle for freedom is to be fought on principle. Slavery is a violation of eternal right. We have temporized with it from the necessities of our condition, but as surely as God reigns and school children read, that black foul lie can never be consecrated into God's hallowed truth.

—ABRAHAM LINCOLN

On July 22, 1862, Lincoln called together perhaps the most remarkable Cabinet meeting of his presidency. Lincoln told them he had a document he wished to share with them. He told them he was now convicted that on January 1, 1863, he should declare the slaves forever free.

There was considerable discussion. Seward contended that to issue such a proclamation in the midst of all their continuing defeats would appear ridiculous to the world. Ultimately, and reluctantly, Lincoln agreed, so the matter was put on hold. Nevertheless, later that year Lincoln announced the Emancipation Proclamation to the nation and promised to sign it on January 1, 1863.

Because Lincoln was so dissatisfied with McClellan's lackluster performance commanding the Union armies, he replaced him with John Pope, who promptly marched into the unmitigated disaster of Second Manassas (or Second Bull Run). The Union lost 16,054 men compared to the South's 9,197. Still Lincoln had not found the man who could lead the Union to victory on the field of battle.

As mentioned in chapter two, Robert E. Lee now concluded that the Confederacy's best chance to win the war hinged on forsaking defense to attack the North. On September 4, he led his men across the Potomac near Leesburg, Virginia, leading to the battle of Antietam, where over 26,000 men fell. Even though it was anything but a victory, to Lincoln it was close enough for his purpose, given that Lee had been forced to withdraw his men back into Virginia.[1]

Artist Frank B. Carpenter, who painted Lincoln signing the Emancipation Proclamation, had plenty of opportunities to ask Cabinet members what had happened during that post-Antietam Cabinet meeting. He was told that on that memorable September 22, 1862, only five days after the terrible battle, the president declared in a grave tone of voice that after wrestling with God over the issue of slavery and the continued casualties and defeats in battle after battle: "I made a solemn vow before God, that if General Lee were driven back from Pennsylvania, I would crown the result with the declaration of freedom for the slaves."[2] Then, knowing the division in the Cabinet, he didn't even take a vote.

The Chains Begin to Fall

Now, when by all these means you have succeeded in dehumanizing the Negro; when you have put him down, and made it forever impossible for him to be but as the beasts of the field; when you have extinguished his soul, and placed him where the ray of hope is blown out in darkness like that which broods over the spirits of the damned—are you quite sure the demon which you have roused will not turn and rend you?

—Abraham Lincoln

Frederick Douglass was born in Maryland to an enslaved black mother and a white man. He grew up on a Maryland plantation with his brothers and sisters, without shoes or stockings even in the snow of the winters, eating from a common trough. As a boy, he was sold to a Baltimore family whose mistress treated him kindly, gave him shoes and stockings, permitted him to eat with a spoon, and had taught him the first four letters of the alphabet when her husband spat out, "Learning would spoil the best nigger in the world; if you teach that nigger how to read the Bible there will be no keeping him. Next he'll want to know how to write and then run away."

Douglass eventually did learn how to spell, read, and write. Then he managed to escape to New England. He became the most popular and widely heard black leader of his time, speaking out as far away as England about the institution of slavery. At home in Rochester, New York, Douglass and his wife were part of the Underground Railroad.

Like most Americans with Negro blood (then and now) Douglass was extremely sensitive to patronizing whites who would espouse the abolitionist cause on principle but would not accept blacks on equal terms when interacting with them personally. What endeared Lincoln to Douglass was that he accepted him not because he was a famous abolitionist but because he was a *brother*, a fellow child of God. Douglass said:

> In all my interviews with Mr. Lincoln I was impressed with his entire freedom from popular prejudice against the colored race. He was the first great man that I talked with in the United States freely, who in no single instance reminded me of the difference between himself and myself, of the difference of color.[3]

THE EMANCIPATION PROCLAMATION

Had Lincoln been able to follow his personal convictions, he would have abolished slavery when yet a teenager. But he had not the power then, and the moment was not right. Even as a young politician he wouldn't have been able to do it. Many of the abolitionists were so vitriolic that to embrace abolitionism was often a political kiss of death.

When he became president, he was still not granted the power instantly to end slavery. In 1860 and early 1861, when peace and war were teetering, a consensus on slavery would have been impossible. Though many in the North despised slavery, they would *never* have responded so magnificently to the call to arms had it been just to free the slaves. What they volunteered to fight for was to save the republic.

The same was true during the early days of the war. Had Lincoln tried to abolish slavery any earlier than he did, he'd have lost not only the vital border states (Delaware, Maryland, West Virginia, Kentucky, Kansas, and Missouri) but also a significant portion of his Northern support, a reality Northern radicals failed to comprehend.

As we've seen, Lincoln did eventually announce the Emancipation Proclamation to the nation, promising to sign it into effect on the first day of 1863. However, some black leaders distrusted the president's commitment to them as a people. They thought that Lincoln's promise to sign the Emancipation Proclamation might be merely a political ploy.

Consequently, across the nation on New Year's Day, 1863, the tension in crowds of abolitionists and blacks mounted as hour after hour passed without any word from Washington. Frederick Douglass, along with a crowd of abolitionists, had been waiting in Boston's Tremont Temple all day—and now it was night. Douglass kept telling the crowd that Lincoln wouldn't let them down, but as day passed into night, even he must have been wondering what would happen. At last, a man ran into the church crying, "It is coming! It is on the wires!"

> Then in a surge of shouting, weeping, and hosannas, the proclamation was read and a colored preacher named Rice led all voices in an anthem: "Sound the loud timbrel o'er Egypt's dark sea, Jehovah has triumphed: His people are free." Douglass took as his text, "This is the year of jubilee." At midnight the crowd adjourned to the Twelfth Baptist Church and held forth till near dawn.[4]

Earlier that day, a big reception was held in the White House. The crowd was so large that by the time he'd finished, the president's arm was all but numb from the number of hands he'd shaken. After the guests had departed, Lincoln walked upstairs to his office where the official Emancipation Proclamation awaited his signature. Sitting down, he waited a few minutes to give his wrist time to recover, then he said to his assembled Cabinet, "If my hand trembles as I sign my name, people will say that I was afraid."

Lincoln's hand did not tremble.

As a result of the Emancipation Proclamation, Abraham Lincoln became almost a messiah to the Negro race. Uncomfortable with such adulation, Lincoln felt it was the fearless abolition leaders who'd paved the way. Furthermore, he said, it was God who deserved all the credit.

Many whites assumed Lincoln would be amused by the devotion of slaves and free blacks. He was not. Typical of such experiences is this one, told by a politician in Negro dialect:

> In a recent Negro camp meeting, a Negro preacher told his congregation that Lincoln's signing the Emancipation Proclamation was

merely an act, something to gain advantage in the war: the president really didn't care about colored people personally. At this, clear in the back stood a patriarch with white, kinky hair. "Bredren!" he shouted, and his voice was so earnest that everyone listened intently, "You don't know nothin' what you talkin' about. Now you jest listen to me. Massa Linkum he everywhar. He know eberyting. He walk de earf like de Lord!" The politician fully expected the president to laugh at how ridiculous the Negro speakers had been, but Lincoln was anything but amused. Instead, he got up from his chair and walked over to the window, an extremely serious look on his face. Finally, he turned to the visitor and said, in a solemn voice, "It is a momentous thing to be the instrument under Providence for the liberation of a race."[5]

However, the patience of even an ultimate forgiver like Lincoln had limits. A petition came to him urging him to pardon a man convicted of commanding a slave ship. He'd been sentenced to several years of imprisonment and a $1,000 fine. He'd served the prison term but could not pay the fine. The letter from the prisoner acknowledged the justice of the sentence but said, since he had no money, he'd have to spend the rest of his life in prison. Lincoln read the letter and the petition, and remarked:

I believe I am kindly enough in nature and can be moved to pity and to pardon the perpetrator of almost the worst crime that the mind of man can conceive or the arm of man can execute; but any man, who, for paltry gain and stimulated only by avarice, can rob Africa of her children to sell into interminable bondage, I never will pardon, and he may stay and rot in jail before he will ever get relief from me.[6]

This was an age in which whites in the South treated blacks with contempt: as less than human. Most whites in the North treated blacks as nonexistent. And yet in this age, when a slave would take off his hat to the president, Lincoln would take off his hat to him. When black children congregated outside the White House hoping to catch a glimpse of him, Lincoln would come out to greet them.

One evening after a White House banquet, Washington's glitterati showed no signs of wanting to leave. Meanwhile, outside a large crowd of blacks had gathered, happy to be this close to their liberator. Finally, several of them dared to venture inside, and others in the crowd timidly followed them. All they wanted was just to look at him. The guests, in their costly attire, scowled, *Who do these ragamuffins think they are, crashing our party!* Suddenly, the president turned, and the intruders froze. What would he say! What followed was one of the most poignant things that ever happened in American history.

The president, forgetting his illustrious guests, moved toward the intruders, a warm smile on his face, and greeted every one, as well as the hundreds who now followed. They were all anxious to meet their president—they, who never dreamed they'd ever have one. Though many of the invited guests now stalked out, thoroughly miffed, others were so deeply moved, they were incapable of speech.

A council of war in Lincoln's steamboat

1863: A LAND AWASH
in Blood

The Almighty has His own purposes.

—ABRAHAM LINCOLN

LINCOLN TAKES THE OFFENSIVE

I hope there will be no trouble; but I will make the South a graveyard rather than see a slavery gospel triumph, or successful secession destroy the Union.

—ABRAHAM LINCOLN

Since visiting General Scott in West Point the year before, Lincoln had deserted his earlier wait-and-see attitude and moved into a high-gear offensive—not just on the military battlefield but on the battlefield of public opinion as well, for if he lost the war there, he'd inevitably lose the war everywhere else as well.

In order to understand fully the impact of the Civil War on its people, it is absolutely essential to incorporate a rule of ten into our research and reading. As a point of reference, approximately three thousand soldiers were lost in the first three years of the Iraq War, with America's total population hovering in the vicinity of 300 million. Those three thousand–plus casualties resulted in a significant backlash against the war.

Step back almost 150 years to the Civil War, when our total population was around 30 million, about one tenth of our current population. The first really bloody battle, Shiloh, had close to 24,000 casualties in two days. Multiply that by ten to find the present-day equivalent, and you learn that this would've been 240,000 lost in two days! The total death count (battle and disease) for the four years of the Civil War was 623,000, which was more than all the rest of our nation's wars put together. Apply the rule of ten, and you see that, in today's numbers, the casualty count would be about 6.2 million lives lost.

How could Lincoln sustain support for the war when so many were dead, wounded (untold thousands of amputees), deathly ill, imprisoned, or just plain "missing in action"? It had been easy to get young men to volunteer at the beginning, before casualty figures skyrocketed; very soon, he knew, the American people would choose peace at any cost over prolonging the horrific casualty count attached to each new battle. Was there any way to sell the continuation of the war to the American people?

James C. Conklin had recently invited Lincoln to address a very large crowd in his home city of Springfield and encourage the attendees to hold the course. Ideally, he'd go—but he knew he didn't have that option. Instead, he wrote an open letter to be read aloud at the rally. Newspapers all over the Union carried it, and Lincoln's well-thought-out words explaining why the war must continue and why it was worth the sacrifice had a significant impact.

The Man without a Country

*I fear you do not fully comprehend . . . the danger of abridging the liberties
of the people. Nothing but the sternest necessity can ever justify it.
A government had better go to the very extreme of toleration, than
do anything that could be construed into an interference with,
or to jeopardize in any degree, the common rights of its citizens.*

—Abraham Lincoln

That spring, Lincoln inherited a public-relations nightmare. Every war has its protestors, and the Civil War was no exception. But what do you do when someone crosses the line? When someone such as Congressman Clement Vallandigham (the leading peace-at-any-price Democrat of Ohio) attacked the president in public speeches and incited soldiers to desert? General Ambrose Burnside had arrested him and charged him with treason. A nation-wide storm of criticism resulted.

Lincoln, caught in the middle, searched his Solomonic mind for a solution. Rather than allowing Vallandigham to remain in an Ohio jail, Lincoln banished him to the Confederacy. Union soldiers escorted him into Tennessee under a flag of truce and handed him over to the rebels. That way, Lincoln said, "his Copperhead body could go to where his heart already was."

The entire country laughed. They laughed even more when the congressman escaped to Canada. But the lesson helped silence extremist rhetoric. The episode even resulted in one of the all-time classic novelettes in American literature: Nathan Hale's *The Man without a Country*, published in 1863. Lincoln also used the event as a springboard for an open letter released to the *New York Tribune*. In it he asked, "Must I shoot a simple-minded soldier boy who deserts, while I must not touch a hair of a wily agitator who induces him to desert?" The letter resulted in plaudits for the president all over the North.[1]

RIPPLES OF THE EMANCIPATION PROCLAMATION

When the president signed that most precious document of the nineteenth century, he set in motion more forces than he realized. Lincoln spoke often of Providence, the Almighty who remains all-powerful behind the scenes. Long since at the end of his own resources, Lincoln made no secret of his conviction that his only bedrock was God.

Perhaps it was during his pivotal visit with General Scott that Lincoln experienced his epiphany of epiphanies: the reason nothing the Union did worked, the reason Union forces quailed in almost every battle, was that the nation had not come to grips with the moral issue of the age: slavery. Saving the Union just to preserve the status quo—which included the continued existence of slavery—gave the North no moral high ground at all, neither on the American continent nor in the rest of the world, nor in the eyes of God.

It was during this crucial period of his journey that Lincoln penned "Meditation on the Divine Will," in which, as we saw in chapter two, he wondered why God refused to bless the efforts of either North or South. "Yet the contest proceeds" was his haunting, inconclusive conclusion.

What is especially fascinating about the war from January 2, 1863 (the day after the Emancipation Proclamation was signed), onward is that Providence appears finally to take sides. Though Confederate victories continued to occur, an ever-so-subtle shift occurred.

The first evidence of this shift was the Battle of Stones River, which was fought from December 31, 1862, to January 2, 1863, near Murfreesboro, Tennessee. What was remarkable about the battle was the very fierceness with which it was fought. It was as if both sides realized a new factor had entered the war on January 1. Suddenly the existence of the Union, the existence of the Confederacy, and the continued institution of slavery in America were *all* at stake.

Every Confederate soldier realized that with one stroke of his pen, Lincoln had made it impossible to ever return to the prewar status quo. If the North won the war, slavery was dead. Only if the North were defeated or worn down to the point of exhaustion would it agree to allow the continued existence of a slave nation next door. In that case, Lincoln's Emancipation Proclamation would be reduced to merely a piece of paper. But if the North won such a clear victory over the Confederacy that full surrender took place, it would be so much more. If that occurred, *all* the slaves would be free. (But to *guarantee* that, a constitutional amendment would be needed.)

Though the North lost 17,287 men at Chancellorsville, compared to the South's 12,463, those figures were deceiving. The most significant outcome of the battle was that Lee's right-hand man, Stonewall Jackson, the brilliant general of the South, was killed on the first evening by friendly fire. The loss was catastrophic to the South. Indeed, it represents the turning point of the war.

The North was thrown into disarray in late June with the news that General Lee had moved his rebel army across the Potomac. Rumor had it that he planned to march up to Harrisburg, take Philadelphia and Baltimore, and circle back to Washington. With Jeb Stuart's (Lee's eyes and ears) hard-riding cavalry on the rampage, Lee had no way of knowing that like two giant crabs, he and General George Meade (who had been given command of the Union forces only hours before) were backing into each other in a little Pennsylvania town few had ever heard of—Gettysburg.

For the first time in the war, nothing would go right for Lee—how terribly he missed Stonewall Jackson! Most damaging of all was the moment when Lee determined to take what he considered the weakest section of Cemetery Ridge.

Mid-afternoon of the third day, after perhaps the fiercest cannonades of the war, into the clearing surged the flower of the Army of Northern Virginia, nine thousand in the first wave, six thousand in the second—a forest of horsemen, slanting rifles glinting in the sunlight, red flags rippling above the columns. Federal artillerymen changed to shrapnel, then to canister. As fast as men fell, others took their places; during the last 200 yards, the meadow ran scarlet with blood. In the end, what was ever after called Pickett's Charge had failed. Futile though it was, it will live forever as one of the most gallant moments in the history of war.[2]

Hours later, on July 3, Lee retreated, his aura of invincibility shattered, and the tilt northward became clear. This pivotal and bloodiest battle of the war (43,000 casualties; 430,000 if we apply the rule of ten) is now considered one of the most significant battles of all time. Here was the high tide of the Confederacy, for had the Civil War ended in a stalemate, the United States, today the world's only superpower, would never have been.

The war began to go well for the North. For seven long months, General Grant and his forces had been vainly attempting to take a city that was considered impregnable: Vicksburg, Mississippi, the Gibraltar of the South. Vicksburg was the land bridge that enabled communication, commerce, and Confederate soldiers to cross back and forth between East and West. Four days after Gettysburg, an aide handed Gideon Welles a telegram from Admiral Porter.

> Welles read the message and almost jumped for joy. *Vicksburg had surrendered to General Grant!* Welles hurried to the White House on pumping legs. Lincoln was sitting at a table tracing certain of Grant's movements on a map for Chase and three or four others. He leaped up at the news and, throwing his arms around the stocky Welles, exclaimed, "What can we do for the Secretary of the Navy for this glorious intelligence? He is always giving us good news. I cannot in words tell you of my joy over this result. It is great, Mr. Welles! It is great!"[3]

At Vicksburg and Port Hudson, Grant had taken almost 38,000 prisoners and 172 guns—38,000 Confederates who would no longer be shooting at federals. With the surrender of Vicksburg, the North now controlled the Mississippi River and had effectively split the Confederacy in two. And Admiral Porter's fleet of ironclads had helped to make such victories possible.

Lincoln spent much time studying maps so that he could follow each movement of Grant's armies. Given that he'd twice made round-trips down the river on rafts and steamboats, each place mentioned in dispatches was familiar to him four times over. Now Lincoln was able to bring the glad news to his people: "The Father of Waters [the Mississippi] once again goes unvexed to the sea."

Down South at Chickamauga, Tennessee, the news appeared dire for the North: General W. S. Rosecrans had been soundly defeated by Confederate troops on September 20. Thirty-three thousand troops had died. Indeed, it appeared the entire Army of the Cumberland might be lost. But General George Thomas (the only Union general never to lose a battle) saved the day and enabled retreating Union troops to reach safety. Ever after, for his brave stand against continual attacks, Thomas was known as "the Rock of Chickamauga."

Stanton and Lincoln immediately ordered Joseph Hooker to the rescue; he moved 20,000 men and 3,000 horses and mules 1,159 miles by railroad in barely a week! Grant, now taking command in the South, moved the expanded army to Chattanooga, where Braxton Bragg's Confederate troops were ensconced in a commanding position stretching from the 2,100-foot-high Lookout Mountain all the way around to Missionary Ridge. *About as impregnable as Vicksburg*, Grant must have thought.

Early in the morning of November 24, the insane order went out to the Union troops to "take Lookout Mountain." Looking up into the thick fog engulfing the heights several thousand feet above, one of General Hooker's troops muttered, "Does the general expect us to fly?"

In the fog above, there was some confusion as Bragg was shifting his forces from one flank to another. That confusion enabled Union troops to reach the top without much resistance. Next day, when the sun finally broke through the fog, there atop Lookout Mountain waved a huge American flag!

On the 400-foot-high Missionary Ridge, the same drama repeated, and the war gave birth to one of the few such spontaneous acts by soldiers in American history. War correspondent Charles Dana wrote in disbelief:

> The storming of their ridge by our troops was one of the greatest miracles in military history. No man who climbs the ascent by any of the roads that wind along its front can believe that 18,000 men were moved up its broken and crumbling face unless it was his fortune to witness the deed. It was as awful as a visible interposition of

God. Neither Grant nor Thomas intended it. . . . The order to storm appears to have been given simultaneously by Generals Sheridan and Wood, because the men were not to be held back. Besides, the generals had caught the inspiration of the men. . . . Bragg was now in full retreat, burning his depots and bridges.

Another officer recalled:

Each soldier moved as his courage and endurance dictated. Confederates in their path had orders to fire and then withdraw to the crest of Missionary Ridge, a misguided tactic that encouraged all the advancing Federals and alarmed Bragg's men up above. "Those defending the heights became more and more desperate as our men approached the top," wrote L. G. Bennett of the 36th Illinois infantry. "They shouted *Chickamauga!* As if the word itself were a weapon. . . . They seized huge stones and threw them, but nothing could stop the force of the desperate charge and one after another the regimental flags were borne over the parapet and the ridge was ours."

Those caught up in these mad rushes said later they could explain neither why nor how they had done it. How was it possible that ordinary men were suddenly and inexplicably endowed with such strength that they hurled themselves up the steep mountain as smoothly and rapidly as though they were plunging downward? For the first time in a large-scale combat, Confederate soldiers had been routed and had run away. What could explain their sudden panic?[4]

Was it God?

Lincoln acting as attorney for an injured soldier

"TO ERR IS HUMAN, *to Forgive, Divine*"

*I am a patient man—always willing to forgive on the Christian
terms of repentance, and also to give ample time for repentance.*

—ABRAHAM LINCOLN

CIVIL WAR MUSIC

The Civil War was the most deeply spiritual war ever fought on American
soil. Both Lincoln and Confederate president Jefferson Davis openly invoked
God's blessing on their people and their cause. When dark days of suffering and pain predominated, they turned to God. Since no other war in our
history has resulted in so many wounded, so many amputations, so much
terminal illness and so much death, it is not surprising that God was always
on their minds.

Many of their troop movements were long and by foot, and marching
songs helped to break up the monotony. Evening campfires brought their
thoughts to family, home, the country, the cause, love, and God. Because of
all this and because the times were Victorian, mothers, and women in general, were idolized. It was our most sentimental war—the last major conflict
in which bands played on the field of combat, musicians relaying orders in
musical code.

It must have been surreal, after slaughtering each other all day, to listen
to the boys in gray singing the same songs as the boys in blue. They were
rarely very far away from each other, and there are documented stories of
opposing camps joining in each others' songs.

Most surreal of all was Christmas singing. Unarmed Union men would
venture into a clearing to be met by unarmed Confederate men. And there

they would harmonize Christmas songs together. Afterward, they talked. Since border states split brothers and cousins, one brother might unknowingly be aiming his gun at his brother. There'd be many inquiries about the whereabouts and latest news of people who were mutually known. Then the bugle would call, they'd say good-bye to one another, return to their respective camps, and reload their rifles.

According to Kenneth W. Osbeck, Julia Ward Howe (1819–1910) was deeply anguished at the conflict between the two sections of her country. One day, as she watched troops marching off to war singing "John Brown's Body" to an old Appalachian camp meeting tune, she felt the music deserved better words. Without knowing what she was doing, she wrote the verses as they came to her, almost without looking at the paper. They first appeared in an 1862 issue of the *Atlantic Monthly* as a battle song for the republic, and almost overnight, the entire nation was singing "The Battle Hymn of the Republic."[1]

And not just the troops were singing it. At one patriotic rally attended by Lincoln, the song was sung as a solo. After the loud and enthusiastic applause, the president, with tears in his eyes, cried out, "Sing it again!" It was:

> *Mine eyes have seen the glory of the coming of the Lord;*
> *He is trampling out the vintage where the grapes of wrath are stored;*
> *He hath loosed the fateful lightning of his terrible quick sword:*
> *His truth is marching on.*
>
> —"Battle Hymn of the Republic" BY JULIA WARD HOWE
>
> *(Civil War marching song)*[2]

A FEW WELL-CHOSEN WORDS AT GETTYSBURG

> *The fact is, General, in the stress and pinch of the campaign there, I went to my room, and got down on my knees and prayed God Almighty for victory at Gettysburg. I told Him that this was His country, and the war was His war, but that we really couldn't stand another Fredericksburg or Chancellorsville. And then and there I made a solemn vow with my Maker that if He would stand by you boys at Gettysburg, I would stand by Him. And He did, and I will. And after this I felt that God Almighty had taken the whole thing into His Hands.*[3]
>
> —ABRAHAM LINCOLN *(said to General Daniel E. Sickles after the Battle of Gettysburg)*

Gettysburg. One word says it all. Though other Civil War battles were almost as bloody, none compares to Gettysburg in terms of the impact on the hearts of Americans that this one word evokes. Perhaps because Lincoln's "few well-chosen words" have in a very special way sanctified this heretofore unknown little town in the rolling hills of Pennsylvania.

Hardly had the reverberating guns faded when David Wills of Gettysburg wrote a letter to Pennsylvania governor Andrew G. Curtin, suggesting that a plot of ground in the midst of the battlefield be at once purchased and designated as a national cemetery, and that the remains of the thousands of bodies be reburied on Cemetery Hill. Governor Curtin promptly did so.

As this was being done, it was also decided to hold a memorial service on November 19, 1863, for all those who had died there. At that time battle followed battle with deadly regularity, and it would have been impossible to grasp the historical significance of Gettysburg. They just knew that Gettysburg had been the bloodiest so far. It would be years later before historians would isolate it as one of the world's most pivotal battles.

Asking Lincoln to come speak at the ceremony was an afterthought. They hoped to land a great orator—Edward Everett of Massachusetts, the nation's greatest—if possible. Formal invitations were also sent to the Cabinet, generals, senators, congressmen, and other VIPs.

Evidently, quite late, someone asked, "What about asking the president to speak?" Not that he would. Lincoln hadn't been known as a speaker since the Douglas debates five years earlier. Who knew whether he was even comfortable speaking in public anymore? After considerable discussion it was decided he could, "by a few appropriate remarks," dedicate the ground to their sacred use. The president promptly accepted.

As he pondered what he might say, Lincoln became convicted that the occasion demanded far more than perfunctory remarks. But not a speech— Everett had been chosen for that.

The next election was also on his mind. Not since Andrew Jackson had a president served two terms. It had almost come to be expected that presidents ought to quit after one term. He also knew that were he to run, his odds of winning looked abysmal. The land was awash in blood, and Northern victories had been all too few. Chase was just one of many who were trying to generate momentum for their own nominations.

So, he must have asked himself, *what will happen when I'm gone? Will any of this have any significance then? Really, what does this terrible war mean to the American people? Perhaps more importantly, what* should *it mean?* With that shift in thinking, he was better able to decide what he should say at Gettysburg. He chose words not just for all those bodies in newly dug graves, but to explain why they were there.

Had he any illusions about the importance his associates placed on his remarks, they would have been quenched by discovering that even though a special train was added, neither Stanton nor Chase was going. Radical abolutionist Thaddeus Stevens considered Lincoln to be, in his words, a "dead card" in the political deck. Hearing that Lincoln and Seward were going, Stevens sarcastically quipped, "The dead going to eulogize the dead."

And yet Lincoln's speech became one of the most famous addresses in history. The essence of the 272 words is this: *All men are created equal.* "All" now included black people. Hundreds of thousands have died, here at Gettysburg and elsewhere in the war. For what? For the dream of a nation based on liberty and equality of all races. Since, by implication, the South does not currently share this dream, the listeners to this speech must resolve that *these men shall not have died in vain!* Should the people of the Union permit a negotiated peace to take place—as so many peace-at-any-price advocates were urging—it would nullify all the sacrifices made, including those in the hundreds of unburied coffins still stacked on the station platform.

In short, the Gettysburg Address was a mandate to the people to hold the course until the job was done, when both halves would come together again, fully committed to the brotherhood of *all* men.

At one of the stops en route to the battlefield, a beautiful little girl was lifted up to the open window of the president's train car. Her four lisped words, "Floweth for the Prethident," instantly brought Lincoln to that window. Accepting with a smile the bouquet of rosebuds she held out to him, he kissed her and said, "You are a sweet little rosebud yourself. I hope your life will open into perpetual beauty and goodness."[4]

Next day, the president mounted a great chestnut horse, "the largest in the Cumberland Valley." His towering figure, crowned with a top hat, made everyone else look small. Seward, Blair, and Lamon rode beside him. Nicolay, Hay, and others came just behind. Minute guns boomed every sixty seconds as the procession moved toward the battlefield.

At the site of the ceremony, Everett, himself almost at the end of his life's journey, psyched himself up for the greatest speech of his long and illustrious life. Though Everett's speech was two hours long, he rarely referenced his notes. By the time he finished, amid great applause, the audience of twenty-five to fifty thousand had been sitting for about four hours.

When Lincoln got up to speak, many assumed another marathon was coming. After all, there had been a marathon opening prayer, a marathon wait for Everett to appear, and Everett's marathon speech. But Lincoln gave his address so quickly that he was done before some were aware he'd even started. In fact, the photographer didn't even have enough time to take a picture. But for the thousands who listened intently to every polished gem of a word, Lincoln's speech was so moving that they felt it almost a sacrilege to clap.

Afterward, Everett wrote Lincoln a note, "I should be glad if I could flatter myself that I came as near the central idea of the occasion in two hours as you did in two minutes," and asked for an autographed copy of Lincoln's speech. Lincoln, supreme master of tact, wrote back to Everett, "In our respective parts yesterday, you could not have been excused to make a short address, nor I a long one."

Today the 272 words of Lincoln's speech are considered to comprise one of the five greatest speeches in human history.[5] Here is the complete text of the Gettysburg Address:

Four score and seven years ago, our fathers brought forth upon this continent a new nation, conceived in Liberty, and dedicated to the proposition that all men are created equal.

Now we are engaged in a great civil war, testing whether that nation, or any nation, so conceived and so dedicated, can long endure. We are met on a great battle-field of that war. We have come to dedicate a portion of that field, as a final resting place for those who here gave their lives, that that nation might live. It is altogether fitting and proper that we should do this.

But, in a larger sense, we can not dedicate—we can not consecrate—we can not hallow—this ground. The brave men, living and dead, who struggled here, have consecrated it, far above our poor power to add or detract. The world will little note, nor long remember what we say here, but it can never forget what they did here. It is for us the living, rather, to be dedicated here to the unfinished work which they who fought here have thus far so nobly advanced.

It is rather for us to be here dedicated to the great task remaining before us—that from these honored dead we take increased devotion to that cause for which they gave the last full measure of devotion—that we here highly resolve that these dead shall not have died in vain—that this nation, under God, shall have a new birth of freedom—and that government of the people, by the people, for the people, shall not perish from the earth.

Chase's Last Resignation

Now, I know meaner things about Governor Chase than any of those men can tell me, but we have stood together in the time of trial, and I should despise myself if I allowed personal differences to affect my judgment of his fitness for office.
—Abraham Lincoln (*explaining why he had nominated Chase to be chief justice of the Supreme Court*)

Salmon Chase saw his own actions through the rosiest of glasses. Many came to the president and asked if he knew Chase was building an empire within the government. Others asked, "Aren't you aware that Chase and his supporters continually find ways to discredit you behind your back?" or "Aren't you aware Chase is using his Cabinet office as a way to supplant you as president?" Yes, the president knew. Not much escaped him.

When John Hay pressed hard as to why he didn't do something about it, Lincoln smiled, saying that Chase's incessant presidential ambitions reminded him of:

Plowing corn on a Kentucky farm with a lazy horse that suddenly sped forward energetically to the end of the furrow. Upon reaching his horse, he discovered an enormous chin-fly fastened upon him, and knocked it off, not wanting the old horse to be bitten in that way. His companion said it was a mistake to knock it off, for "that's all that made him go."

"Now," Lincoln concluded, "if Mr. Chase has a presidential chin-fly biting him, I'm not going to knock it off, if it will only make his department go."[6]

Relations between the two men continued to erode, and Chase all but ceased attending Cabinet meetings. But Lincoln did nothing until he was renominated. Once that took place, he was ready to make his move against Chase, his secretary of the Treasury. The opportunity came in June of 1864, when Chase tried to get Lincoln to agree to an unwise staff promotion. When Lincoln balked, Chase, who assumed he was indispensable, used his favorite ploy: offering his resignation. He was stunned when Lincoln accepted it—his resignation tantrums had always worked before. But this time Lincoln replaced him with William Pitt Fessenden, who did a splendid job.

With Chief Justice Taney's death on October 12, 1864, the only other office Chase had ever lusted for became vacant. When Chase asked some of his friends to intervene with the president for him, some looked at him as though he'd lost his mind—he, who'd tried to sabotage the president's reelection! Besides, other well-qualified people also wanted the job. In fact, it was the *only* job Stanton had ever really wanted. Edward Bates wanted it, too, and Francis Blair implored Lincoln to give it to his son. Many were openly snickering: *Finally, that sneaky Chase is going to get what's coming to him! If he'd remained loyal to his chief, he'd now have an inside track. But not now!*

Those in the know couldn't believe their eyes when, right after his reelection, Lincoln nominated Chase as the new chief justice. Lincoln had previously told Chittenden that in spite of Chase's disloyalty, "Yet there is not a man in the Union who would make as good a chief justice as Chase. . . . And, if I have the opportunity, I will make him Chief Justice of the United States."

Even though he'd promised Lincoln confidentiality, Chittenden admits in his book that he failed Lincoln that time:

> I had the satisfaction of informing the chief justice that his appointment had been decided upon the 30th of the previous June, after which the president had never contemplated any other. Not many days afterwards I was shown a copy of a letter to the president, written by Mr. Chase, in which he expressed his gratitude for the appointment which, he said, he desired more than any other. Thus was the *entente cordiale* restored between these two eminent Americans, never again to be broken or interrupted. Among the sorrowing hearts around the bed of the republic's greatest president, there was none more affectionate than that of his Chief Justice and his first Secretary of the Treasury.[7]

The Sleeping Sentinel—the Story of William Scott

There are many fictional stories about Lincoln forgiving soldiers who fell asleep on sentinel duty. (An excellent example can be found in Appendix C.) The question sometimes arises: Are these stories authentic? Or are they out of character? Let's find out.

Early in the war, Chittenden, upon reaching his office one morning, found a group of excited Vermont soldiers waiting for him. Finally calming them down, he got their story. William Scott, a fellow Vermonter who'd volunteered to do picket duty for a sick comrade, had himself fallen asleep during his own watch the following night. He was due to be shot within hours. What could they do to save his life? Knowing his commander General W. F. Smith as a by-the-book officer, Chittenden knew there was no hope there.

"Come, I said, there is only one man on earth who can save your comrade. Fortunately, he is the best man on the continent. We will go to President Lincoln."

I went swiftly out of the Treasury over to the White House, and up the stairway to the little office where the president was writing. The boys followed in a procession. I did not give the thought time to get any hold on me that I, an officer of the government, was committing an impropriety in thus rushing a matter upon the president's attention. The president was the first to speak.

"What is this?" he asked. "An expedition to kidnap somebody, or to get another brigadier appointed, or for a furlough to go home to vote? I cannot do it, gentlemen. Brigadiers are thicker than drummajors, and I couldn't get a furlough for myself if I asked it from the War Department."

There was hope in the tone in which he spoke. I went straight to my point. "Mr. President," I said, "these men want nothing for themselves. They are Green Mountain boys of the Third Vermont, who have come to stay as long as you need good soldiers. They don't want promotion until they earn it. But they do want something you alone can give them—the life of a comrade."

"What has he done?" asked the president. "You Vermonters are not a bad lot, generally. Has he committed murder or mutiny?"

"Tell him," I whispered to the captain.

"I cannot! I cannot! I should stammer like a fool! You can do it better!"

"Captain," I said, pushing him forward, "Scott's life depends on you. You must tell the president the story. I only know it by hearsay."

He commenced like the man by the Sea of Galilee, who had an impediment in his speech; but very soon the string of his tongue was loosened, and he spoke plain. He began to word-paint a picture with the hand of a master. As the words burst from his lips they stirred my own blood. He gave a graphic account of the whole story, and ended by saying, "He is as brave a boy as there is in your army, sir. Scott is no coward. Our mountains breed no cowards. They are the homes of thirty thousand men who voted for Abraham Lincoln. They will not be able to see that the best thing to be done with William Scott will be to shoot him like a traitor and bury him like a dog! Oh, Mr. Lincoln, can you?"

"No, I can't!" exclaimed the president. It was one of the moments when his countenance became such a remarkable study. It had become very earnest as the captain rose with his subject; then it took on that melancholy expression which, later in his life, became so infinitely touching. I thought I could detect a mist in the deep cavities of his eyes. Then, in a flash, there was a total change. He smiled, and finally broke into a hearty laugh, as he asked me,

"Do your Green Mountain boys fight as well as they talk? If they do, I don't wonder at the legends about Ethan Allen." Then his face softened as he said, "But what can I do? What do you expect me to do? As you know, I have not much influence with the departments."

"I have not thought the matter out," I said. "I feel deep interest in saving young Scott's life. I think I knew the boy's father. It is useless to apply to General Smith. An application to Secretary Stanton would only be referred to General Smith. The only thing to be done was to apply to you. It seems to me that, if you would sign an order suspending Scott's execution until his friends can have his case examined, I might carry it to the War Department, and so insure the delivery of the order to General Smith to-day, through the regular channels of the War Office."

"No! I do not think that course would be safe. You do not know these officers of the regular army. They are a law unto themselves. They sincerely think it is good policy occasionally to shoot a soldier. I can see it, where a soldier deserts or commits a crime, but I cannot in such a case as Scott's. They say I am always interfering with the discipline of the army. Well, I can't help it, so I shall have to go right on doing wrong. I do not think an honest, brave soldier, conscious of no crime but sleeping when he was weary, ought to be shot or hung. The country has better uses for him."

"Captain," continued the president, "your boy shall not be shot—that is, not tomorrow, nor until I know more about his case." To me he said, "I will have to attend to this matter myself. I have for some time intended to go up to the Chain Bridge. I will do so today. I shall then know that there is no mistake in suspending the execution."

I remarked that he was undertaking a burden which we had no right to impose; that it was asking too much of the president in behalf of a private soldier.

"Scott's life is as valuable to him as that of any person in the land," he said. "You remember the remark of a Scotchman about the head of a nobleman who was decapitated. It was a small matter of a head, but it was valuable to him, poor fellow, for it was the only one he had."

I saw that remonstrance was in vain. I suppressed the rising gratitude of the soldiers, and we took our leave. Two members of the committee remained to watch events in the city, while the others returned to carry news of their success to Scott and to the camp. Later in the day the two members reported that the president had started in the direction of the camp.

Within a day or two the newspapers reported that a soldier, sentenced to be shot for sleeping on his post, had been pardoned by the president and returned to his regiment. Other duties pressed me, and it was December before I heard anything further from Scott. Then another elderly soldier of the same company, whose health had failed, and who was arranging for his own discharge, called upon me, and I made inquiry about Scott. The soldier gave an enthusiastic account of him. He was in splendid health, was very athletic, popular with everybody, and had the reputation of being the best all-around soldier in the company, if not in the regiment. His mate was the elderly soldier who had visited me with the party in September, who would be able to tell me all about him. To him I sent a message, asking him to see me when he was next in the city.

Not long afterwards he called at my office, and, as his leave permitted, I kept him overnight at my house, and gathered from him the following facts about Scott. He said that, as we supposed, the president went to the camp, had a long conversation with Scott, at the end of which he was sent back to his company a free man. The president had given him a paper, which he preserved very carefully, which was supposed to be his discharge from the sentence. A regular order for his pardon had been read in the presence of the regiment, signed by General McClellan, but every one knew his life had been saved by the president.

From that day Scott was the most industrious man in the company. He was always at work, generally helping some other soldier. His arms and his dress were neat and clean; he took charge of policing the company's quarters; was never absent at roll-call, and always on hand if there was any work to be done. He was very strong, and practiced feats of strength until he could pick up a man lying on the ground and carry him away on his shoulders. He was of great use in the hospital, and in all the serious cases sought employment as a nurse, because it trained him in night-work and keeping awake at night. He soon attracted attention. He was offered promotion, which, for some reason, he declined.

It was a long time before he would speak of his interview with Mr. Lincoln. One night, when he had received a long letter from home, Scott opened his heart, and told Evans the story.

Scott said: "The president was the kindest man I had ever seen; I knew him at once, by a Lincoln medal I had long worn. I was scared at first, for I had never before talked with a great man. But Mr. Lincoln was so easy with me, so gentle, that I soon forgot my fright. He asked me all about the people at home, the neighbors, the farm, where I went to school, and who my schoolmates were. Then he asked me about mother, and how she looked, and I was glad I could pull out her photograph and show it to him. He said how thankful I ought to be that my mother still lived, and how, if he was in my place, he would try to make her a proud mother, and never cause her a sorrow or a tear. I cannot remember it all, but every word was so kind.

"He had said nothing yet about that dreadful next morning. I thought it must be that he was so kindhearted he didn't like to speak of it. But why did he say so much about my mother, and my not causing her sorrow or a tear when I knew I must die the next morning? But I supposed that was something that would have to go unexplained, and so I determined to brace up, and tell him I did not feel a bit guilty, and ask him wouldn't he fix it so the firing-party would not be from our regiment! That was going to be the hardest of all—to die by the hands of my comrades. Just as I was going to ask him this favor, he stood up, and he says to me, 'My boy, stand up here and look me in the face.' I did as he bade me. 'My boy,' he said, 'you are not going to be shot tomorrow, I believe you when you tell me you could not keep awake. I am going to trust you, and send you back to your regiment. But I have been put to a good deal of trouble on your account. I have had to come up here from Washington when I have got a great deal to do; and what I want to know is, how you are going to pay my bill?' There was a big lump in my throat; I could scarcely speak. I had expected to die, you see, and had kind of got used to thinking that way. To have it all changed in a minute! But I managed to say, 'I am grateful, Mr. Lincoln! I hope I am as grateful as ever a man can be to you for saving my life. But it comes upon me sudden and unexpected like. I didn't lay out for it at all. But there is some way to pay you, and I will find it after a little. There is the bounty in the savings-bank. I guess we could borrow some money on the mortgage of the farm.' There was my pay, and if he would wait until payday I was sure the boys would help, so I thought we could make it up, if it wasn't more than five or six hundred dollars. 'But it is a great deal more than that,' he said. Then I said I didn't see how, but I was sure I would find some way—if I lived.

"Then Mr. Lincoln put his hands on my shoulders and looked into my face as if he was sorry, and said, 'My boy, my bill is a very large one. Your friends cannot pay it, nor your bounty, nor the farm, nor all your comrades! There is only one man in all the world who can pay it, and his name is William Scott! If from this day William Scott does his duty, so that, if I was there when he comes to die, he can look me in the face as he does now, and say, "I have kept my promise, and I have done my duty as a soldier," then my debt will be paid. Will you make that promise and try to keep it?'

"I said I would make the promise, and, with God's help, I would keep it. I could not say any more. I wanted to tell him how hard I would try to do all he wanted; but the words would not come, so I had to let it all go unsaid. He went away, out of my sight forever. I know I shall never see him again; but may God forget me if I ever forget his kind words or my promise."

This was the end of the story of Evans, who got his discharge, and went home at the close of the year. I heard from Scott occasionally afterwards. He was gaining a wonderful reputation as an athlete. He was the strongest man in the regiment. The regiment was engaged in two or three reconnaissances in force, in which he performed the most exposed service with singular bravery. If any man was in trouble, Scott was his good Samaritan; if any soldier was sick, Scott was his nurse. He was ready to volunteer for any extra service or labor—he had done some difficult and useful scouting. He still refused promotion, saying he had done nothing worthy of it. The final result was that he was the general favorite of all his comrades, the most popular man in the regiment, and modest, unassuming, and unspoiled by his success.

The next scene in this drama opens on the Peninsula, between the York and the James rivers, in March, 1862. The sluggish Warwick River runs from its source, near Yorktown, across the Peninsula to its discharge. It formed at that time a line of defense, which had been fortified by General Magruder, and was held by him with a force of some twelve thousand Confederates. Yorktown was an important position to the Confederates.

On the 15th of April the division of General Smith was ordered to stop the enemy's work on the entrenchments at Lee's Mills, the strongest position on the Warwick River. His force consisted of the Vermont brigade of five regiments, and three batteries of artillery. After a lively skirmish, which occupied the greater part of the forenoon, this order was executed, and should have ended the movement.

But about noon General McClellan with his staff, including the French princes, came upon the scene, and ordered General Smith to assault and capture the rebel works on the opposite bank. Some discretion was given to General Smith, who was directed not to bring on a general engagement, but to withdraw his men if he found the defense too strong to be overcome. This discretion cost many lives when the moment came for its exercise.

General Smith disposed his forces for the assault, which was made by Companies D, E, F, and K of the Third Vermont Regiment, covered by the artillery, with the Vermont brigade in reserve. About four o'clock in the afternoon the charge was ordered. Unclasping their belts, and holding their guns and cartridge-boxes above their heads, the Vermonters dashed into and across the stream at Dam Number One, the strongest position in the Confederate line, and cleared out the rifle-pits. But the earthworks were held by an overwhelming force of rebels, and proved impregnable. After a dashing attack upon them, the Vermonters were repulsed, and were ordered to retire across the river. They retreated under a heavy fire, leaving nearly half their number dead or wounded in the river and on the opposite shore.

Every member of these four companies was a brave man. But all the eye-witnesses agreed that among those who in this, their first hard battle, faced death without blanching, there was none braver or more efficient than William Scott, of Company K, debtor for his own life to President Lincoln. He was almost the first to reach the south bank of the river, the first in the rifle-pits, and the last to retreat. He recrossed the river with a wounded officer on his back—he carried him to a place of safety, and returned to assist his comrades, who did not agree on the number of wounded men saved by him from drowning or capture, but all agreed he had carried the last wounded man from the south bank, and was nearly across the stream, when the fire of the rebels was concentrated upon him; he staggered with his living burden to the shore and fell.

An account of the closing scene in the life of William Scott was given me by a wounded comrade, as he lay upon his cot in a hospital tent, near Columbia College, in Washington, after the retreat of the army from the Peninsula. "He was shot all to pieces," said Private H. "We carried him back, out of the line of fire and laid him on the grass to die. His body was shot through and through, and the blood was pouring from his many wounds. But his strength was great, and such a powerful man was hard to kill. The surgeons checked the flow of blood—they said he had rallied from the shock; we laid him on a cot in a hospital tent, and the boys crowded around him, until the doctors said they must leave if he was to have any chance at all. We all knew he must die. We dropped on to the ground wherever we could, and fell into a broken slumber—wounded and well side by side. Just at daylight word was passed that Scott wanted to see us all. We went into his tent and stood around his cot. His face was bright and his voice cheerful. 'Boys,' he said, 'I shall never see another battle. I supposed this would be my last. I haven't much to say. You all know what you can tell them at home about me. I have *tried* to do the right thing! I am almost certain you will all say *that.*' Then while his strength was failing, his life ebbing away, and we looked to see his voice sink into a whisper, his face lighted up and his voice came out natural and clear as he said: 'If any of you ever have the chance, I wish you would tell President Lincoln that I have never forgotten the kind words he said to me at the Chain Bridge—that I have tried to be a good soldier and true to the flag—that I should have paid my whole debt to him if I had lived; and that now, when I know that I am dying, I think of his kind face and thank him again, because he gave me the chance to fall like a soldier in battle, and not like a coward by the hands of my comrades.'

"His face, as he uttered these words, was that of a happy man.

Not a groan or an expression of pain, not a word of complaint or regret came from his lips. 'Goodbye, boys,' he said, cheerily. Then he closed his own eyes, crossed his hands on his breast, and—and—that was all. His face was at rest, and we all said it was beautiful. Strong men stood around his bed; they had seen their comrades fall, and had been very near to death themselves: such men are accustomed to control their feelings; but now they wept like children. One only spoke, as if to himself, 'Thank God, I know now how a brave man dies.'

"Scott would have been satisfied to rest in the same grave with his comrades," the wounded soldier continued. "But we wanted to know where he lay. There was a small grove of cherry-trees just in the rear of the camp, with a noble oak in its center. At the foot of this oak we dug his grave. There we laid him, with his empty rifle and accouterments by his side. Deep into the oak we cut the initials, W. S., and under it the words, 'A brave soldier.' Our chaplain said a short prayer. We fired a volley over his grave. Will you carry his last message to the president?" I answered, "Yes."

Some days passed before I again met the president. When I saw him I asked if he remembered William Scott?

"Of Company K, Third Vermont Volunteers?" he answered. "Certainly I do. He was the boy that Baldy Smith wanted to shoot at the Chain Bridge. What about William Scott?"

"He is dead. He was killed on the Peninsula," I answered. "I have a message from him for you, which I have promised one of his comrades to deliver."

A look of tenderness swept over his face as he exclaimed, "Poor boy! Poor boy! And so he is dead. And he sent me a message! Well, I think I will not have it now. I will come and see you."

He kept his promise. Before many days he made one of his welcome visits to my office. He said he had come to hear Scott's message. I gave it as nearly as possible in Scott's own words. Mr. Lincoln had perfect control of his own countenance: when he chose, he could make it a blank; when he did not care to control it, his was the most readable of speaking human faces. He drew out from me all I knew about Scott and about the people among whom he lived. When I spoke of the intensity of their sympathies, especially in sorrow and trouble, as a characteristic trait of mountaineers, he interrupted me and said, "It is equally common on the prairies. It is the privilege of the poor. I know all about it from experience, and I hope I have my full share of it. Yes, I can sympathize with sorrow."

"Mr. President," I said, "I have never ceased to reproach myself for thrusting Scott's case so unceremoniously before you—for causing you to take so much trouble for a private soldier. But I gave way to an impulse—I could not endure the thought that Scott should be shot. He was a fellow-Vermonter—and I knew there was no other way to save his life."

"I advise you always to yield to such impulses," he said. "You did me as great a favor as the boy. It was a new experience for me—a study that was interesting, though I have had more to do with people of his class than any other. Did you know that Scott and I had a long visit? I was much interested in the boy. I am truly sorry that he is dead, for he was a good boy—too good a boy to be shot for obeying nature. I am glad I interfered."[8]

THE LAST FULL MEASURE

Now the war had turned firmly in favor of the Union. From September 1864 to March 1865, Phil Sheridan's men ravaged the breadbasket of the South, the Shenandoah Valley, so that Confederate armies would find food hard to get.

During 1864, Grant, now supreme Union general, trailed Lee into Virginia's wilderness—just like Joel Chandler Harris's Brer Rabbit, Lee loved to lure Union generals into the wilderness. The wilderness would now claim almost a hundred thousand more, with neither side giving in.

Ever the strategist, and desperately hoping to get Grant to overreact, Lee sent Early north with seventeen to twenty thousand men at a half-trot to take Washington, which was then only lightly protected. Only General Lew Wallace (who would later write *Ben-Hur*) stood in the way, with barely three thousand men. The best he could hope to do would be to delay the rebel force for a day. But that one day's delay saved Washington.

With no good war news coming from Grant lately, Lincoln hoped Sherman would do better. For if he did not, the president's reelection bid would be doomed. But Joseph Johnston had always given Sherman fits. Not only could Sherman not gain an edge on him, he was forced to siphon off badly needed troops just to protect his railroad supply line. Consequently, his original fighting force of 98,000 kept shrinking, while Johnston was able continually to pick up new troops as he fell back. His force increased from 45,000 to 62,000.

It was at this crucial juncture that Jefferson Davis lost the war for the Confederacy. Distressed by Johnston's purely defensive strategy, Davis demoted Johnston, whom he had never liked much, anyway, and handed the command over to John B. Hood. Hood, though a good general, stepped into very big boots. Without Johnston to keep him on guard, Sherman was able to wear Hood down in a series of extremely bloody battles. After the last defining one, Sherman wired Washington: "Atlanta is ours and fairly won."

That victory, coupled with the fall of the port of Mobile to Admiral Farragut, sewed up Lincoln's reelection. Like punctured balloons, the air went out of George McClellan's and John C. Fremont's campaigns.[9] On November 8, 1864, Lincoln was reelected—the first reelection of a president since Andrew Jackson thirty-two years before.

Sherman next marched sixty thousand plus men across Georgia to the sea, just to show the world that Davis could no longer protect his own. Then Sherman marched north through the Carolinas, leaving precious little in the way of food for either civilians or soldiers.

Back in Tennessee, Hood next led his battered army to the outskirts of Nashville, hoping to catch General George Thomas napping. Though Grant urged Thomas to strike immediately and grew angry enough to remove him from command when he didn't, none of that altered Thomas's timetable. Thomas, the most painstaking of Union generals, never struck except for the kill. After waiting out an ice storm, on December 15, 1864, Thomas's army gave Hood the battle he'd been hoping for. So thoroughly did they thrash Hood's army during a forty-eight-hour period that his Army of Tennessee was crushed, losing six thousand men. The Battle of Nashville proved to be the only Civil War battle in which one army virtually annihilated another.[10]

The telegram announcing Thomas's great victory reached Stanton in the middle of the night. Hurriedly he raced to the White House and had the president awakened. What a sight Lincoln made: standing at the top of the stairs, in his night attire, lighted candle in his hand, and face transformed by joy.[11] How Lincoln felt about Thomas's victory is perhaps best shown in one of his stories:

> When Hood's army had been scattered into fragments, President Lincoln, elated by the defeat of what had so long been a menacing force on the borders of Tennessee, was reminded by its collapse of the fate of a savage dog belonging to one of his frontier neighbors. "The dog," he said, "was the terror of the neighborhood, and its owner, a churlish and quarrelsome fellow, took pleasure in the brute's forcible attitude.
>
> "Finally, all other means having failed to subdue the creature, a man loaded a lump of meat with a charge of powder, to which was attached a slow fuse; this was dropped where the dreaded dog would find it, and the animal gulped down the tempting bait.
>
> "There was a dull rumbling, a muffled explosion, and fragments of the dog were seen flying in every direction. The grieved owner, picking up the shattered remains of his cruel favorite, said: 'He was a good dog, but as a dog, his days of usefulness are over.' Hood's army was a good army," said Lincoln, by way of comment, "and we were all afraid of it, but as an army, its usefulness is gone."[12]

After the battle Sherman and his sixty thousand men disappeared from sight. Not even Lincoln knew where he was for well over a month. At Christmas, however, Sherman telegraphed a welcome message to the worried president: "I beg to present you, as a Christmas gift, the city of Savannah, with 150 heavy guns and plenty of ammunition, and also about 25,000 bales of cotton."[13]

With that, the Civil War was effectively won.

*Lincoln and Grant viewing captured Confederate soldiers at Peters-
burg front, 1861*

O CAPTAIN!
My Captain!

O Captain! my Captain! our fearful trip is done,
The ship has weather'd every rack, the prize we sought is won,
The port is near, the bells I hear, the people all exulting,
While follow eyes the steady keel, the vessel grim and daring;
But O heart! heart! heart!
O the bleeding drops of red,
Where on the deck my Captain lies,
Fallen cold and dead.

O Captain! my Captain! rise up and hear the bells;
Rise up—for you the flag is flung—for you the bugle trills,
For you bouquets and ribbon'd wreaths—for you the shores a'crowding,
For you they call, the swaying mass, their eager faces turning;
Here Captain! dear father!
The arm is beneath your head!
It is some dream that on the deck,
You've fallen cold and dead.

My Captain does not answer, his lips are pale and still,
My father does not feel my arm, he has no pulse nor will,
The ship is anchor'd safe and sound, its voyage closed and done,
From fearful trip the victor ship comes in with object won;
Exult O shores, and ring O bells!
But I with mournful tread,
Walk the deck my Captain lies,
Fallen cold and dead.

—"O Captain! My Captain!" BY WALT WHITMAN[1]

*I do not consider that I have ever accomplished anything without God;
and if it is His will that I must die by the hands of an assassin, I must
be resigned. I must do my duty as I see it, and leave the rest
with God. I go to amusements very much against my inclinations.
I go because I must have change. I laugh because I must not weep.*

—ABRAHAM LINCOLN

HAMPTON ROADS

With the fall of the last seaport still in Confederate hands (Wilmington, North Carolina), there was no longer any way to move goods in and out of the Confederate states. Even the Mississippi was now controlled by Union gunboats. Though battles continued to be fought, and men continued to die, eventual Union victory now seemed likely.

Jefferson Davis, almost in desperation, sent a peace team headed by Confederate vice president Alexander Stephens to dialogue with Lincoln. Lincoln and Seward met with them on the *River Queen* on the Mississippi on February 3, 1865. Stephens and Lincoln had been good friends back when Lincoln was in Congress, but they hadn't seen each other for many years.

Stephens had always been a tiny man, weighing less than a hundred pounds. When he arrived for these talks, it appeared to Lincoln that the war had been good to him in that he'd gained a lot of weight. But as Stephens now divested himself of shawls and one overcoat after another, Lincoln had to laugh, saying in an aside to Seward, "That is the largest shucking for so small a nubbin that I ever saw."[2]

The two old friends picked up where they'd left off long ago. Eventually, however, the subject of the hour came up. Lincoln and Seward had earlier determined that they'd never recognized the Confederacy as a separate nation and certainly wouldn't acknowledge it as such for the purpose of the negotiations. Davis had known this before he'd sent his team, but he'd hoped that Lincoln and the once-conciliatory Seward would be willing to negotiate. So the conference came to naught—except two old friends, long estranged by the war, got to see each other again—for the last time.

A month later, Davis tried again, this time through General Lee, to get concessions by means of a convention with Grant. When Stanton brought

Lincoln a telegram in which Grant informed him of the request, a no-nonsense telegraph was wired back:

> The president directs me to say to you that he wishes you to have no conference with Lee unless it be for the capitulation of Gen. Lee's army or for some minor, and purely military, matter.[3]

With Malice toward None

I love the Southern people more than they love me. My desire is to restore the Union. I do not intend to hurt the hair of a single person in the South if it can possibly be avoided.

—Abraham Lincoln

For the first time in thirty-two years, crowds gathered for the second inaugural address of a president. Never before had so many people poured into Washington for an inauguration. Greeting them was a band playing "The Battle Cry of Freedom." A sight never seen by an inaugural crowd before was the great dome of the Capitol, completed at last. Lincoln had insisted work be continued on it during the war.

After the swearing in of Vice President Andrew Johnson in the Senate chamber, the nation's leaders now came outside. A photograph of the event shows that up behind the right buttress stood a man later identified as the actor John Wilkes Booth. When Lincoln was introduced, "a roar of applause shook the air, and again, and again repeated. The military band played 'Hail to the Chief,' helping to build the enthusiasm for the gathering." When the waves of applause finally subsided, Lincoln stood and put on his steel-rimmed glasses.

Precisely as Lincoln began to speak, the sun broke through the clouds, and a star, brilliant even in the daylight, cast its radiance over the Capitol. People would talk about that celestial phenomenon for years to come.

As we saw in chapter two, in Lincoln's six-minute, 703-word address, there was no gloating over victories or accomplishments, no castigating of the South. Instead, Lincoln stated that *both* sides were responsible for the evils of slavery, both had been punished by God for that collusion, and how much longer that punishment would continue, only the Almighty would know.[4] And then came that incredibly moving last paragraph:

With malice toward none, with charity for all; with firmness in the right, as God gives us to see the right, let us strive on to finish the work we are in; to bind up the nation's wounds; to care for him who shall have borne the battle, and for his widow, and his orphan—to do all which may achieve and cherish a just, and a lasting peace, among ourselves, and with all nations.

That night at a White House reception the president sought out Frederick Douglass, who'd been at the Capitol that morning. So had thousands of black men, women, and children—half the crowd, it was estimated. These former slaves, now full citizens of the republic themselves, came to celebrate their long-delayed jubilee. It had been 247 years since they had last stood tall in their native Africa. They were there now to listen to the president—*their* president. Lincoln now said to Douglass:

"I saw you in the crowd today, listening to my inaugural address. How did you like it?"

Douglass demurred. "I must not detain you with my poor opinion," he said. But Lincoln pressed on.

"There is no man in the country whose opinions I value more than yours," he said. "I want to know what you think of it."

"Mr. Lincoln," Douglass replied, "that was a sacred effort."[5]

RICHMOND

*Thank God that I have lived to see this! It seems to me that
I have been dreaming a horrid dream for four years,
and now the nightmare is gone. I want to see Richmond.*

—ABRAHAM LINCOLN

Lincoln was sadly in need of a vacation. As he once said, "I sincerely wish war was an easier and pleasanter business than it is, but it does not admit of holidays." His first presidential term had been stressful almost beyond belief. And now it seemed as though his second was going to be more of the same.

Though a bill proposing the Thirteenth Amendment (emancipation of the slaves) had passed with the necessary two-thirds vote in the Senate, it had failed in the House. In his December message to Congress, Lincoln urged the House to reconsider. When the proposal was reintroduced on January 6, 1865, Lincoln began an all-out blitz of individual congressmen, for if it failed to pass, the emancipation of the slaves would be put at risk.

Finally, thanks to five Democrats who changed their votes, the measure passed. When Speaker Schuyler Colfax stood to announce the results, his voice was shaking. There followed an explosion of cheers, then a roar of artillery from Capitol Hill announcing the glad news—the firing went on a long time.

Far to the north, the fiery abolitionist editor William Lloyd Garrison (who'd often had harsh words for Lincoln's slowness in freeing the slaves), addressing a jubilant Boston crowd, posed the question as to whom the credit for the victory over slavery should go. Then he answered in ringing tones: "I believe I may confidently answer—to the humble railsplitter of Illinois—to the presidential chain-breaker for millions of the oppressed—to Abraham Lincoln!"[6]

One early March morning, Julia Grant (wife of General Ulysses Grant) lowered a newspaper and suggested that her husband invite the president to pay them a visit in City Point, Virginia, command headquarters for the Union armies. She felt the exhausted president needed some time away from the pressures of the White House. Grant extended the invitation and Lincoln accepted, against the counsel of military leaders such as Stanton, who worried that City Point's proximity to battles still being fought might place the president's life in jeopardy.

The next day Mary Lincoln insisted she come along. The stay proved to be everything the Grants had hoped for, as Lincoln appeared more rejuvenated each day that passed. Mary's visit, however, was an entirely different matter. When one day she noticed General Edward Ord's lovely wife, Mary, riding a horse not far from the president's, she flew into a jealous rage and caused such a scene that everyone in the party was aghast. When Julia Grant stood up for Mrs. Ord, Mary Lincoln turned on her as well. Mary then accused Julia of secretly planning to usurp her position as First Lady. From that time on Julia Grant stayed out of Mary's vicinity completely. Only days later that decision would save Julia Grant's husband's life.

On April 3, 1865, glad news reached Stanton by telegram: "Richmond has fallen." Huge crowds gathered in Washington streets to celebrate. Across the Chesapeake in City Point, Lincoln's jubilation over the fall of the Confederate capital turned into a yearning desire to see Richmond himself.

Disregarding those who urged him to wait until Union forces more fully controlled the still-smoldering ruined city, the very next day the presidential party reached the Richmond landing. No sooner had Lincoln stepped ashore than he was engulfed by freed slaves who now shouted their joy: "Bress de Lord! . . . dere is de great Messiah! . . . Glory, Hallelujah!" A number fell to their knees. Lincoln insisted they rise, saying, "Don't kneel to me. . . . You must kneel to God only, and thank Him for your liberty!"

Back at the City Point encampment, Lincoln visited the hundreds of injured soldiers, speaking words of encouragement to each one—Confederates as well as Union troops.

THE PREMONITIONS BEGIN

I long ago made up my mind that if anybody wants to kill me he will do it.
If I wore a shirt of mail and kept myself surrounded by bodyguards,
it would all be the same. There are a thousand ways of
getting at a man if it is desirable that he should be killed.

—ABRAHAM LINCOLN

In 1859 Dan Emmet and Collin Coe's adaptation of a catchy minstrel tune, "Dixie," had swept the nation, with everybody playing, humming, or singing, "I wish I was in de land ob cotton." Only two years later, all Southern songs became taboo in the North.

But that didn't mean the Kentucky-born president didn't long to hear them.

Just before leaving City Point for Washington on April 8, 1865, the president turned to the military band and asked if they'd mind playing two numbers: the "Marseillaise," in honor of his guest, the Marquis de Chambrun; and, for him, "Dixie." As once again the soldiers heard the strains of "Dixie," many surreptitiously wiped away the tears: If the president of the United States requested that "Dixie" be performed for him, could peace be far away?

On the slow river trip back to Washington, Lincoln was unnaturally silent and contemplative, unwilling to discuss anything bordering on the political. Instead, he turned the discussion to literary subjects, especially the works of Shakespeare. From the play *Macbeth* Lincoln chose to read lines uttered by Macbeth, who had murdered his predecessor, Duncan, only to find it impossible to escape tormenting guilt:

> . . . *we will eat our meal in fear, and sleep*
> *in the affliction of these terrible dreams,*
> *That shake us nightly: better be with the dead . . .*
> *Than on the torture of the mind to lie*
> *In restless ecstasy. Duncan is in his grave:*
> *After life's fitful fever he sleeps well,*
> *Treason has done his worst; nor steel, nor poison,*
> *Malice domestic, foreign levy, nothing*
> *Can touch him further.*

David Donald then notes that:

> Struck by the weird beauty of the lines, Lincoln paused, as Chambrun recalled, and "began to explain to us how true a description of the murderer that one was; when, the dark deed achieved, its tortured perpetrator came to envy the sleep of his victim; and he read over again the same scene."[7]

LEE'S VALLEY FORGE

> *It [Robert E. Lee's face] is a good face; it is the face of a noble,*
> *noble, brave man. I am glad that the war is over at last.*
>
> —ABRAHAM LINCOLN

For Lee and his dwindling army, it had been a winter from hell. They were assailed by Union forces from every side. It was bitterly cold, and many of the soldiers were without coats, shoes, or blankets. All were on the verge of starvation. It was indeed the South's Valley Forge. Lee himself subsisted on only a little parched corn each day.

For weeks now, Lee had known it would come to this. The cause was hopeless, and the Confederacy was crumbling around him. With Sherman's army having moved up from the Carolinas, Grant now had a hundred thousand more men than Lee had with him.

He might just as well admit it: it was over. But for this proud yet humble descendant of the Washingtons and the Lees, the mere thought of the humiliating surrender ahead was more than his malnourished body could handle. After talking the matter over with General James Longstreet and other officers, it was obvious they, too, recognized checkmate: the last pawn had been taken, the final move was Grant's. Lee said, his voice choking, "There is nothing left for me to do but to go and see General Grant, and I would rather die a thousand deaths."

He now wrote a note asking Grant for an interview, "with reference to the surrender of my army," and sent it by courier with a flag of truce. Grant quickly responded, asking Lee to name the meeting place. Lee suggested the courthouse of the little Virginia town of Appomattox.

For Grant, the night before had been tough. He'd been staying in the saddle night and day, living on scant meals. He was worn to a frazzle. He'd bathed his feet in hot water and mustard, also applying mustard plasters on his wrists and the back of his neck, but he hadn't been able to get much sleep. Now, though, receiving the letter, the pain in his body seemed magically to disappear.

As he rode his horse down the dusty road to Appomattox with his aides, Grant couldn't help thinking about what an answer to prayer Lee's note was. His deepest fear—and Lincoln's—had been that Lee would escape, join forces with Joseph Johnston's still-viable force, hide out in a wilderness somewhere, and prolong the war indefinitely.

Grant thought, too, of what the troops had endured—especially Sherman and his men, who'd joined him only days before. What stories Sherman had to tell him! Twenty-five hundred miles they'd marched! Fording streams and flooded rivers, through rainstorms and hot sun, across mountains and through swamps even Johnston had said were impassible in the spring.

What a sight they were. More than half had marched through their shoes and were barefoot (the feet of many being so sore and bleeding that they had wrapped pieces of blanket around their feet), their trousers were so shredded by brush and brambles that they barely hung together. How they'd shouted for joy when food and clothing had caught up with them at Goldsboro!

But then Grant thought of the nineteen thousand bedraggled prisoners that had come his way from Lee's army during the last few weeks. They'd been in even worse shape than Sherman's men, for they were starving as well. The torching of the Shenandoah Valley, the taking of Wilmington and Fort Fisher, the effectiveness of the blockade, the destruction of central Georgia and the Carolina coast—it had all done what they hoped it would do, judging by the condition of Lee's men.

Reaching the little country courthouse and seeing Lee and his officers, Grant's mind returned to business. As his eyes took in the aristocratic-looking Lee in his impeccably clean uniform, the forty-two-year-old Grant ruefully looked down at his dusty, battle-worn clothes.

They small-talked their way through their mutual experiences in the Mexican War, Grant feeling hesitant to bring up the real reasons they were in this little building together. As Grant looked over to the splendid-looking man in the gray uniform sitting at the other table, he had to have thought, *Ah! the fortunes of war! It could just as easily have been me sitting over there, dying inside every minute, all my dreams shattered.* This perception, his own inherently kind nature, and Lincoln's repeated injunctions to be kind, caused his voice to soften even more as he moved to the acceptable terms of surrender.

Lee nodded, pleased the surrender terms were no worse. Officers and men would surrender, to be paroled and disqualified from taking up arms again until properly exchanged. All arms, ammunition, and supplies had to be turned over as captured property. Lee had been afraid they'd all be marched off to prison as traitors. Now he actually began to smile.

Grant asked Lee if he had any further suggestions. Yes, Lee had one. In the army, cavalrymen and artillerists provided their own horses. If they couldn't take them home with them, they'd have no way to do their spring plowing. Grant hadn't known that. He now added to the surrender terms a line indicating all those who owned a horse or mule could take the animals home with them. Lee showed even greater relief.

Lee almost left without asking for anything else—but thinking of his troops, as he always did, he remarked to Grant that his men hadn't had anything to eat but parched corn for a long time. Almost immediately, Grant directed 25,000 rations be sent to Lee's men.

Lee wrote an acceptance, signed it, and at 3:45 P.M. on Palm Sunday, April 9, 1865, the documents of surrender were finalized. There remained only the formalities of roll call and the stacking of arms. When Grant noticed Union gunners getting ready to fire a great salute of triumph, he stopped them. There would be no gloating over a brave and courageous opponent who was no longer an enemy.

Afterward, Lee:

> rode among his men—who crowded around him crying, "We'll fight 'em yet"—and exclaimed, with tears and in a choked voice, that they had fought the war together, he had done his best, and it was over. Many were dazed. Some wept. Others cursed. . . . The army could die but never surrender, they had hoped. Yet they still worshiped Lee. They touched his hands, his uniform; they petted Traveler and smoothed his flanks with their hands.

The next day Grant and Lee sat upon their horses while the Confederate men stacked their arms. Of the 28,231 parolees, only about 10,000 were still capable of fighting. Already the blue and gray were fraternizing with each other. Already the yawning chasm between North and South was beginning to contract. In only days, Joseph Johnston and his men would also lay down their arms. And the land would begin to heal.

Lincoln, back in Washington from City Point, was in the White House when Stanton burst in with Grant's telegram: "General Lee surrendered the Army of Northern Virginia this afternoon upon terms proposed by myself."[8]

The Civil War was officially over.

The nation, still celebrating the fall of Richmond, now went wild, and the only noise loud enough to adequately express the unbridled joy came from cannons and church bells. At long last, they were one nation again!

"The Dream Was Prophetic!"

If I am killed, I can die but once; but to live in
constant dread of it is to die over and over.

—Abraham Lincoln

Ward Hill Lamon, marshal of Washington, a close friend from the Illinois days, and Lincoln's personal bodyguard, wrote several books after Lincoln's death about his experiences with Lincoln. Especially pertinent to Lincoln's premonitions are these observations:

> From early youth he seemed conscious of a high mission. . . . He believed that he was destined to rise to a great height . . . that from a lofty station he would fall. . . . The plain people with whom his life was spent, and with whom he was in cordial sympathy, believed also in the marvelous as revealed in presentiments and dreams; and so Mr. Lincoln drifted on through years of toil and exceptional hardship, struggling with a noble spirit for honest promotion—meditative, aspiring, certain of his star, but appalled at times by its malignant aspect. Many times prior to his election as president he was both elated and alarmed by what seemed to him a rent in the veil which hides from mortal view what the future holds. He saw, or thought he saw, a vision of glory and blood, himself the central figure in a scene which his fancy transformed from giddy enchantment to the most appalling tragedy.[9]

Just after his election as president in 1860, Lincoln, lying on a lounge in his Springfield bedchamber one day, looked up into a mirror and saw a strange double reflection of himself looking back. One of these two images was:

> reflecting the full glow of health and hopeful life; and in the same mirror, at the same moment of time, was his face revealing a ghostly paleness. On trying the experiment at other times, as confirmatory tests, the illusion reappeared, and then vanished as before.
>
> Later, he'd tried the experiment a number of times in the Executive Mansion, but without success. Over time, he wrestled with the double-imagery, certain it had a meaning. Finally, he came to the conclusion that the life-like image foretold a safe-passage through his first term as president; the ghostly one: that he would surely hear the fatal summons from the silent shore during his second term. With that firm conviction, which no philosophy could shake, Mr.

Lincoln moved on through a maze of mighty events, calmly awaiting the inevitable hour of his fall by a murderous hand.

There was also the account of a certain dream Lincoln had. Lamon records it like this:

But the most startling incident in the life of Mr. Lincoln was a dream he had only a few days before his assassination. To him it was a thing of deadly import, and certainly no vision was ever fashioned more exactly like a dread reality. Coupled with other dreams, with the mirror-scene and with other incidents, there was something about it so amazingly real, so true to the actual tragedy which occurred soon after, that more than mortal strength and wisdom would have been required to let it pass without a shudder or a pang. After worrying over it for some days, Mr. Lincoln seemed no longer able to keep the secret. I give it as nearly in his own words as I can, from notes which I made immediately after its recital. There were only two or three persons present. The president was in a melancholy, meditative mood, and had been silent for some time. Mrs. Lincoln, who was present, rallied him on his solemn visage and want of spirit. This seemed to arouse him, and without seeming to notice her sally he said, in slow and measured tones:

"It seems strange how much there is in the Bible about dreams. There are, I think, some sixteen chapters in the Old Testament and four or five in the New in which dreams are mentioned; and there are many other passages scattered throughout the book which refer to visions. If we believe the Bible, we must accept the fact that in the old days God and His angels came to men in their sleep and made themselves known in dreams. Nowadays dreams are regarded as very foolish, and are seldom told, except by old women and by young men and maidens in love."

Mrs. Lincoln here remarked: "Why, you look dreadfully solemn; do *you* believe in dreams?"

"I can't say that I do," returned Mr. Lincoln; "but I had one the other night which has haunted me ever since. After it occurred, the first time I opened the Bible, strange as it may appear, it was at the twenty-eighth chapter of Genesis, which relates the wonderful dream Jacob had. I turned to other passages, and seemed to encounter a dream or a vision wherever I looked. I kept on turning the leaves of the old book, and everywhere my eye fell upon passages recording matters strangely in keeping with my own thoughts—supernatural visitations, dreams, visions, etc."

He now looked so serious and disturbed that Mrs. Lincoln exclaimed: "You frighten me! What is the matter?"

"I am afraid," said Mr. Lincoln, observing the effect his words had upon his wife, "that I have done wrong to mention the subject at all; but somehow the thing has got possession of me, and, like Banquo's ghost, it will not down."

This only inflamed Mrs. Lincoln's curiosity the more, and while bravely disclaiming any belief in dreams, she strongly urged him to tell the dream which seemed to have such a hold upon him, being seconded in this by another listener. Mr. Lincoln hesitated, but at length commenced very deliberately, his brow overcast with a shade of melancholy.

"About ten days ago," said he, "I retired very late. I had been up waiting for important dispatches from the front. I could not have been long in bed when I fell into a slumber, for I was weary. I soon began to dream. There seemed to be a death-like stillness about me. Then I heard subdued sobs, as if a number of people were weeping. I thought I left my bed and wandered downstairs. There the silence was broken by the same pitiful sobbing, but the mourners were invisible. I went from room to room; no living person was in sight, but the same mournful sounds of distress met me as I passed along. It was light in all the rooms; every object was familiar to me; but where were all the people who were grieving as if their hearts would break? I was puzzled and alarmed. What could be the meaning of all this? Determined to find the cause of a state of things so mysterious and so shocking, I kept on until I arrived at the East Room, which I entered. There I met with a sickening surprise. Before me was a catafalque, on which rested a corpse wrapped in funeral vestments. Around it were stationed soldiers who were acting as guards; and there was a throng of people, some gazing mournfully upon the corpse, whose face was covered, others weeping pitifully. 'Who is dead in the White House?' I demanded of one of the soldiers. 'The president,' was his answer; 'he was killed by an assassin!' Then came a loud burst of grief from the crowd, which awoke me from my dream. I slept no more that night; and although it was only a dream, I have been strangely annoyed by it ever since."

"That is horrid!" said Mrs. Lincoln. "I wish you had not told it. I am glad I don't believe in dreams, or I should be in terror from this time forth."

"Well," responded Mr. Lincoln, thoughtfully, "it is only a dream, Mary. Let us say no more about it, and try to forget it."[10]

Friday, April 14, 1865—Good Friday—was an exceedingly busy day for the president. In a Cabinet meeting that morning, with General Grant present, Lincoln asked Grant if he had any news from Sherman, who was negotiating with General Joseph Johnston. Grant said no, but he expected to receive a dispatch at any moment announcing Johnston's surrender.

According to Lamon, Lincoln then with great impressiveness said:

"We shall hear very soon, and the news will be important." General Grant asked him why he thought so. "Because," said Mr. Lincoln, "I had a dream last night; and ever since this war began I have had the same dream just before every event of great national importance. It portends some important event that will happen very soon."

This particular dream was always an omen of a Union victory and came with unerring certainty just before every military or naval engagement where our arms were crowned with success. In this dream he saw a ship sailing away rapidly, badly damaged, and our victorious vessels in close pursuit. He saw, also, the close of a battle on land, the enemy routed, and our forces in possession of vantage ground of incalculable importance. Mr. Lincoln stated it as a fact that he had this dream just before the battles of Antietam, Gettysburg, and other signal engagements throughout the war.[11]

After the Cabinet meeting, the president went for a ride with Mary, uncharacteristically insisting that no one else accompany them. On that ride, the traumas of the last four years seemed to be dissipating and he seemed almost happy. "Mary," he said, "we have had a hard time of it since we came to Washington, but the war is over, and with God's blessing we may hope for four years of peace and happiness, and then we will go back to Illinois and pass the rest of our lives in quiet." They also discussed traveling to California and Europe. Almost, it seemed, he could imagine getting on with his life and marriage.

THE BLACK DAY

The Lincolns loved to attend dramatic productions, and the president felt that they now deserved some relaxation. They invited the Grants to go with them, but because Mary had been so insolent to her, Julia Grant refused to go. To put another front on the refusal, the Grants booked a berth on a train that night. In their place, Mary invited Miss Harris, the daughter of Senator Ira Harris, and her fiancé, Major Rathbone.

Lamon, Lincoln's bodyguard, was away on a trip. Before leaving he had begged the president not to attend a play while he was gone. There were too many ugly assassination rumors floating around right then for him to feel good about the president's taking such a risk. But the Lincolns went anyway.

Presidential guard William H. Crook later declared it was his impression that Lincoln vaguely felt an attempt would be made on his life that night. Why would he go then? "He was human," Crook answered. "He shrank from it. But he was characterized by what some men call fatalism; others, devotion to duty; still others, religious faith."[12]

So Abraham and Mary Lincoln went that night to Ford's Theater to take in a performance of *Our American Cousin*.

As did John Wilkes Booth, who'd been stalking the president for four years now. Booth, a Southern sympathizer, yearned to be famous like his brother, famed tragedian Edwin Booth. And what better way of achieving fame than killing a president—in as dramatic a setting as possible? The beauty of having it happen in a play was that it would then become a play within a play, and thereby make him doubly famous.

Since John Wilkes Booth was fairly well known as an actor, Ford's Theater personnel permitted him to prowl around at will. Having heard the president would be there that night with the Grants, he planned to kill both men. He'd been able to fasten a simple mortise in the angle of the wall and door so that when a device was slid into the aperture, the door could not be opened from the hallway. He'd also bored a small hole in the door so he could observe the occupants of the presidential box before entering.

His murderous plan might work, provided he could first overpower the presidential guard. As fate would have it, on duty that night was the least reliable guard in the White House rotation. This man wandered outside instead of remaining at his post.

It all worked perfectly. And horribly. Holding a pistol in one hand and a knife in the other, Booth sneaked into the presidential box, put the pistol to the president's head, and fired.

Major Rathbone leaped up to grapple with him, but Booth savagely ripped his arm open with the knife.

Rushing forward, Booth vaulted from the box to the stage floor. It was a high leap, but he was known for frequently making such dramatic leaps. Unfortunately for the artistic effect he wanted, his spur caught in the flag draped over the front of the box, causing him to fall and break a leg. After brandishing his bloody knife, he shouted, *"Sic semper tyrannis!"*—a line from *Julius Caesar* meaning "Thus ever it be with tyrants!" Booth then fled as fast as he could with a broken leg, climbed on his rented horse, and was off into the night.

His accomplices were supposed simultaneously to murder Seward, Stanton, and Vice President Johnson. Seward was slashed again and again, as was his son, Frederick, the assistant secretary of state, though both survived. Providentially, Stanton's life was saved because his doorbell cord had broken recently. Johnson's attacker got cold feet.

Julia Grant later got goose bumps when, seeing Booth's face in a newspaper, she recognized him as someone who had shadowed her earlier the day of the assassination. In the train that night, someone had jiggled the latch to the Grants' compartment several times, but the latch held, so the attacker gave up. But rumors across the country had it that the president and his entire Cabinet had been assassinated.

THE DEATH OF ABRAHAM LINCOLN

The president was carried across the street to the Peterson house. All through the night, family, close friends, and Cabinet members came in and out of the room that held Lincoln. The doctors told them there was no hope: the wound was mortal. All they could do was wait. The first words out of Mary's lips after Booth's attack were, "The dream was prophetic!"[13] In the room with Lincoln, Mary went into hysterics and had to be moved into an adjoining room.

The president never regained consciousness. Senator Sumner came in and wept, like so many others. Stanton took charge, and for the rest of that terrible night was acting president of the nation, setting up a police and military network to track down the killer or killers—since no one yet knew for sure who they were.

At 7:22 A.M. Saturday, April 15, Abraham Lincoln breathed his last breath. Stanton, who had earlier declared "There lies the most perfect leader of men who ever lived," now spoke again, this time with words that have become immortal: "Now he belongs to the ages."

The Long Good-Bye

When he died the veil that hid his greatness was torn aside, and the country then knew what it had possessed and lost in him.

—William Herndon and Jesse Weik

It was later called a "Night of Madness." The wildest rumors ran rampant, like the unfounded story that the president had been murdered through a vast Confederate conspiracy. Thousands wanted that rumor to be true so that they could hate where Lincoln had asked them to love.

When Andrew Johnson had been chosen as vice president, apparently nobody even dreamed he'd ever be president. Lincoln himself generally steered clear of him. And Johnson's drunkenness at the inauguration had done little to elevate his status. Stanton, who had in the vacuum caused by Booth's bullet so ably managed the crisis, showed no inclination to turn over the reins of the government to Johnson. Apparently, Johnson did spend several minutes at Lincoln's bedside during that night, however.

Only when the president was pronounced dead did Senator Solomon Foot of Vermont, head of the Republican caucus, round up Chief Justice Chase and, in a rattletrap hack, haul him over to the Kirkwood House to rouse the bleary-eyed Johnson with the news that he was now president. Chase then swore him in as the seventeenth president of the United States.

Lloyd Lewis notes that:

> Just as the joyous news of Lee's surrender had come smashing into the cities of the north on the tongues of bells Palm Sunday night, so did the awful word of Lincoln's death come on Good Friday night. And the religious folk who saw in one the triumph of Jesus, saw in

the other the crucifixion. Where the bells of Sunday had exalted, the bells of Saturday tolled a funeral song.

By Saturday morning the entire North was in mourning. The flags, arches, and bunting that had gone up five days before as the people celebrated their jubilation were now taken down and replaced with black crêpe. When the stores sold out of black fabric, old black dresses were cut up for bunting. Anyone who failed to drape his home in black was accused of being a traitor.

In the frenzy of grief and rage that followed, mobs threatened the lives of those accused of being Southern sympathizers. By Saturday night all chance of Lincolnian mercy toward the South was gone.

The cold rain stopped on Sunday morning, and the sun finally came out. Though it was Easter Sunday, there was little joy in the North that day. "Black Easter" they called it in years to come. People thronged into churches in numbers not seen since before the war. They'd come for solace. Instead, in thousands of churches ministers called for vengeance, playing into the hands of the Radical Republicans who would propel the nation into the twelve-year-long horror of "Reconstruction." Rare indeed was Lincoln's spirit of tolerance that Sunday morning.

The people of Washington wanted Lincoln to be buried there. So did the people of New York. But in the end the prairie people of Illinois staked their claim, and Mary Lincoln, ever after a recluse, confirmed that the president had yearned to return to the serenity of the plains he so loved.

The longest funeral in world history—seventeen hundred miles long—was orchestrated by Stanton. On Tuesday, April 18, the White House doors were opened, and the people flooded in. The masses inched past the coffin, many weeping: 25,000 filed past before the doors were closed.

On Wednesday came the military funeral, attended by every dignitary with rank high enough to gain admission. By the casket stood Grant, the hero of Appomattox, wearing a white sash across his breast, indicating that he was the head pallbearer. Beside him stood Admiral Farragut and other top generals, flanked by foreign ambassadors. Lonely and lost in the august assemblage were Robert Lincoln, in his captain's uniform, and Tad, his face swollen from tears. With them were many of the Todds—but not Mary.

After the service, according to Lloyd Lewis (the best chronicler of this period), "Abraham Lincoln's trip to mythland began."

The instant the pallbearers came through the White House doors, all the church bells in Washington, Georgetown, and Alexandria began to toll. From the fortresses ringing the city, minute guns began to boom. A vast crowd gathered along Pennsylvania Avenue. At 2:00 P.M., the black-tassled hearse, pulled by six white horses, began to move, accompanied by drums, the clanging bells, the minute guns, the pop of horses' hooves on cobblestones, and the tramp, tramp, tramp of soldiers' shoes. So enormous was the pressing crowd that it took an hour for the hearse to reach the Capitol building, where the pallbearers carried the casket up into the rotunda.

At 10:00 A.M. on Thursday, wounded soldiers were the first to enter, followed by 3,000 people an hour—25,000 were allowed in before the doors closed. Before sunup on Friday, seven days after Lincoln's death, the coffin was closed, and Dr. Phineas D. Gurley, Lincoln's pastor, prayed.

In the train yards the funeral train was ready: eight coaches swathed in black (six for the mourners, one for the guard of honor, one for the bier). At the foot of the big casket rested the little coffin of Willie Lincoln. It had been disinterred in order for the son to accompany his father back to Illinois. Between regiments at present-arms, the funeral train began to move, with a pilot engine ten miles ahead to ensure a clear track. For the entire 1,600-mile journey, the train would move at a steady pace of twenty miles per hour.

As the train slowly moved through Maryland, not even Stanton had any idea of what awaited them. At 10:00 A.M., the *Edward H. Jones* engine slowed to a stop in Baltimore, the city having been packed since dawn. In the three hours permitted, ten thousand people shoved their way past the coffin. Stanton had insisted Lincoln's face not be prettied up, but marks of the wound would remain. All during this time, bells tolled and guns boomed once every minute.

As the train moved out of Maryland into Pennsylvania, crowds thickened along the tracks. Farmers stood with their wives and children, silently staring; each crêpe-bedecked town was a sea of people with town bands playing dirges. The official party in the train was stunned as the crowds increased with every mile, and every farmhouse wore black. At Harrisburg, a huge crowd waited through torrential rain. All day they streamed by the bier—until midnight. Armies of farmers from outlying regions sat up all night in order to be there when the doors opened at 7:00 A.M. Lancaster, too, was a sea of black.

As the cortege neared Philadelphia, solid walls of people lined the tracks. In the city, half a million mourners jammed the streets. Outside Independence Hall, a line of mourners three miles long waited to see the bier. And, as continued to be true for the entire journey, in every city were the everlasting bells and minute guns. At midnight the doors were closed, but thousands remained outside all night. By 3:00 A.M. on Sunday morning, the crowd was even larger than it had been the day before. The crush was so great that many fainted in line. Hundreds were injured. Nor had the crowds decreased by 2:00 A.M. the following morning, when the hearse was taken to the railroad amid the resuming bells and guns.

The country had gone wild. Newspaper editors and writers were stunned. By dawn, all New Jersey appeared to have gathered along the tracks. In Jersey City, a great choir of Germans sang hymns as the casket was carried onto a boat for its journey to New York, where an even bigger crowd awaited.

For hours the streets of New York had been so jammed that nothing moved. The police and military fought desperately to keep lanes open. A giant new hearse pulled by sixteen white horses carried the casket onto Broadway, where the funeral party gasped. It was the greatest sight New York had ever seen: 160,000 people marched in the parade itself. Incredibly, except for the incessant bells and guns, the crowd was deathly silent as the catafalque passed. In City Hall, 150,000 looked at Lincoln's face.

On Monday night, embalmers restored Lincoln's face. It had become unlifelike through exposure. For twenty-four hours crowds poured through City Hall in double file. When at noon on Tuesday the casket was closed, three hundred thousand people were turned away. At 12:30 P.M., a parade of one hundred thousand people accompanied the catafalque, with half a million looking on. No one would ever know just how many people jammed those New York streets, but the general estimate was upwards of 1.5 million.

At the station waited the locomotive *Union*, the same engine that had brought Lincoln into New York in 1861. At Albany, sixty thousand people waited—four thousand an hour went by the open coffin all afternoon and all night. By now, each city, hearing about all that had gone on before, tried to outdo what any other city had done. "The thing had become half circus, half heartbreak," concluded Lewis.

By the time Lincoln's casket was opened in Springfield, well over 7 million people (a third of the total population of the nation) had looked upon the hearse or the coffin, with 1.5 million having looked upon his face.

But now, in Illinois:

In the House of Representatives where Lincoln, long before, had pronounced doom upon slavery . . . for twenty-four hours, was heard the steady tramp of feet—the feet of prairie people, farmers, atheistic lawyers, fanatic circuit-preachers, rail-splitters, crippled soldiers, shysters Lincoln had tricked, mothers he had protected, politicians he had disappointed, bullies he had whipped, girls to whom he had sold sugar, loafers who had laughed at his stories—the feet of prairie people.

It was 10:00 A.M. on May 4, 1865, and time for the last service, then the last parade. General Joe Hooker rode ahead of the hearse, and "Old Bob," the aging bay horse that had borne Lincoln over the circuit, was led behind, riderless.

A long parade, bannered, mottoed, costumed like the rest, but with some new and terrible woe, as of family grief in it, wound out two miles to Oak Ridge Cemetery. Prayers, oratory, religious hymns, boys falling with breaking boughs, apple blossoms in the wind.

And the long journey was over. Abraham Lincoln had come home.[14]

Daniel Chester French's sculptured heads of Lincoln for the Lincoln Memorial

Epilogue

Flags remained at half-mast in the nation's capital until the last week in May. For days the trains had been packed with people from all across the country, all with one purpose: to witness the "farewell march" of the nearly two hundred thousand Union soldiers who would soon disband and return to civilian life. The master choreographer himself, Edwin Stanton, was orchestrating this as well. Never in the history of Washington had there been such an enormous influx of visitors.

The weather cooperated; it was perfect. Reviewing stands had been built all along Pennsylvania Avenue and a covered platform was reserved for President Johnson, General Grant, and other luminaries.

Over a million Union men would soon be reduced to a peacetime force of only twenty-five thousand. Because of the sheer number of soldiers involved, Stanton decided to schedule the march over a two-day period. The first day: the Army of the Potomac—its cavalry, mounted artillery engineering brigades, "each with their distinctive uniforms and badges, accompanied by 'the clatter of hoofs, the clank of sabers, and the shrill call of bugles.'" The second day: the Army of the West, marching solemnly behind General Sherman.

Nor should we forget the brave men in gray south of the Potomac who did not march down Pennsylvania Avenue. Their decimated ranks, too, were mourned all across the South. They were part of the 623,000 men who had paid the ultimate sacrifice for a cause they believed in. And 623,000 men cast an awfully long shadow.

THE REST OF THE STORY

Before completing our story, let's bring closure to the lives of the key players.

Almost unbelievably, both Seward and his son Frederick eventually recovered from their terrible injuries during what has since been called "the Night of Horrors"—the single most eventful twenty-four hours in the history of our nation. But the toll was too much for Frances Seward: six weeks later, she died. Their daughter Fanny so weakened her constitution caring for her father and mother that she succumbed to tuberculosis and died at age twenty-one. Seward would remain secretary of state under Johnson and be responsible for the purchase of Alaska from Russia. He died peacefully in 1872.

Stanton, lacking a strong hand on the rudder, did not flourish under Johnson. In fact, he barricaded himself in his office for weeks after Johnson asked for his resignation. After Johnson escaped impeachment by one slim vote (the Radicals turned on Johnson in fury when he attempted to continue Lincoln's policy of kindness to the South), Stanton resigned. Three days after Ulysses Grant, who became the eighteenth president of the United States, nominated him to the Supreme Court, he died of an asthma attack. He was only fifty-three.

Salmon Chase, as Lincoln had predicted, never did overcome his infection with the "presidential bug." He made unsuccessful bids for the nomination in 1868 and 1872. Weakened by disappointment and depression, a heart attack, and a stroke, he died in 1873.

Lincoln's personal secretaries, John Nicolay and John Hay, remained friends until the end of their lives, coauthoring the greatest of Lincoln biographies. Hay would go on to serve as secretary of state under Presidents William McKinley and Theodore Roosevelt.

Mary Lincoln never recovered from her husband's death. Without him, she felt life was not worth living—she continued only for Tad. The two traveled to Europe in order to get away from their terrible memories. After returning to America, Tad, never very strong, died of "compression of the heart" at eighteen. After his death, Mary's increasingly erratic behavior got so bad that Robert had her committed to a state hospital for the insane. Four months later, she was released into the care of her sister Elizabeth in Springfield. She never forgave Robert for committing her.

She would spend the rest of her life—except for a final trip to Europe—obsessing over not having enough money (which was not true), existing in dark rooms, wishing she'd die. She finally got her wish in 1882. She was sixty-three.

Robert Lincoln had a very successful life: as ambassador to England, secretary of war, and president of the Pullman Company. Yet he never really felt successful. Always he felt that these positions fell into his lap merely because he was Abraham Lincoln's son. In public, he tried to keep a low profile. Though Robert and his wife, Mary, had children and grandchildren, there were no descendants beyond them. Robert died in 1926 at the age of eighty-two.[1]

LAST THOUGHTS: RELEVANCE OF LINCOLN TODAY

We've come to the end of this book and my thoughts swirl like windswept autumn leaves. Chief among them: So what does all this men in the twenty-first century? What do we gain by this nineteenth-century archaeological dig? What parts of it are still relevant to the daunting day-to-day problems we now face?

I submit that there are many reasons Lincoln remains relevant today. First and foremost, no matter what assails us—even Hell itself—God is our only bedrock. The only eternal source of power and comfort during our few ephemeral days on this troubled planet. Not surprisingly, mankind tends to distance itself from God during good times, only to come crawling back during tough times.

Second, in this age of T. S. Eliot's Hollow Men, true integrity sometimes seems like a vanishing species. Integrity that cannot be bought or sold for any amount of money. Robert Penn Warren, in *All the King's Men*, famously postulated that we all have our breaking points: all it takes is stress enough, incentive enough, temptation enough, and we break. Lincoln did not break, even under superhuman stress.

Third, Lincoln never lost the common touch. He would shake his head at the imperial presidencies of our age. He was accessible to everyone, rich or poor; white, brown, or black—none received preferential treatment, and he was kind to all. Lincoln would never have permitted "security" to bar him from daily interaction with his people, convicted as he was that a higher power would protect him until his time came.

Fourth, Lincoln also insisted that his voice was not for sale. Unlike leaders during the last half century, his speeches represented his own thoughts and convictions; so did his letters. What huge opportunity is lost today (in terms of moral impact upon an age) by presidents who permit others to write their speeches, letters, and books. Even their signatures are churned out by mechanical signature machines! In future generations' books, who will ever believe that the words are theirs rather than some speechwriter's?

Fifth, Lincoln would curl his lip in scorn at poll-driven government. He has another increasingly rare quality today: true courage. Courage to do what he perceived to be the right thing regardless of consequences.

Sixth, Lincoln believed in accountability. Leaders who fail to lead are being led by others. Where a leader fails to lead, chaos inevitably results. He believed in surrounding himself with a team of the nation's strongest leaders and permitting them to lead, with one proviso: so great was his moral authority that all instinctively recognized that his was the last word, his the ultimate responsibility.

Seventh, Lincoln believed that God holds nations as well as individuals accountable for their actions. Consequently, he led out during his years in office as did the prophet-kings in Old Testament times, God being the ultimate authority in everything.

Might there not be food for thought here in our own times? For all of us—not just national leaders? Indeed, Lincoln reminds us of the worth of each individual—nay, more than that: each created being, from a mistreated turtle to a baby bird fallen from its nest to a drunk dying from the cold in a pool of icy water. In God's sight, all are interconnected.

Funeral car that carried Lincoln's body to Illinois

WHEN LINCOLN PASSED
Mabel McKee

Young Richard Trowbridge, kin to the queen of England, vowed that someday the suspicious innkeeper would pay for doubting his word.

But then, sitting on top a stagecoach with a tall ungainly stranger—who kept him laughing at his stories—his own slights began to dim. And he watched as this strangely attractive ugly stranger went out of his way to serve two judges who had gone out of their way to be rude to him.

Young Trowbridge had no way of knowing that this humble man, this serving man, would someday be considered the greatest man of his age.

When Richard Trowbridge walked across the dining room of the Eagle and Lion Inn that morning, Ezra Ross, the merchant, thought of a young prince. The youth carried his head like one. His dark eyes flashed as if giving a challenge to A. Beste, the innkeeper, who gave him some terse orders about directing the service in the room.

But Ezra Ross didn't dream that the lad who was serving him was related to a king. The flash in the boy's eyes merely accompanied a bitter surging in his heart because he had to take orders from the innkeeper. Though no one knew it, the surging promised a time of reckoning with the man who had refused the boy credit at his inn until his uncle could arrive. Instead, the innkeeper had told him that he would have to work for his room and board or find other lodgings.

Black Cindy came in from the kitchen to gather up the empty dishes on the table. Then Ezra Ross left the room, Richard Trowbridge following a little later. His work was over until dinnertime. He wandered out to sit on a bench in front of the tavern and watch the stagecoaches come in.

Two judges walked up and down in front of the inn, discussing politics. They talked of the Kansas-Nebraska bill and the new party—Republican, its supporters called it. Often both of them quoted Colonel Richard Thompson's opinion of different leaders in those turbulent times.

Mention of Colonel Richard Thompson brought a smile to Richard's lips. When his uncle or the colonel arrived, it would become known who he was. He imagined these men, who had called him "Boy" and ordered him to do their most menial tasks, would treat him with honor. His heart beat exultantly. *I, who am related to a king, will then come into my own,* he thought proudly.

His uncle wanted Richard to read law in Colonel Thompson's office when they had become settled. He himself was to buy one of the packing houses on the other side of the river. An advertisement that it was for sale had been inserted in a Philadelphia newspaper, and this it was that had interested John Seymour in the little town on the Wabash. Long before his nephew had come from England, John had wanted to leave New York City and Philadelphia and journey to the Northwest Territory, reported by Western settlers to be the garden spot of the world.

Suddenly there was a commotion among the men in front of the inn. A cloud of dust from down the street, the scattering of small boys playing in the road, and the rushing of the Negroes who carried the luggage of travelers into the inn told the story—the coach from the West had been sighted.

A few minutes later it was in front of the inn. A wave of disappointment went through the crowd of watchers. There was only one occupant, a man asleep on the back seat. Scant attention was given him by the young dandies who were watching for the return of the town's two belles. Immediately they scattered, and the two watching boys ran around the tavern to play in the backyard. Richard Trowbridge, the habitual "loafers," and the judges were the only watchers left. Richard turned toward Charles Lesser, the driver of the coach, who had started to climb from his high seat to get water for his horses.

He slumped into a heap when his feet touched the ground. One of the men and Richard ran to him. The boy who was related to a king liked the kindly stage driver. He had brought him on the last lap of his journey to the Wabash and allowed him to drive his horses much of the way. His illness now distressed Richard.

The blueness of the driver's face and trembling of his hands told the story. He had contracted that deadly disease of early settlers along the river—the ague. His teeth chattered so, they could hardly understand his request for a driver to take the coach on to Indianapolis. Finally he managed to ask, "Will you drive it, young mister?"

Unconsciously Richard threw up his shoulder. "Young Mister" was a title the old driver had given him on their trip over as the boy drove and the old man pointed out different trails along the way. Now he answered in a sturdy fashion, "I'll be glad to drive for you." His dark eyes flashed with pride. "You know I can manage the horses, sir. I'll see that they have food and water and care exactly as you do."

The old man was helped into the inn, and Richard made ready to mount the driver's seat. But just then he became aware of some commotion at the coach itself. The two judges who were going to Indianapolis had opened the door and were surveying a great, long, lanky Westerner who was asleep, sprawled on the backseat. Another traveler had climbed on the front seat. Their intention of talking politics on their way to the capital city could not be carried out if they were required to occupy different seats.

One of them prodded the sleeping man—prodded him until he awoke with a jump. He yawned, and it seemed to Richard that his mouth was at least a yard wide. Then he smiled sleepily, and instantly his homely face became beautiful to the boy.

He drawled out in nasal tones that grated on one's nerves, "Howdy, friends? What can I do for you?"

Rather imperiously, Judge Hammond stated their request for the backseat of the coach, so their talk would not be interrupted. He suggested that the stranger sit on the front seat with the other passenger. His request brought a still broader smile to the Westerner's lips. Slowly and with difficulty he managed to move his long legs and then the rest of his body from the coach. He reached under the seat and brought out a stovepipe hat which he fitted on his head.

Tall, lanky, with ill-fitting clothes, the man stood then. His rugged features were crooked and angular and indescribably homely. His shoes were ill-fitting. So was the collar of his shirt. His neck was extremely long and reached far above it. His hands hung from his sleeves and dangled like those of a scarecrow. Many of the people who were coming out of the candy store across the street stopped in front of it to stare at the strange-looking person.

Richard was sure he would never forget this man so long as he lived. He had seen no other that looked like him. He visualized the word "Yankee," which he had heard applied contemptuously in New York to the pioneers of the Middle West.

The tall man, who had started to climb into the coach's front seat, suddenly stopped. "Why, here's a new driver," he exclaimed, and smiled his rare smile again. "He doubtless will need some instruction about the road. I'll ride with you, young man, if you don't object."

He swung himself onto the high seat beside Richard, and soon they were driving down the dusty road, past children who shouted at them and women who stared and waved. The beautiful bay horses pranced as if on parade. Richard lifted his head with the same pride he had shown back in England when he and his mother had driven with their cousins to Buckingham Palace to see their relative, the queen.

Soon they were out of the town and passing through a woods of sycamore and poplar trees. Thick underbrush grew all around. Wild vines covered the trunks of the trees nearest the road, which was so rough that Richard on the high driver's seat had a terrible time keeping his balance. After a time they reached a district in which it had rained the night before. Soon they were in a region where the road was muddy and water stood in the deep ruts.

Once Richard gave a terrific lurch, and just then the tall, ungainly man reached out his strong hand and clutched him. "Sit closer to me, son," he said kindly. "It takes more than a jolt to unseat a backwoodsman. That made me think of Tom Harden and the time he tried to ride the oxen. Never heard that story, I reckon?"

He himself laughed at the story of disaster and fun he told. His voice was squeaky at times, then deep and soft again. His laugh was still stranger than his voice. But his story was good and told so well that Richard laughed uproariously and forgot all his former troubles.

Ahead of them lay a stretch of corduroy road. The tall man told Richard that it had been built by laying logs crosswise in the road where swampy land prevented filling in. He told of cutting down the trunks of such trees and of splitting rails for all the fences on his father's farm.

"Pretty nice little village, that Terry Hut," he said after a time. "Reckon you're going to live there. I went through there when I was a boy, moving a family from Boonville over to Illinois. I made three dollars that way. I stayed all night in the Spencer wagon yard. I reckon it's still there?"

Richard was interested in this man in spite of himself. The expression "wagon yard" had caught his fancy back at the inn when he first heard it. He had gone down to the place they called wagon yards, watched the farmers drive their loads of corn and other produce into them for the night, and make their beds in the wagons filled with straw. It was always amusing to see them crawl into this straw, drawing heavy covers around them, ready to sleep all night.

He could imagine the tall stranger crawling into such a wagon bed, folding up his legs for the night, and then sleeping soundly the sleep of the just.

On and on the stranger talked, telling stories about the people who had lived in Hoosier county, which had been his boyhood home, and about the men who kept store or were attorneys in Springfield, Illinois, which was then his home. When he mentioned the fact that he, too, was a lawyer, Richard sat up straight. "Do you know Colonel Richard Thompson?" he asked excitedly. "He's a lawyer back there where we came from."

"Dick Thompson!" chuckled the stranger. "Reckon I do know him. He's the brightest, keenest lawyer in the whole Middle West. He's up at Indianapolis now, lookin' after the legislature there, I should say."

"I'm going to read law in his office." Richard raised his head proudly. "My uncle, who met him while he was in Washington, arranged for that."

"You are!" The tall Yankee seemed delighted. "Reckon you'll know all the rudiments of law then. Up at Indianapolis they say what law Dick don't know ain't ever been written. That reminds me of a story Abner Williams told about his schoolteacher. Don't suppose you ever heard that?"

Dick shook his head. When it was finished and the boy had laughed many hearty laughs, he in turn began to talk. He went back to England, told of his royal relations there, of the death of his parents, and the urge for adventure which had brought him to America. He told of his journey across the prairies to Indiana and of the innkeeper who had made him work when his money gave out. He admitted that he was too proud to ask for credit in his uncle's name at the packing establishment. Almost vindictively he added the information that his uncle would see that this innkeeper was properly humiliated for his treatment of him.

"Reckon I wouldn't do that, son," the tall man spoke slowly, persuasively, sweetly. A beautiful smile came over his rugged face. "He didn't mean to be rude to you. He's often been cheated that way. When people have been cheated, they can't be blamed for doing as he did. Guess he didn't know the story about the man who went to a feast and took a high seat only to be sent down lower, and about the one who took a low seat and was sent higher. That's in the Bible, son. Think you'd better read it some day."

At his own suggestion, Richard allowed the man to take the lines. He drove like an experienced horseman, not talking much, but watching the rough, muddy road ahead of him. When he did speak, he told of how the national highway over which they were driving had been built and improved during the last twenty years.

Once they stopped the coach at a little gully to get a drink. The tall driver told Richard the spring was the finest in that district. He led the way through a thicket where tall ferns grew and to the rocks from which trickled a stream of cold water. They drank from their hands like boys. When they came back to the coach, Judge Hammond had his head out of the window, frowning impatiently. "We want to get to Indianapolis before dark," he said. "Will we have time to stop at the Half-Way House for dinner, do you think?"

Richard hesitated. He had almost forgotten there was a hostelry by this name on the road. The tall stranger, who was studying the position of the sun, finally answered. "Reckon we shall, judge. They'll have dinner ready any time they see us." He added to Richard: "We'd better eat there, too. I'm as hungry as Enoch Rent's bear. Now I must tell you that story."

After they had climbed back onto the top of the coach, they heard Judge Hammond's stentorian voice talking about "Whigs" and "Butternuts" and "slaves."

"Slaves! Men and women and children sold like cattle!" And the man who was driving grew stern. "The judge says they should be allowed in Indiana to work in the fields. Slaves here! The ordinance of the Northwest Territory fixed that." [The Northwest Ordinance of 1787 mandated that no slavery would be permitted in future states].

Richard was completely absorbed in the man's talk. He would have to know about Indiana's laws and ordinances if he became an attorney like the famous Colonel Thompson, as his uncle desired.

Finally they were at the Half-Way Inn—a long, low, frame-and-log build-

ing, set back in a big yard. Here all coaches that traveled along the National Road stopped for meals or to stay overnight. A fat, jolly-looking host ran out to ring a dinner bell. He waved his hand at the coach, calling a greeting to the old driver who he thought was driving. The tall stranger waved back, cordially, cheerfully, kindly.

Richard had driven the coach as near the side of the yard as he could, but still a muddy space intervened between it and some boards that were laid to the inn door. Before he could descend from the high seat to open the door of the coach for his passengers, the tall man was out of the seat, onto the ground. He jumped across the mud puddle, spattering his long coat, and was in the yard where some loose boards lay. He picked up two or three, carried them to the end of the boardwalk, and made an extension to the coach door so the passengers were able to walk to the inn without getting their feet muddy.

When Judge Hammond complained of a touch of ague and said that the drizzling rain would make him bedfast, the tall man ran back to the inn and came back carrying a heavy coat to him.

Who is he, anyway? Richard asked himself. *He acts like a servant, but speaks like an educated person. I wonder if it would be rude to ask his name. I told him mine, but he didn't offer to tell me his. I'll wait a little while longer. Perhaps he'll tell me later.*

Surmising that the boy had no money, the tall man graciously asked him to be his guest for dinner, and together they went into the dining room.

The rest of the trip was a quieter one for the man and the youth. The drizzle became a slow, pronounced rain, which seemed to sadden the tall man still more. He dropped into a silence, broken suddenly when his voice seemed fairly to wail, "I can't bear to think of the rain falling on the lonely graves of the people you love."

Richard's eyes filled with quick tears as he thought of the two new graves in England which held his father and mother. He drove on and on, through mud puddles and water at times. Trees loomed tall on each side of the road. Sometimes the woods were so dense that it seemed like night as they passed through them. The coach jolted from one side of the road to the other. A feeling of elation rose in the boy's heart as he thought of the two pompous men inside the coach, still talking politics. He hoped they were jolting from one side of the seat to the other.

Just before they reached Indianapolis, the stranger talked again. Richard, according to his advice, was not to worry if his uncle didn't arrive soon. The work at the hotel was not hard. Indiana was a democratic state; and when he did get started in law, people would give him extra praise for having worked his way in time of emergency. "Remember this, son," he added with a kindly smile, "if you try always to serve like a king, you can't go wrong."

Richard noticed the man's awkward hands, showing by their calloused spots and their roughness that their owner had worked at the hardest manual labor. He listened with more interest then as the stranger spoke of honest labor scars.

Soon they were at the little hostelry in the capital city at which the coach stopped. Richard noticed that the tall man remained in his seat while he sprang to the ground and opened the coach door for his passengers. They hurried toward a distinguished-looking little man whom every one seemed to know.

While he was watching the three talk together, Richard noticed that his tall, ungainly friend was unfolding his legs and coming to the ground with a single jump. The noise of his landing drew the attention of other people in front of the inn, particularly that of the distinguished-looking man who was talking to the judges. Hurriedly he came toward Richard's friend. "Why, Mr. Lincoln," he began, "I had no notion you were coming stagecoach."

"Dick Thompson!" the tall man clutched his hand, and his face was wreathed with a hundred smiles. "I'm glad to meet you so soon. And here"—his other hand reached out for Richard's—"is my young friend who has come all the way from England to see you. Since I've come only from Illinois, I reckon that gives him the first chance to talk to you."

Richard Thompson, who had heard that the young Britisher was coming and who knew all his sad history since the death of his parents, at once gave the boy a cordial handclasp. "Abraham Lincoln," he said, turning to the tall stranger, "is the best lawyer and the most intelligent man in the country. You'll always be glad to have him for a friend."

Judge Hammond and his companion were staring at the Westerner with open mouths. Abraham Lincoln, the lawyer who was then stirring the country through his debates with Stephen Douglas, had given them his seat in the coach at their request. He had carried boards and made a walk so they would not step in the mud. They could not speak, so great were their amazement and confusion.

Richard stood speechless, too. But through his heart went one sentence: *He served like a king.*

Some years later Richard Trowbridge stood in Indianapolis again. This time he was a man, with a pretty young woman, dressed in long, hooped skirts, tight basque, and tiny hat, clinging to one arm as they waited at the station. The sleeve which should have held his other arm hung empty. He had left that at Gettysburg.

It was raining as it had been that day back in the long ago when Richard had driven the coach along the National Road. Crowds thronged the station—crowds which were tragically silent and restless. Women sobbed and men were grief-stricken.

Abraham Lincoln was passing—on his last journey from Washington to his hometown, Springfield, Illinois. He was coming more quietly than he had ever traveled before, coming in a casket wrapped in flags, for he had been killed by an assassin's deadly bullet. Richard Trowbridge turned to his wife. "I shall never forget how he carried that board to the coach," he said softly. "I shall never forget that he told me always to serve like a king."

A sound of weeping rose, mingled with the noise of an engine. Slowly it came—the dark, snorting steel creature back of which Abraham Lincoln lay. Richard Trowbridge saw it through the mourning people around him and the station building, draped in black. And he said softly to himself more than to the woman by him, "Years from now they'll know that the greatest American of them all is now passing."

"When Lincoln Passed," by Mabel McKee. Published in *The Youth's Instructor,* February 4, 1930. Reprinted by permission of Joe Wheeler (P.O. Box 1246, Conifer, CO 80433), Review and Herald Publishing Association, Hagerstown, MD 21740, and Fleming H. Revell, a division of Baker Book House.

Lincoln and Julia carrying his valise

THE MISSIONARY MONEY
by Olive Vincent Marsh

This is a true story of a little girl who refused to accept a contribution from Abraham Lincoln because all the money in her missionary box had to be *earned*.

After little Julia grew up, and many years went by, she shared this story with Helen Nicolay, who then published it about a hundred years ago in the pages of the greatest child magazine of all time, *St. Nicholas*. It took place sometime between 1861 and 1864.

Once upon a time, as all the good fairy stories begin—only I must warn you that the fairy in this story was a very big fairy indeed, and very real—there lived a little girl in a little town in New York State. I know that she was a bright and happy and altogether delightful little girl, because now that she is growing old she is bright and happy and altogether delightful.

She lived with her father and her mother and her brothers in a real, old-fashioned, homey home, where guests liked to come. One of the guests who liked to come was the great Abraham Lincoln, president of the United States. The little girl was always very happy when he came, and she used to like to sit in his lap and talk to him. She called him "Uncle Abe," and he often called her "Sissy," though her real name was Julia.

One time when the president was visiting at Julia's home and the family were all gathered in the sitting room in the evening, Julia was counting the money in her missionary box, at one end of the table. Mr. Lincoln watched her for a moment and then asked, "What are you doing over there?"

"I'm counting my missionary money, Uncle Abe," replied Julia.

Mr. Lincoln put his hand in his pocket and pulled out something and held it toward Julia. Julia drew back her box.

"Oh, no, I can't take that, Uncle Abe," she said earnestly; "I have to *earn* all the money I put in this box."

"That so?" said Mr. Lincoln thoughtfully and, making no further comment, he put his hand back into his pocket again.

The next day, when he was ready to start for the train, he said to Julia, "I wonder if you couldn't walk down to the depot with me, Julia?"

"Oh, yes, I'd love to!" cried Julia, and she ran for her hat.

As they started down the street together, Abraham Lincoln shifted his valise to the other hand. It was an old-fashioned valise with two handles. He looked down from his great height at his little companion.

"Do you suppose," he said, "that you could help me carry my valise? It's pretty heavy."

Julia was a little surprised, for Mr. Lincoln had never asked her to help him carry his valise before; but she took hold of one of the handles, and they carried it between them all the way to the depot, talking gaily as they went. At the depot the president took the valise and pulled a shining coin out of his pocket, holding it out to the little girl.

"There, Julia," he said, "now you've earned your missionary money."

Julia was very much surprised, for she had not thought of such a thing as earning money while she was helping her friend carry his valise, but she saw that she really had earned it. Mr. Lincoln had found a way. Her face lighted up as she exclaimed joyfully, "Oh, *thank* you, Uncle Abe!"

And then he went away on the train, and Julia ran home with the shining coin clutched tight in her hand. She thought it was the very brightest penny she had ever seen and she hurried to put it into the missionary box, where it would be safe and sound.

The next Sunday at Sunday school, when the missionary boxes were opened, Julia was called out into another room. There sat the superintendent and there were her father and one of her brothers, and there on the table was her missionary box. Everybody looked very serious.

"How much money did you have in your missionary box, Julia?" asked the superintendent.

"Eighty-two cents," answered the little girl, without any hesitation.

"I knew it was a mistake. It's not her box," said her father.

"Are you sure that was all you had? Where did *this* come from?" she was asked, and she saw the bright penny that the president had given her.

"Oh, that's the money Uncle Abe gave me!" she answered eagerly. "I earned it helping him carry his valise."

The shining coin was a five-dollar gold-piece, and this is a true story of how Abraham Lincoln helped a little girl to earn her missionary money. I know that it is true because the little girl, who is a little girl no longer, told me the story herself.[1]

"The Missionary Money," by Olive Vincent Marsh. Reprinted in *St. Nicholas*, February 1918.

Lincoln with boy at the White House

A LESSON in FORGIVENESS
by T. Morris Longstreth

T. Morris Longstreth wrote several stories about Lincoln during his long writing career, but none are more moving than this one. The time: July 7, 1863, four days after the Battle of Gettysburg. Two people, a man and a boy, are faced with a terrible decision on the same hot summer night.

The Ripley brothers were as different in nearly every way as are the rapids and still pools of a mountain stream. Perhaps that is why they loved each other in a way not usually meant by "brotherly love."

Will Ripley was the "still pool." He was thoughtful to the point of appearing drowsy, honest as daylight, mild-tempered, and twenty. He was up north in Pennsylvania somewhere, either alive or dead, for the date of this story is July 7, 1863, which means, as you can read in the dispatches of the time, that the terrible Battle of Gettysburg was just over. The Ripleys, on their farm near Washington, had not heard from him for some time.

Although Will was no soldier at heart, he had responded to Lincoln's call for more men two years before, leaving his young brother, Dan, at home to help his father and mother. Dan was now fourteen, a high-strung, impetuous, outspoken lad of quick actions and hasty decisions. He was the "laughing rapid." But for all his hastiness, he had a head, and a heart that could be appealed to, usually.

The only thing to which he could not reconcile himself was the separation from Will. Even Will's weekly letters—which had seldom missed coming until recently, and which always sent messages of love to Dan, coupled with encouragement to stay on the farm as the best way to aid the cause—scarcely kept him from running away and hunting up his brother. Dan knew that he and his collie, Jack, were needed to look after the sheep; he knew that his father, who was little more than an invalid, must have help. But to see the soldiers marching set him wild to be off with them. In fact, Jack seemed to be the anchor which held him. Dan sometimes even thought that he loved Jack next to Will.

The summer of '63 had been unbearably hot. There had been an increasingly ominous list of military disasters. Even the loyal were beginning to murmur against Lincoln's management of the war. Then Will's letters had ceased, and Mr. Ripley could get no satisfaction from headquarters.

Dan was irritable with fatigue and his secret worry; his family was nearly sick with the heat and the tension.

The climax to this state came from an unforeseen event. Jack, crazed either by the heat or by some secret taste for blood, ran amuck one night, stampeded the sheep, and did grievous damage. Farmer Ripley doubtless acted on what he considered the most merciful course by having Jack done away with and buried before Dan got back from an errand to the city. But to Dan it seemed, in the first agony of his broken heart, an unforgivable thing. Weariness, worry, and now this knife-sharp woe changed the boy into a heartsick being who flung himself on the fresh mound behind the barn and stayed there the whole day, despite the entreaties of his mother and the commands of his father.

That evening his mother carried some food out to him. He did not touch it; he would not talk to her.

Some time later, as the night wore on, he stole into the house, tied up some clothes into a bundle, took the food at hand, and crept out of his home. Once more he went to the grave of his slain pal. What he said there, aloud but quietly, need not be told. Sufficient it is to know that a burning resentment toward his father filled him, coupled with a sickening longing to be with his brother Will. Ill with his hasty anger, he thought that Will was the only one in the world who loved or understood him.

In the wee hours of morning he left the farm, forever, as he thought, and turned down the road which led to the soldiers' home, not far away, where he hoped to find someone who could tell him how to get to Will's regiment. The sultry, starless heat of a Washington midsummer enclosed him; the wood was very dark and breathless; his head throbbed. But he pushed on, high-tempered, unforgiving; he would show them all!

Suddenly he remembered that he had not said the Lord's Prayer that night. Dan had been reared strictly. He tried saying it walking. But that seemed sacrilegious. He knelt in the dark and tried. But when he got to "as we forgive our debtors," he stopped, for he was an honest lad. This new gulf of mental distress was too much for him; it brought the tears. There in the dark by the roadside, Dan lay and bitterly cried himself into an exhausted sleep.

At the same hour another worn person, a tall, lean-faced man with eyes full of unspeakable sorrow, was pacing the chamber of the White House in the nearby city. The rebellion had reached its flood tide at Gettysburg three days before. The president had stayed the flood, bearing in tireless sympathy the weight of countless responsibilities. Now, all day long, decisions of affairs had been borne down upon him—decisions that concerned not only armies, but races; not only races, but principles of human welfare. He was grief-stricken still from his son Willie's death, and his secretary in the room downstairs, listening unconsciously to the steady march of steps overhead, read into them the pulse beats of human progress. Lincoln had given instructions that no one was to interrupt him. He was having one of his great heart battles.

Finally, shortly before dawn, the footsteps stopped, the secretary's door opened, and the gaunt, gray face looked in. "Stoddard, do you want anything more from me tonight?"

The secretary rose. "I want you in bed, sir. Mrs. Lincoln should not have gone away; you are not fair with her or us."

"Don't reproach me, Stoddard," said Lincoln, kindly: "it had to be settled, and with God's help, it has been. Now I can sleep. But I must have a breath of air first. There's nothing?"

"Only the matter of those deserters, sir, and that can wait."

The president passed his hands over his deep-lined face. "Only!" he murmured. "Only! How wicked this war is! It leads us to consider lives by the dozen, by the bale, wholesale. How many in this batch, Stoddard?"

The secretary turned some papers. "Twenty-four, sir. You remember the interview with General Scanlon yesterday."

Lincoln hesitated, saying, "Twenty-four! Yes, I remember. Scanlon said that lenience to the few was injustice to the many. He is right, too." Lincoln held out his hand for the papers, then drew it back and looked up at Stoddard. "I can't decide," he said in a low voice, "not now. Stoddard, you see a weak man. But I want to thresh this out a little longer. I must walk. These cases are killing me; I must get out."

"Let me call an attendant, Mr. Lincoln."

"They're all asleep. No, I'll take my chances with God. If anybody wants to kill me, he will do it. You must go to bed, Stoddard."

The two men, each concerned for the other, shook hands in good night, and Lincoln slipped out into the dark, his long legs bearing him rapidly northward. During the heat he usually slept at the soldiers' home, being escorted thither by cavalry with sabers drawn. But he hated the noise of it, and during Mrs. Lincoln's absence was playing truant to her rules. When he neared the home, he felt slightly refreshed and turned into a wood road. The sky to his right began to lighten.

By the time dawn showed the ruts in the road, Lincoln realized that he was tired. "Abe, Abe," he said half aloud, "they tell me you used to be great at splitting rails, and now a five-mile stroll before breakfast—well! What have we here?"

The exclamation was occasioned by his nearly stepping on a lone youngster lying in the road. The boy raised his head from a small bundle of clothes. The tall man stooped with tenderness, saying, "Hello, sonny. So you got old Mother Earth to make your bed for you! How's the mattress?"

Dan sat and rubbed his eyes. "What are you doin'?" he asked.

"I appear to be waking you, and making a bad job of it," said Lincoln.

"You didn't come to take me, then," exclaimed Dan, greatly relieved. "I wouldn't'a gone!" he added defiantly.

Lincoln looked at him sharply, his interest aroused by the trace of tears in the boy's eyes and the bravado in his voice. "There's a misunderstanding here," said Lincoln, "almost as bad a misunderstanding as Mamie and her mother had over Mr. Riggs, who was the undertaker back home." Here the gaunt man gave a preliminary chuckle. "Ever hear that story, sonny?"

Dan shook his head, wondering how such a homely man could sound so likable. Lincoln seated himself on a fallen tree trunk. "Well, it was this way—" And he told the story.

Dan's quick, impetuous laugh might have disturbed the early-rising birds. Lincoln joined in, and for an instant Dan completely forgot dead Jack and his deserted home. For the same fleet instant Lincoln forgot his troubles in Dan's laugh. The boy chuckled again. "I'll have to tell that to fa—" He didn't finish the word, remembering with a pang that he was not going to see his father again.

Lincoln caught the swift change on his face, and it was his turn to wonder. He knew better than to ask questions. You can't fish for a boy's heart with question marks, neat little fishhooks though they be. So he said, "Our sitting here when we ought to be getting back home reminds me of another story."

"Tell me," said Dan, well won already to this man, despite the gray, lined cheeks and the sadness that colored his voice. Dan didn't know yet who he was. He had not seen the cartoons that flooded the country during election. He was too young to go in alone to the inauguration, and the idea of the president of the United States sitting with him in the woods was too preposterous to cross his mind.

When Dan had laughed heartily over the second story, Lincoln said, "Well, sonny, I reckon we ought to be moving, don't you?" He helped the lad with his bundle.

"Are you going to the war, too?" asked Dan. "I am."

"You!" exclaimed Lincoln, "why, you're no bigger than my own tadpole, and he's only a wriggler yet. Does your father know?"

"I reckon he does by now," said the boy, darkly. "Father's an early riser. You see, he killed my dog without my knowin', and so I left without *his* knowin'."

The hardness of the boy's voice hurt Lincoln, who said, "What's your father's name, sonny?"

"William Ripley—that is, senior. Will, that's junior, my brother, is off at the war. I'm Dan. I'm going to find my brother. I don't care if I never come back. I loved Jack better than—than—" His voice choked.

Lincoln put his hand on the boy's shoulder. He was getting the situation. "Jack was your dog?" asked the big man, as gently as a mother.

"Yeh. And father shouldn't'a killed him unbeknownst to me. I'll never forgive him that, never!"

"Quite right," said the wise man, walking with him. "Don't you ever forgive him, Dan. Or don't ever forget it—under one condition."

"What's that?" asked the boy, a trifle puzzled at the unexpected compliance of his elder with his own unforgiving mood.

"Why, that you also never forget all the kind and just things that your father has done for you. Why did he kill the dog, Dan?"

"Well—he—killed—some sheep," said the boy. He would be honest with this tall, gentle, and grave person who understood so readily.

"How old are you, Dan?"

"Fourteen, going on fifteen."

"That's quite a heap," said Lincoln, musingly, "quite a heap! In fourteen years a father can pile up a lot of good deeds. But I suppose he's done a lot of mean ones to cancel 'em off, has he?"

"No," admitted Dan.

His frankness pleased the president. "I congratulate you, Dan. You're honest. I want to be honest with you, and tell you a story that isn't funny, for we're both in the same boat, as I size up this proposition—yes, both in the same boat. I am in the army, in a way. At least, I'm called commander in chief, and occasionally they let me meddle in a little with things."

"Honest?" said Dan, opening his eyes very wide. He had been so absorbed in his own disasters that he had accepted this strange, friendly acquaintance without question. But now, although the forefront of his consciousness was very active with the conversation, the misty background was trying to make him compare this man with a certain picture in the big family album, with another one pasted on the dining room cupboard door, the same loose-hung person, only this one had a living rawness—maybe it was bigness—about him that the pictures didn't give, like a tree, perhaps. But it *couldn't be* the president talking to him, Dan. If it was, what would the folks at home—and again his thought stopped. There were to be no more "folks at home" for him.

"Honestly, Dan. But sometimes they don't like it when I do meddle. There's a case on now. Last night I pretty nearly had twenty-four men shot."

"Whew!"

"But I hadn't quite decided, and that's the reason I came out here in God's own woods. And I'm glad I came, for you've helped me decide."

"I have!" said Dan, astonished, "to shoot them?"

"No! Not to. You showed me the case in a new light. Here you are, deserting home, deserting your father, bringing sorrow to him and to your mother, who have sorrowed enough with Will in danger and all; you're punishing your father because he did one deed that he couldn't very well help, just as if he'd been a mean man all his life. And it's like that with my twenty-four deserters, Dan, very much like that. They've served for years, faithfully. Then, can any one thing they do be so gross, so enormously bad, as to blot out all the rest, including probably a lifetime of decent living? I think not. Is a man to blame for having a pair of legs that play coward once? I think not, Dan. I tell you what I'll do, sonny," and the tall man stopped in the road, a new light shining in his cavernous, sad eyes, "I'll make a bargain with you. If you'll go home and forgive your father, I'll go home and forgive my twenty-four deserters. Is that a bargain?"

The boy had been shaken, but it was difficult to change all at once. "It is hard to forgive," he murmured.

"Someday you'll find it hard not to," said the great man, putting out his huge palm for the boy to shake. "Isn't that a pretty good bargain, Dan? By going home, by ceasing to be a deserter yourself, you will save the lives of twenty-four men. Won't you be merciful? God will remember and perhaps forgive you some trespass sometime even as you forgive now."

Something of last night's horror, when he could not say that prayer, and something of the melting gentleness of the new friend before him touched the boy. He took Lincoln's hand, saying, "All right. That's a go."

"Yes, a go home," smiled Lincoln. "I suppose I'll have to turn, now."

"Where's your home?" asked the boy, knowing yet wishing to hear the truth, to be very sure; for now he *could* tell the folks at home.

"The White House," replied Lincoln, "but I wish I were going back to the farm with you."

The boy heard him vaguely; his jaw was sagging. "Then you—are the president?"

Lincoln nodded, enjoying the boy's wonder. "And your servant, don't forget," added Lincoln. "You have been a help to me in a hard hour, Dan. General or no generals, I'll spare those men. Any time I can do anything for you, drop in, now that you know where to find me."

The boy was still speechless with his assured elation.

"But you'd better—Wait," and Lincoln began hunting through his pockets; "you'd better let me give you a latchkey. The man at the door's a stubborn fellow, for the folks will bother him. Here—"

And finding a card and a stub of a pencil, he wrote:

Please admit Dan'l Ripley on demand.

A. LINCOLN.

"How's that?"

"Thank you," said Dan, proudly. "I reckon I should'a guessed it was you, but those stories you told kind o' put me off."

"That's sometimes why I tell them." And Lincoln smiled again. "It's not a bad morning's work—twenty-four lives saved before breakfast, Dan. You and I ought to be able to eat a comfortable meal. Good-bye, sonny."

And so they parted. The man strode back the way he had come; the boy stood looking, looking, and then swiftly wheeled and sped. He had been talking to the president, to Abraham Lincoln, and hearing such talk as he never had heard before; but especially the words, "You have been a help to me in a hard hour, Dan"—those words trod a regular path to his brain. He ran, eager to get to the very home he had been so eager to leave. Forgiveness was in his heart, but chiefly there was a warm pride. He had been praised by Abraham Lincoln! Of this day he would talk to the end of his days. Dan did not know that the major part of the day, the greatest in his life, was still to come. Certainly the dawning of it had been very beautiful.

Breathless and with eyes bright in anticipation of telling his tale, he leaped the fences, ran up to the back door, and plunged into the house. The kitchen was quiet. A misgiving ran over him. Were they all out in search of him? Would he have to postpone his triumph?

In the dining room a half-eaten meal was cooling. He explored on, and coming out to the spacious front of the house, found them—found them in an inexplicable group around a uniformed officer. Tears were streaming down his mother's cheeks. His father, still pale from his accident, looked ashen and shriveled. They turned at Dan's approach. He expected that this scene of anguish would turn to smiles upon his arrival. He was amazed to find that his return gave them the merest flurry of relief and alleviated their sorrow not at all.

"Danny, dear, where have you been?" asked his mother.

"The Lord must have sent you home in answer to our prayers," said his father.

Then they turned back to the officer, pleading, both talking at once, weeping. Dan felt hurt. Did his return, his forgiveness, mean so little to them? He might as well have gone on. Then he caught the officer's words, "Colonel Scott can do no more, madam. The president cannot see him, and more pardons are not to be hoped for."

Mrs. Ripley turned and threw her arm across Dan's shoulders. "Danny—Danny—you are our only son now. Will was—" and she broke down completely.

"Will was found asleep while on duty, Dan, and—"

"Is to be shot?" asked the boy. "I wonder if he was one of the twenty-four." They looked at him, not understanding.

"The Lord has restored you to us. If we could only pray in sufficient faith, He could restore Will," said Farmer Ripley, devoutly. "Dear, let us go in and pray. We should release this gentleman to his duty. We can talk to the Father about it."

Dan realized with a sudden clearness that his brother, his beloved, was to be taken from him as Jack had been taken. It shook his brain dizzy for a moment; but he knew that he must hold onto his wits—must think. There was Abraham Lincoln, *his friend*!

"You pray," he cried to his father, shrilly, "and I'll run."

"Run where, dear? Will is in Pennsylvania."

"To the White House, mother. He said, 'Any time I can do anything for you, drop in.' *Anything*, mother. Surely he'll—"

"Who?" cried both his parents.

"Why, the president, Mr. Lincoln!"

"But the president is busy, dear."

"He'll see me—I know he will!" said Dan. "Look! We have a secret together, the president and I have." And the boy showed his card and poured out his story.

The mother saw a break in her gray heaven, saw the bright blue of hope.

"We must go at once," she said. "Father, you are not able to come with us, but pray here for us."

"Please take my horse and carriage," said the officer.

"Yes," said Dan, "let's hurry. Oh, I'm glad, I'm so glad!" And the joy at his lucky turning back shone in his face as he helped his mother into the vehicle.

"May God help you!" said the officer.

"He does," said the boy, thinking.

It was high noon when the doorkeeper of the White House, hardened into a very stony guard by the daily onslaught of Lincoln seekers, saw an impetuous youth leap from a light carriage and help a woman up the portico steps toward him.

"In which room is the president?" asked Dan.

"He's very busy," said the doorkeeper, probably for the five hundredth time that morning. "Have you an appointment?"

"No, but he said I should drop in when I wanted to; and what's more, here's my 'latchkey'"; and Dan, trembling a little with haste and pride, showed him the card "A. Lincoln" had written.

The man looked quizzically at it and at him. "In that case," he said, dryly, "you'd better step into the waiting room there."

There must have been forty or fifty people crowded into the anteroom, each on some urgent errand. Some were in uniform; all looked tired, impatient, important. Dan saw the situation, and knew that Lincoln could never see them all. He whispered to his mother and showed her to a chair, then went up to the doorboy and asked if the president was in the next room. The boy admitted the fact, but would not admit anything further, including Dan. The annoyed looks on the faces of the waiting people deepened. *Does this urchin* [said their looks] *expect to see the president today, when so many more important persons (such as we) are kept waiting?*

Dan, not caring for etiquette when his brother might be shot at any moment, slipped under the arm of the doorboy and bolted into the room.

Lincoln was standing by the window. He looked around in surprise at the noise of Dan Ripley's entry. He recognized his walking partner, made a motion for the doorboy, who had one irate hand on Dan, to withdraw, and said: "Why, Dan, I'm glad to see you so soon again. You're just in time to back me up. Let me introduce you to General Scanlon."

Dan looked into the amazed and angry eyes of a Union general who, practically ignoring the boy, went on to say: "Mr. President, I repeat that unless these men are made an example of, the army itself may be in danger. Mercy to these twenty-four means cruelty to near a million."

The president, worn not only from his sleepless night, but from the incessant strain of things, looked grave, for the general spoke truth. He turned to Dan, "Did you go home, sonny?"

Dan nodded.

"Then I shall keep my half of the bargain. General, this boy and I each walked the woods half the night carrying similar troubles, trying to decide whether it was best to forgive. We decided that it was best, as the Bible says, even to seventy times seven. Dan, how did your folks take it?"

Dan spoke quickly. "It would'a killed them if I'd run off for good, for they just got word that my brother Will—you know I told you about him—is to be shot for sleeping on watch. I just know he was tired out—he didn't go to sleep on purpose. I told my mother that you wouldn't let him be shot, if you knew."

Lincoln groaned audibly and turned away to the window for a moment. The general snorted.

"I brought my mother in to see you, too," said Dan, "seeing as she wouldn't quite believe what I said about our agreement."

Lincoln looked at the boy, and his sunken eyes glistened. "I agreed for twenty-four lives," he said; "but I don't mind throwing in an extra one for you, Dan."

And this time the general groaned.

"Stoddard," added the president, "will you see if there is a Will Ripley on file?"

The secretary left the room. Lincoln turned abruptly to the general. "You have heard me," he said. "I, with the help of God and this boy, threshed out the matter to a conclusion, and we only waste time to discuss it further. If I pardon these deserters, it surely becomes a better investment for the United States than if I had them shot—twenty-four live fighters in the ranks, instead of that many corpses underground. There are too many weeping widows now. Don't ask me to add to that number, *for I won't do it!*"

It was rarely that Lincoln was so stirred. There was a strange silence. Then the secretary entered with, "Yes, sir, a Will Ripley is to be executed tomorrow, for sleeping on duty. The case was buried in the files; it should have been brought to you earlier."

"Better for the case to be buried than the boy," said the president. "Give me the paper, Stoddard."

"Then you will!" said Dan, trembling with joy.

"I don't believe that shooting the boy will do him any good," said Lincoln, as the pen traced the letters of his name beneath this message, "Will Ripley is not to be shot until further orders from me."

Dan looked at it. "Oh, thank you!" he said. "Can I bring mother in to see it—and to see you?" he asked.

The president looked down into the shining face and could not refuse. In a moment, Dan's mother was in the room. She was all confused; the general was red with irritation.

She read the message. It didn't seem quite clear to her. "Is that a pardon? Does that mean that he won't be shot at all?"

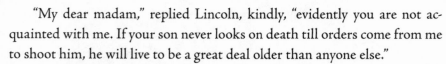

"My dear madam," replied Lincoln, kindly, "evidently you are not acquainted with me. If your son never looks on death till orders come from me to shoot him, he will live to be a great deal older than anyone else."

She stretched out both her hands, crying, "I want to thank you, sir. Oh, thank you, thank you!"

"Thank Dan here," said Lincoln. "If he had not let the warmth of forgiveness soften his heart, Will Ripley would have died. And perhaps, if I had not met him in the woods at dawn, I might have gone into eternity with the blood of these twenty-four men on my hands. Dan helped me.

"True, they are erring soldiers, Mrs. Ripley. But we must consider what they have done and what they will do as intently as we consider the wrong of the moment. Good-bye, Dan; we shall both remember today with easy consciences."

The waiting crowd in the anteroom could not understand, of course, why that intruder of a boy who had fairly dragged the woman in to see the president so unceremoniously should bring her out on his arm with such conscious pride. They could not understand why the tears were rolling down her cheeks at the same time that a smile glorified her face. They did not see that the boy was walking on air, on light. But the dullest of them could see that he was radiant with a great happiness.

And if they could have looked past him and pierced the door of the inner room with their wondering glances, they would have seen a reflection of Dan's joy still shining on the somber, deep-lined face of the man who had again indulged himself—in mercy.

"A Lesson in Forgiveness," by T. Morris Longstreth. Published in *The Youth's Instructor*, February 10, 1925. Reprinted by permission of Joe Wheeler (P.O. Box 1246, Conifer, CO 80433) and Review and Herald Publishing Association, Hagerstown, MD 21740.

Volk's life-mask of Lincoln

Notes

INTRODUCTION

1. *"It was not until,"* in Lloyd Lewis's *Myths after Lincoln* (New York: Grosset & Dunlap, 1929), 351–52.
2. *Lewis noted that,* in Lewis, 353.

CHAPTER ONE: ABRAHAM LINCOLN'S WORLD

1. *"The American rarely expected to stay,"* in Henry Steele Commanger's *The American Mind* (New Haven, CT: Yale University Press, 1950, 1968), 18.

CHAPTER TWO: THE FAITH OF ABRAHAM LINCOLN

1. *"I have never denied the truth,"* in Elton Trueblood's *Abraham Lincoln: Theologian of American Anguish* (New York: Harper & Row Publishers, 1973), 15.
2. *"I sincerely hope father may,"* in William Barton's *The Soul of Abraham Lincoln* (New York: George H. Doran Company, 1920), 77.
3. *"Lincoln was the most original,"* in Trueblood, VII.
4. *"Lincoln was drawn to the Bible,"* in Trueblood, 62.
5. *"Man's glory lies not,"* in Trueblood, 65.
6. *"My friends, no one, not,"* in John Nicolay and John Hay's *Abraham Lincoln: A History,* reprinted in *Century Magazine* (December 1887), 265.
7. *"The family retired to an,"* in Barton, *The Soul of Abraham Lincoln,* 86.
8. *By this time, war clouds were hovering,* in Trueblood, 24.
9. *"And whereas when our beloved,"* in Trueblood, 86.
10. *"Lincoln knelt beside him,"* in Barton, *The Soul of Abraham Lincoln,* 87.
11. *"The will of God prevails,"* in Trueblood, 8.
12. *"When Lee crossed the Potomac,"* in Trueblood, 41.
13. *"Lincoln's final emergence,"* in Trueblood, 31–32.
14. *After the Battle of Gettysburg,* in Barton's *The Soul of Abraham Lincoln,* 201–202.
15. *"Lincoln was taking seriously the idea,"* in Trueblood, 90–92.

279

16. *"What is increasingly obvious,"* in Trueblood, 94.

17. *"chose to speak,"* in Trueblood, 132.

18. *"As Lincoln rose,"* in Ronald C. White, Jr.'s "Absence of Malice," *Smithsonian* (April 2002), 109–19.

19. *"Both parties deprecated war,"* in White, 119.

20. *"of the Guiding Hand of God,"* in Trueblood, 136.

21. "We cannot read it," in Trueblood, 137.

22. *"the death of Lincoln,"* in Trueblood, 135–41.

23. *"Events marched rapidly,"* in Joseph Fort Newton's *Lincoln and Herndon* (Cedar Rapids, IA: Torch Press, 1910), 349–50.

CHAPTER THREE: A CHILD OF THE FRONTIER

1. *One of their sons,* in Ida M. Tarbell's *In the Footsteps of the Lincolns* (New York: Harper & Brothers, 1924), 1–60.

2. *Bathsheba had no way,* in Nicolay and Hay (July 1887), 6–7, 13–14.

3. *At first he thought,* in Carl Sandburg's, *Abraham Lincoln: The Prairie Years,* (New York: Charles Scribner's Sons, 1942), I1: 65–66.

4. *"She'd been looking for a man,"* in Tarbell, 77.

5. *"A little later that morning,"* in Paul Angle's *The Lincoln Reader* (New Brunswick, NJ: Rutgers University Press, 1947), 6–7.

6. *It was a self-contained world,* in Angle, 7–9.

7. *"'Abe' and I played all day,"* in Alexander McClure's *Abe Lincoln's Yarns and Stories* (Chicago: Thompson & Thomas, 1901), 302.

8. Pigeon Creek, Indiana Section, in Angle, 18–20.

9. *"She knew she was going to die,"* in Trueblood, 72–73.

10. *The following Sunday,* in W. M. Thayer's *The Pioneer Boy and How He Became President* (London: Hodder and Stoughton, 1882), 50–64.

CHAPTER FOUR: A NEW BEGINNING

1. *"Miss Johnston, I have no wife,"* in Sandburg, I: 42.

2. Arrival of Sally Johnston Lincoln section, in Thayer, 74–77; William O. Stoddard's *Abraham Lincoln: The True Story of a Great Life* (New York: Fords, Howard & Hulbert, 1890), 21–24.

3. *Well, almost everything,* in William H. Herndon and Jesse William Weik's *Herndon's Lincoln: The True Story of a Great Life* (Scituate, MA: Digital Scanning, Inc., 1999), 33, 34.

4. *"Yes, that would be,"* in Herndon and Weik, 33, 34.

5. *"She was my best friend,"* in Albert J. Beveridge's *Abraham Lincoln: 1809–1858* (Boston: Houghton Mifflin, 1928), I: 67.

6. *"In a few weeks all had changed,"* in Thayer, 77.

7. *"He read diligently,"* in Thayer, 79–88.

8. *One such book*, in Thayer, 89–90.

9. *One day, in a spelldown*, in McClure, 291.

10. *Mr. Gordon, the miller*, in William Barton's *The Life of Abraham Lincoln*, (Indianapolis: Bobbs-Merrill, 1925), 135–36.

11. "*Abe saved my life*," in McClure, 384.

12. "*The Chronicles of Reuben*" section, in Beveridge, I: 91–94; McClure, 149–51.

13. *They woke to find seven Negro*, in Thayer, 130–33.

Chapter Five: The Village of New Salem

1. "Time, what an empty vapor tis," by Abraham Lincoln, in Beveridge, I: 64–65.

2. "*I s'pose Abe is still fooling*," in Sandburg, *Abraham Lincoln: The Prairie Years*, I: 111.

3. *Clary's Grove Boys* section, in McClure, 287; *After striving a long time*, in Beveridge, I: 111.

4. "*Most astonishing to his militant*," in Beveridge, I: 113.

5. *It is intriguing to note*, in Angle, 531.

6. "*held it at arm's length*," in Doris Kearns Goodwin's *Team of Rivals* (New York: Simon & Schuster, 2005), 436–37.

7. "*In those wilderness days*," in Angle, 39–40.

8. *Lincoln threw his old straw hat*, in McClure, 429.

9. "*The red light of the morning sun*," in McClure, 401.

10. *So who would repay*, in Angle, 51–55.

11. *The line was "skewed*," in McClure, 139.

12. *In 1828, the chief topic*, in Beveridge, I: 90–91.

13. *Ann Rutledge* section, in Tarbell, 220.

14. "Oh! Why Should the Spirit of Mortal Be Proud?" in William Knox's Oh, Why Should the Spirit of Mortal Be Proud? (Boston: Lee and Shepard, 1882), no numbering on pages.

Chapter Six: Life Goes On

1. "[I'm reminded] of a fellow," in Barton, *The Life of Abraham Lincoln*, II: 396.

2. *Thirty years later*, in Herndon and Weik, II: 396.

3. "*I can loan you the money*," in McClure, 75–76.

4. *Lincoln as a dancer* section, in McClure, 384.

5. "*I am now the most miserable*," in David Herbert Donald's *Lincoln* (New York: Simon & Schuster, 1995), 88.

6. *Lincoln had always been*, in Barton, *The Life of Abraham Lincoln*, 244–45.

7. *Duel with Shields* section in Donald, 91; Beveridge, II: 36–56.

8. "*Logan was perhaps the most constructive influence*," in Albert A. Woldman's *Lawyer Lincoln* (Boston: Houghton Mifflin, 1936), 38–39.

9. "*I loved the woman*," in Donald, 57–58.

10. *"Though the Globe Tavern room,"* in Donald, 94–96.
11. *"In December 1847, the Lincolns journeyed to Washington,"* in Beveridge, II: 100–105.

CHAPTER SEVEN: THE ROAD BACK TO GOD

1. *"His political fortune at low ebb,"* in Woldman, 76.
2. *"Lawyers were learning that a broad,"* in Woldman, 78.
3. *"The faculty which he had before,"* in Godfrey Rathbone Benson Charnwood's *Abraham Lincoln,* (New York: Pocket Books, 1948), 112.
4. *"his constitutional interpretations, his understanding,"* in Woldman, vi.
5. *Mary, who'd been nursing Eddie night and day,* in Stephen B. Oates's *With Malice Toward None: A Life of Abraham Lincoln* (New York: HarperCollins, 1994), 94.
6. *Not that they were the exception,* in Trueblood, 96.
7. *"a very unprogressive type of preaching,"* in Barton, *The Soul of Abraham Lincoln,* 48.
8. *"In New Salem, Baptists, Methodists,"* in Donald, 48.
9. *"The Reverend Dr. James Smith,"* in Barton, *The Soul of Abraham Lincoln,* 159–63.
10. *"The State's star witness was,"* in Woldman, 111–16.
11. *"the lawyers who followed the presiding,"* in Woldman, 82–87.

CHAPTER EIGHT: COUNTDOWN TO THE CIVIL WAR

1. *"The distinct and emphatic idea,"* in Beveridge, III: 137.
2. *"So you're the little woman who wrote,"* in Carl Sandburg's *Abraham Lincoln: The War Years* (New York: Harcourt, Brace, 1939), II: 20.
3. *"For four hours the circuit-riding lawyer,"* in Angle, 206–207.
4. *"had to use the passions of the crowd,"* in Beveridge, IV: 11–18.

CHAPTER NINE: TO THE WHITE HOUSE

1. *"It was unquestionably a factor in shaping,"* in Benjamin Thomas's *Abraham Lincoln* (New York: Barnes & Noble Books, 1994), 91.
2. *"The whole country knows me,"* in Beveridge, IV: 268.
3. *"On August 21, 1858, the sun,"* in Beveridge, IV: 283–85.
4. *"I believe this government,"* in Donald, 206.
5. *"Gentlemen, I am killing larger game,"* in Nicolay and Hay (July 1887), 393.
6. *The high tide of Lincoln's elocutionary,* in Woldman, 261; in Donald, 237–40.
7. *"They have gambled me all around,"* in J. G. Randall's *Lincoln the President* (New York: Dodd Mead, 1946), 1:170.
8. *"There was then living in Chicago,"* in Isaac Arnold's, *The Life of Abraham Lincoln* (Chicago: A. C. McClurg, 1891), 167.
9. *"The shouting was absolutely frantic, shrill,"* in Randall, 1:166.
10. *"There is a little woman,"* in Arnold, 169.

11. *"This Presidential campaign has had,"* in Arnold, 170.

12. *When John Nicolay and John Hay researched this* (October 1887), 822.

13. *"Buchanan . . . is giving away,"* in McClure, 130.

CHAPTER TEN: IN THE MIDST OF ENEMIES

1. *Now, on January 31, 1860 after traveling,* in Donald, 271.

2. *"Let it hang there undisturbed,"* in Angle, 307–308.

3. *"It was a cloudy, stormy morning,"* in Nicolay and Hay (December 1887), 265.

4. *"I have a correspondent in this place,"* in Sandburg, *Abraham Lincoln: The War Years,* I:51.

5. This section, in L. E. Chittenden's *Recollections of President Lincoln and His Administration* (New York: Harper & Brothers, 1891), 40–46.

6. *Nine days later, Scott affected,* in Donald, 277.

7. *"One of them is an actor,"* in Chittenden, 58–64.

8. *"the most subtle juggler of words,"* in Nicolay and Hay (November 1887), 79.

CHAPTER ELEVEN: SUNLIGHT AND SHADOW

1. *"Nothing more conclusively showed,"* in Angle, 318.

2. This section: beginning with, *barricade cables had been stretched on either,* in Chittenden, 84–92.

3. Sumter section, in Nicolay and Hay (March 1888), 707–16; Neil Kagan's *Eyewitness to the Civil War* (Washington, D.C.: National Geographic, 2006), 48–49, 56–61.

4. *"When he finally gave the order that,"* in Nicolay and Hay (March 1888), 716.

5. The "Washington cut off" section, in Nicolay and Hay (April 1888), 908–22.

CHAPTER TWELVE: LIFE IN THE WHITE HOUSE

1. *"When the Lincolns had moved,"* in Donald, 309.

2. Boys in the White House section, in Ruth Painter Randall's *Lincon's Sons,* pp. 70–90.

CHAPTER THIRTEEN: THE EARLY WAR YEARS

1. *"Where did that long-armed baboon,"* in Sandburg, *Abraham Lincoln: The Prairie Years,* I: 41–42.

2. *"a frail, aristocratic woman,"* in Oates, 299.

3. *"mother, wife, and children of a man,"* in Goodwin, 671.

4. *"Mr. Lovejoy, heading a committee,"* in McClure, 163.

5. Death of Willie Lincoln section, in Ruth Painter Randall, 99–109; Angle, 427–32; Donald, 336–38; Goodwin, 415–23; Michael Burlingame's *With Lincoln in the White House: Letters, Memoranda, and Other Writings of John G. Nicolay,*

1860–1865 (Carbondale, IL: Southern Illinois Press, 2000), 71; Oates, 293; Thomas, 483.

6. *"The defiant courage with which she had faced,"* in Thomas, 480.

7. *It was because of this fierce inner need,* in Ronald G. White's *The Eloquent President* (New York: Random House, 2005), 169.

CHAPTER FOURTEEN: ANXIOUS TO MEET *Their* PRESIDENT

1. *Robert E. Lee now concluded that,* in Kagan, 155–69.

2. *"I made a solemn vow before God,"* in Barton, *The Soul of Abraham Lincoln,* 285.

3. *"In all my interviews with Mr. Lincoln,"* in Allen Thorndike's *Reminiscences of Abraham Lincoln* (New York: North American Review, 1888), 193.

4. *"Then in a surge of shouting,"* in Sandburg, *Abraham Lincoln: The War Years,* II: 184.

5. *In a recent Negro camp meeting,* in McClure, 417.

6. *even an ultimate forgiver,* in Rice, 582–83.

CHAPTER FIFTEEN: 1863: A LAND AWASH IN BLOOD

1. *That spring, Lincoln inherited,* in Goodwin, 522–24.

2. *Pickett's Charge section,* in Thomas, 384–86; Barton, *The Life of Abraham Lincoln,* II:180–183.

3. *"Welles read the message and almost jumped,"* in Thomas, 387.

4. Chattanooga section, in Kagan, 276–82; Thomas, 403–404; Sandburg, *Abraham Lincoln: The War Years,* II: 478–79.

CHAPTER SIXTEEN: TO ERR IS HUMAN, TO FORGIVE, DIVINE

1. *deeply anguished at the conflict,* in Kenneth W. Osbeck's Amazing Grace: 366 Inspiring Hymn Stories for Daily Devotions (Grand Rapids, MI: Kregel Publications, 1990), 165.

2. "Battle Hymn of the Republic," in *Heart Songs Dear to the American People* (Boston: Chapple Publishing, 1909), 312.

3. *"The fact is, General,"* in McClure, 418.

4. *"You are a sweet little rosebud,"* in McClure, 351–58.

5. Gettysburg Address section, in Donald, 460–66; White, 251–59; Sandburg, *Abraham Lincoln: The War Years,* II: 460, 461, 464–71, 474–75; Angle, 439–49.

6. *"Plowing corn on a Kentucky farm,"* in McClure, 565.

7. *"I had the satisfaction of informing,"* in Chittenden, 375–84.

8. "The Sleeping Sentinel," in Chittenden, 265–83.

9. Battle of Atlanta section, in Kagan, 316–33.

10. *Back in Tennessee,* in Ernest B. Furgurson's "Catching Up With 'Old Slow Trot,'" *Smithsonian* (March 2007), 57.

11. *The telegram announcing Thomas's,* in Goodwin, 685.

12. *"When Hood's army had been scattered,"* in McClure, 159.

13. Sherman's March to the Sea section, in Kagan, 340; J. G. Randall's *The Civil War and Reconstruction* (Boston: D. C. Heath, 1937, 1953), 550–64.

Chapter Seventeen: O Captain! My Captain!

1. "O Captain! My Captain!" in Leslie Lee Culpepper and Mildred McClary Tymeson's *American Authors* (Takoma Park, MD: Review and Herald Publishing Association, 1944), 163.

2. *"That is the largest shucking,"* in McClure, 255–56.

3. *"The president directs me to say,"* in Thomas, 503.

4. Excerpts from the Second Inaugural, in Ronald C. White's "Absence of Malice," *Smithsonian* (April 2002), 109.

5. *That night, at a White House,* in Ronald C. White's "Absence of Malice," 119.

6. *"I believe I may confidently answer,"* in Goodwin, 686–90.

7. *Struck by the weird beauty,* in Donald, 580.

8. Appomattox section, in Sandburg's *Abraham Lincoln: The War Years,* 136–39, 198–206.

9. *"From early youth he seemed,"* in Ward Hill Lamon's *Recollections of Abraham Lincoln* (Washington, D.C.: Private Printing, 1911), 110–14.

10. *"But the most startling incident,"* in Lamon, 114–17.

11. *"We shall hear very soon,"* in Lamon, 118–19.

12. *"He was human,"* in Sandburg's *Abraham Lincoln: The War Years,* IV: 338.

13. *"The dream was prophetic,"* in Lamon, 120.

14. The long good-bye section, in Lewis, 54–130.

Epilogue

1. This biographical section, in Goodwin, 751–54; Ruth Painter Randall, 253–63.

Appendix B: The Missionary Money

1. "The Missionary Money," by Olive Vincent Marsh. Reprinted in *St. Nicholas,* February 1918.

1784 1809 1818 1828 1831 1835 1842
1778 1806 1816 1819 1830 1834 1837

KEY EVENTS IN
Lincoln's Life Story

1778 – Thomas Lincoln is born in Rockingham County, Virginia.

1784 – Nancy Hanks is born in Western Virginia.

1806 – Thomas Lincoln and Nancy Hanks are married near Springfield, Kentucky.

1809 – Abraham Lincoln is born in Hardin County, Kentucky.

1816 – Thomas and Nancy Lincoln leave Knob Creek, Kentucky, and move to Pigeon Creek, Indiana.

1818 – Nancy Hanks Lincoln dies.

1819 – Thomas Lincoln and Sarah Bush Johnston marry.

1828 – Sarah Lincoln Grigsby dies in childbirth.
Abraham Lincoln makes first trip on flatboat to New Orleans.

1830 – Thomas and Sarah Lincoln move to Illinois.

1831 – Abraham Lincoln makes second flatboat trip to New Orleans.
Abraham Lincoln moves to New Salem, Illinois.

1834 – Abraham Lincoln is elected to the Illinois Legislature.

1835 – Ann Rutledge dies.

1837 – Lincoln moves to Springfield, Illinois.

1842 – Lincoln and Mary Todd are married.

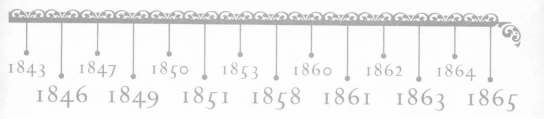

1843 1846 1847 1849 1850 1851 1853 1858 1860 1861 1862 1863 1864 1865

1843 – Robert Todd Lincoln is born.

1846 – Edward Baker Lincoln is born.

1847 – Lincoln takes his seat in the Thirtieth Congress.

1849 – Lincoln returns home to Springfield.

1850 – Edward Baker Lincoln dies.
       William Wallace Lincoln is born.

1851 – Thomas Lincoln dies in Coles County, Illinois.

1853 – Thomas (Tad) Lincoln is born.

1858 – The Lincoln-Douglas debates take place.

1860 – Lincoln, on the Republican ticket, is elected president of the
       United States.

1861 – Lincoln is inaugurated as the sixteenth president.
       Fort Sumter, in Charleston harbor, surrenders to Confederate
         forces.
       The Civil War begins.

1862 – William Wallace Lincoln dies.
       Lee's invasion of the North is turned back at Antietam.

1863 – Lincoln issues the Emancipation Proclamation.
       Lee's second invasion of the North is turned back at Gettysburg.
       The first national observance of Thanksgiving takes place.

1864 – Lincoln is reelected president.

1865   Lincoln is inaugurated for his second term.
       Lee surrenders to Grant at Appomattox.
       Lincoln is assassinated in Ford's Theater by John Wilkes Booth.

The Cast

Anderson, Robert —————— Union Commander of Fort Sumter

Arnold, Isaac ————————— Lincoln's Assistant Secretary

Bates, Edward ————————— Attorney General in Lincoln's Cabinet

Beauregard, P. G. T. ————— Confederate General

Booth, John Wilkes ————— Murderer of Lincoln; brother of Edwin
Booth

Brady, Mathew B. ————— Famed Civil War photographer

Buchanan, James ————— Fifteenth President of the United States

Burnsides, Ambrose ————— Union General

Cameron, Simon ————— Secretary of War in Lincoln's Cabinet

Chase, Salmon ————— Secretary of the Treasury in Lincoln's
Cabinet; later Chief Justice

Davis, David ————— Judge with whom Lincoln traveled the
circuit; later Justice of the Supreme
Court

Davis, Jefferson ————— President of the Confederacy

Douglas, Stephen ————— Senator from Illinois; debate partner
with Lincoln; presidential nominee

Douglass, Frederick ————— Notable abolitionist

Farragut, David ————— Union Admiral

Forrest, Nathan Bedford ——— Confederate General

Fremont, John ————— Union General

Grant, Ulysses S. ————— Chief Union General

Greeley, Horace ————— Famed New York newspaper publisher

Hackett, Henry ————— Lincoln's military Chief of Staff

Hamlin, Hannibal ————— Lincoln's first Vice President

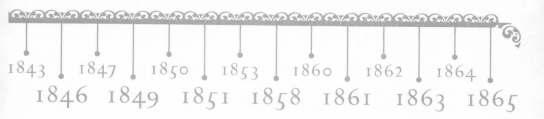

1843   1847   1850   1853   1860   1862   1864
1846   1849   1851   1858   1861   1863   1865

1843 – Robert Todd Lincoln is born.

1846 – Edward Baker Lincoln is born.

1847 – Lincoln takes his seat in the Thirtieth Congress.

1849 – Lincoln returns home to Springfield.

1850 – Edward Baker Lincoln dies.
       William Wallace Lincoln is born.

1851 – Thomas Lincoln dies in Coles County, Illinois.

1853 – Thomas (Tad) Lincoln is born.

1858 – The Lincoln-Douglas debates take place.

1860 – Lincoln, on the Republican ticket, is elected president of the
       United States.

1861 – Lincoln is inaugurated as the sixteenth president.
       Fort Sumter, in Charleston harbor, surrenders to Confederate
         forces.
       The Civil War begins.

1862 – William Wallace Lincoln dies.
       Lee's invasion of the North is turned back at Antietam.

1863 – Lincoln issues the Emancipation Proclamation.
       Lee's second invasion of the North is turned back at Gettysburg.
       The first national observance of Thanksgiving takes place.

1864 – Lincoln is reelected president.

1865   Lincoln is inaugurated for his second term.
       Lee surrenders to Grant at Appomattox.
       Lincoln is assassinated in Ford's Theater by John Wilkes Booth.

The Cast

Anderson, Robert————— Union Commander of Fort Sumter

Arnold, Isaac ————— Lincoln's Assistant Secretary

Bates, Edward ————— Attorney General in Lincoln's Cabinet

Beauregard, P. G. T. ————— Confederate General

Booth, John Wilkes ————— Murderer of Lincoln; brother of Edwin Booth

Brady, Mathew B.————— Famed Civil War photographer

Buchanan, James ————— Fifteenth President of the United States

Burnsides, Ambrose ————— Union General

Cameron, Simon ————— Secretary of War in Lincoln's Cabinet

Chase, Salmon ————— Secretary of the Treasury in Lincoln's Cabinet; later Chief Justice

Davis, David————— Judge with whom Lincoln traveled the circuit; later Justice of the Supreme Court

Davis, Jefferson————— President of the Confederacy

Douglas, Stephen ————— Senator from Illinois; debate partner with Lincoln; presidential nominee

Douglass, Frederick ————— Notable abolitionist

Farragut, David ————— Union Admiral

Forrest, Nathan Bedford ——— Confederate General

Fremont, John ————— Union General

Grant, Ulysses S. ————— Chief Union General

Greeley, Horace ————— Famed New York newspaper publisher

Hackett, Henry ————— Lincoln's military Chief of Staff

Hamlin, Hannibal ————— Lincoln's first Vice President

10. *Back in Tennessee*, in Ernest B. Furgurson's "Catching Up With 'Old Slow Trot,'" *Smithsonian* (March 2007), 57.

11. *The telegram announcing Thomas's*, in Goodwin, 685.

12. *"When Hood's army had been scattered,"* in McClure, 159.

13. Sherman's March to the Sea section, in Kagan, 340; J. G. Randall's *The Civil War and Reconstruction* (Boston: D. C. Heath, 1937, 1953), 550–64.

CHAPTER SEVENTEEN: O CAPTAIN! MY CAPTAIN!

1. "O Captain! My Captain!" in Leslie Lee Culpepper and Mildred McClary Tymeson's *American Authors* (Takoma Park, MD: Review and Herald Publishing Association, 1944), 163.

2. *"That is the largest shucking,"* in McClure, 255–56.

3. *"The president directs me to say,"* in Thomas, 503.

4. Excerpts from the Second Inaugural, in Ronald C. White's "Absence of Malice," *Smithsonian* (April 2002), 109.

5. *That night, at a White House*, in Ronald C. White's "Absence of Malice," 119.

6. *"I believe I may confidently answer,"* in Goodwin, 686–90.

7. *Struck by the weird beauty*, in Donald, 580.

8. Appomattox section, in Sandburg's *Abraham Lincoln: The War Years*, 136–39, 198–206.

9. *"From early youth he seemed,"* in Ward Hill Lamon's *Recollections of Abraham Lincoln* (Washington, D.C.: Private Printing, 1911), 110–14.

10. *"But the most startling incident,"* in Lamon, 114–17.

11. *"We shall hear very soon,"* in Lamon, 118–19.

12. *"He was human,"* in Sandburg's *Abraham Lincoln: The War Years*, IV: 338.

13. *"The dream was prophetic,"* in Lamon, 120.

14. The long good-bye section, in Lewis, 54–130.

EPILOGUE

1. This biographical section, in Goodwin, 751–54; Ruth Painter Randall, 253–63.

APPENDIX B: THE MISSIONARY MONEY

1. "The Missionary Money," by Olive Vincent Marsh. Reprinted in *St. Nicholas*, February 1918.

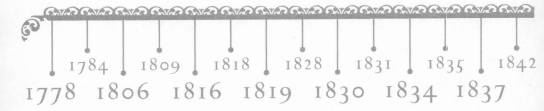

1784   1809   1818   1828   1831   1835   1842
1778 1806 1816 1819 1830 1834 1837

KEY EVENTS IN
Lincoln's Life Story

1778 – Thomas Lincoln is born in Rockingham County, Virginia.

1784 – Nancy Hanks is born in Western Virginia.

1806 – Thomas Lincoln and Nancy Hanks are married near Springfield, Kentucky.

1809 – Abraham Lincoln is born in Hardin County, Kentucky.

1816 – Thomas and Nancy Lincoln leave Knob Creek, Kentucky, and move to Pigeon Creek, Indiana.

1818 – Nancy Hanks Lincoln dies.

1819 – Thomas Lincoln and Sarah Bush Johnston marry.

1828 – Sarah Lincoln Grigsby dies in childbirth.
Abraham Lincoln makes first trip on flatboat to New Orleans.

1830 – Thomas and Sarah Lincoln move to Illinois.

1831 – Abraham Lincoln makes second flatboat trip to New Orleans.
Abraham Lincoln moves to New Salem, Illinois.

1834 – Abraham Lincoln is elected to the Illinois Legislature.

1835 – Ann Rutledge dies.

1837 – Lincoln moves to Springfield, Illinois.

1842 – Lincoln and Mary Todd are married.

Hay, John ——————————— Lincoln's Secretary

Herndon, William ————— Lincoln's longtime law partner

Hood, John Bell ————— Confederate General

Hooker, Joseph———————— Union General

Jackson, Andrew ————— President who appointed Lincoln
Postmaster of New Salem

Jackson, Thomas "Stonewall" — Confederate General

Johnson, Andrew ————— Lincoln's second Vice President;
seventeenth President of the United
States

Johnston, Joseph E. ————— Confederate General

Lamon, Ward Hill ————— Marshal of Washington; bodyguard;
friend of Lincoln

Lee, Robert E. ————— Chief Confederate General

Lincoln, Abraham ————— Lincoln's grandfather

Lincoln, Edward ————— Son of Abraham and Mary Lincoln; died
at age four

Lincoln, Mary Todd ————— Lincoln's wife

Lincoln, Nancy Hanks ————— Lincoln's mother

Lincoln, Robert Todd ———— Oldest son of Abraham and Mary Lincoln

Lincoln Grigsby, Sarah ———— Lincoln's sister

Lincoln, Sarah Bush ———— Lincoln's stepmother

Lincoln, Thomas ————— Lincoln's father

Lincoln, Thomas (Tad)———— Son of Abraham and Mary Lincoln; died
at age eighteen

Lincoln, William Wallace——— Son of Abraham and Mary Lincoln; died
at age twelve

Logan, Stephen T. ————— Lincoln's law partner

McClellan, George B. ———— Union General

Meade, George G. ———— Union General

Nicolay, John ————— Lincoln's Secretary

Owens, Mary ————— Courted by Lincoln

Pope, John ————— Union General

Rosecrans, W. S. ————— Union General

Scott, Winfield———————— Union General (Supreme Commander)

Seward, William H. ———— Secretary of State in Lincoln's Cabinet

Sheridan, Philip Henry ——— Union General

Sherman, William Tecumseh — Union General

Speed, Joshua ———————— Lincoln's closest friend

Stanton, Edwin ————————— Lincoln's second Secretary of State

Stephens, Alexander————————— Vice President of the Confederacy

Stuart, John Todd ————— Lincoln's law partner

Sumner, Charles ————————— Senator attacked on the Senate floor

Stowe, Harriet Beecher ——— Author of *Uncle Tom's Cabin*

Swett, Leonard———————— Lincoln's close friend and law associate

Taney, Roger —————————— Chief Justice

Vallandigham, Clement ——— Peace-Democrat Congressman turned
over by Lincoln to the Confederacy

Wallace, Lew ——————————— Union General and author of *Ben-Hur*

Weed, Thurlow "Boss" ————— New York political boss

Welles, Gideon———————— Secretary of the Navy in Lincoln's Cabinet